Visions of Struggle in Women's Filmmaking
in the Mediterranean

Comparative Feminist Studies Series
*Chandra Talpade Mohanty, Series Editor*


Published by Palgrave Macmillan:

*Sexuality, Obscenity, Community:*
*Women, Muslims, and the Hindu Public in Colonial India*
     by Charu Gupta

*Twenty-First-Century Feminist Classrooms:*
*Pedagogies of Identity and Difference*
     edited by Amie A. Macdonald and Susan Sánchez-Casal

*Reading across Borders:*
*Storytelling and Knowledges of Resistance*
     by Shari Stone-Mediatore

*Made in India:*
*Decolonizations, Queer Sexualities, Trans/national Projects*
     by Suparna Bhaskaran

*Dialogue and Difference:*
*Feminisms Challenge Globalization*
     edited by Marguerite Waller and Sylvia Marcos

*Engendering Human Rights:*
*Cultural and Socio-Economic Realities in Africa*
     edited by Obioma Nnaemeka and Joy Ezeilo

*Women's Sexualities and Masculinities in a Globalizing Asia*
     edited by Saskia E. Wieringa, Evelyn
     Blackwood, and Abha Bhaiya

*Gender, Race, and Nationalism in Contemporary Black Politics*
     by Nikol G. Alexander-Floyd

*Gender, Identity, and Imperialism:*
*Women Development Workers in Pakistan*
     by Nancy Cook

*Transnational Feminism in Film and Media*
     edited by Katarzyna Marciniak, Anikó Imre, and Áine O'Healy

*Gendered Citizenships:*
*Transnational Perspectives on Knowledge Production,*
*Political Activism, and Culture*
     edited by Kia Lilly Caldwell, Kathleen Coll, Tracy Fisher,
     Renya K. Ramirez, and Lok Siu

*Visions of Struggle in Women's Filmmaking in the Mediterranean*
     edited by Flavia Laviosa; Foreword by Laura Mulvey

# Visions of Struggle in Women's Filmmaking in the Mediterranean

*Edited by*
*Flavia Laviosa*

*Foreword by*
*Laura Mulvey*

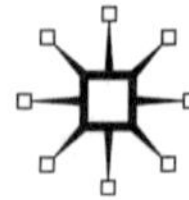

VISIONS OF STRUGGLE IN WOMEN'S FILMMAKING IN THE MEDITERRANEAN
Copyright © Flavia Laviosa, 2010.



First published in 2010 by
PALGRAVE MACMILLAN®
in the United States—a division of St. Martin's Press LLC,
175 Fifth Avenue, New York, NY 10010.

Where this book is distributed in the UK, Europe and the rest of the world,
this is by Palgrave Macmillan, a division of Macmillan Publishers Limited,
registered in England, company number 785998, of Houndmills,
Basingstoke, Hampshire RG21 6XS.

Palgrave Macmillan is the global academic imprint of the above companies
and has companies and representatives throughout the world.

Palgrave® and Macmillan® are registered trademarks in the United States,
the United Kingdom, Europe and other countries.

ISBN: 978–0–230–61736–0

Library of Congress Cataloging-in-Publication Data

Visions of struggle in women's filmmaking in the Mediterranean /
edited by Flavia Laviosa.
    p. cm.—(Comparative Feminist Studies)
    ISBN 978–0–230–61736–0 (alk. paper)
    1. Feminist films—Mediterranean Region—History and criticism.
2. Women in motion pictures. 3. Women motion picture producers and
directors—Mediterranean Region—Biography. I. Laviosa, Flavia.

PN1995.9.W6V57 2009
791.43′63522091822—dc22                     2009021445

A catalogue record of the book is available from the British Library.

Design by Newgen Imaging Systems (P) Ltd., Chennai, India.

First edition: February 2010

10  9  8  7  6  5  4  3  2  1

Printed in the United States of America.

*For my parents*
*Volumnia and Giuseppe*

# Contents



## Israel: Orientalism and Europeanness



## Maghreb: Political and Transcultural Resistance



## Spain: Domestic Violence



## France: Body Mutilation



## Italy: Women of the Mafia

## The Balkans: Peacekeeping and Women's (In)security



## Greece: Women's New Roles and Identities



## Turkey: Harsh Living Conditions



## Syria: Female Identities and Political Resistance



## Turkey, Jordan, Palestine: Honor Killings

# Illustrations

# Series Editor's Foreword

The *New York Times* (August 23, 2009) just declared "the oppression of women worldwide" to be the "human rights cause of our time," claiming that women's liberation would "solve many of the world's problems!" Some years ago, then U.N. Secretary-General Kofi Anan announced that the status of women was the key indicator of the "development" of a nation. These pronouncements supposedly recognize the global crises in women's lives, but they also reflect a history of women's struggles and feminist movements around the globe. The Comparative Feminist Studies (CFS) series is designed to foreground writing, organizing, and reflection on feminist trajectories across the historical and cultural borders of nation-states. It takes up fundamental analytic and political issues involved in the cross-cultural production of knowledge about women and feminism, examining the politics of scholarship and knowledge in relation to feminist organizing and social justice movements. Drawing on feminist thinking in a number of fields, the CFS series targets innovative, comparative feminist scholarship, pedagogical and curricular strategies, and community organizing and political education. It explores a comparative feminist praxis that addresses some of the most urgent questions facing progressive critical thinkers and activists today. *Visions of Struggle in Women's Filmmaking in the Mediterranean* is an excellent example of such comparative feminist praxis. It is located at the intersection of feminist film and visual studies, and struggles for human rights and social justice in countries of the southern European Union, southwestern Balkans, North Africa, and the Middle East—a post-cold war economic and political landscape of the Mediterranean. *Visions of Struggle in Women's Filmmaking in the Mediterranean* is a unique collection in geopolitical and comparative terms.

Over the past many decades, feminists across the globe have had varying degrees of success at addressing fundamental issues of oppression and liberation. In our search for gender justice in the early twenty-first century, however, we inherit a number of the challenges our mothers and grandmothers faced. But there are also new challenges to face as we attempt to make sense of a world indelibly marked by the failure of postcolonial (and advanced) capitalist and communist nation-states to provide for the social, economic, spiritual, and psychic needs of the majority of the world's population. In the year 2009, globalization has come to represent the interests of corporations and the free market rather than self-determination and freedom from political, cultural, and economic domination for all the world's peoples. The project of the U.S. Empire building, alongside the dominance of corporate capitalism, kills, disenfranchises, and impoverishes women everywhere. Militarization, environmental degradation, heterosexist state practices, religious fundamentalisms, sustained migrations of peoples across the borders of nations and geopolitical regions, environmental crises, and the exploitation of women's labor by capital all pose profound challenges for feminists at this time. Recovering and remembering insurgent histories and seeking new understandings of political subjectivities and citizenship have never been so important at a time marked by social amnesia, global consumer culture, and the world-wide mobilization of fascist notions of "national security." The year 2009 also heralds changes in the political landscapes of many nations, with Barack Obama as the first African American president of the United States and numerous female heads of state around the world, including Ellen Johnson of Liberia, Michelle Bachelet Jeria of Chile, Mary McAleese of Ireland, Sheikh Hasina Wajed of Bangladesh, and Angela Merkel of Germany. However, whether these political shifts in governance at the top actually lead to deep and transformative changes in the economic, social, and cultural marginalization faced by communities around the globe and whether the contours of gendered and racialized citizenship change remain to be seen.

These are some of the very challenges the CFS series is designed to address. The series takes as its fundamental premise the need for feminist engagement with global as well as local ideological, historical, economic, and political processes, and the urgency of transnational dialogue in building an ethical culture capable of withstanding and transforming the commodified and exploitative practices of global governance structures, culture, and economics. Individual volumes in the CFS series provide systemic and challenging interventions into the (still) largely Euro-Western feminist studies knowledge base, while simultaneously highlighting the work that can and needs to be done to envision and enact cross-cultural, multiracial, feminist solidarity.

*Visions of Struggle in Women's Filmmaking in the Mediterranean* extends, complicates, and pushes the range of scholarship in the CFS series to another level. The volume focuses on an examination of films by women filmmakers in the particular geographical areas that constitute the Mediterranean, creating a dialogue between these cultures and nations about fundamental issues of women's human rights.

Drawing on a range of feminist critiques of violence, and the consequences of masculinist cultures and practices in the lives of women, the book maps a cartography of "the hybrid expressions of modernity" (Introduction, 3) manifested in women's lives. In addition, the films analyzed foreground the political militancy that accompanies struggles for women's liberation, and highlight the significance of a "collective space" as Laura Mulvey suggests in her foreword. Individual chapters examine films by women filmmakers from Israel, Turkey, Jordan, Palestine, Spain, France, Italy, Greece, Syria, The Balkans, Algeria, Morocco, and Tunisia.

*Visions of Struggle in Women's Filmmaking in the Mediterranean* showcases the kind of scholarship that can create the ground for cross-racial /cross-national dialogue among and between feminist scholars and activists in regional as well as global contexts. The book will be of interest to a wide range of feminist scholars, activists, and cultural critics. It embodies the comparative praxis and vision of transnational knowledge production that is a hallmark of the CFS series.

CHANDRA TALPADE MOHANTY

# *Foreword*

This fascinating collection of chapters analyzes films made by women brought together by their geographical location: the Mediterranean. Even at first glance, this point of departure arouses curiosity as to how the widely different social and historical nations and communities grouped around the sea might or might not be using film to trace themes that connect the arbitrariness of geography with wider questions confronting women in the early twenty-first century. On closer examination, however, the unifying geographical space provides more than an actual topography, a first organizing principle; space widens out of the literal, and resonates across multiple layers of reference from the social to the metaphoric, from the lived and the everyday to the screen space of the cinema. The chapters in this work, taken together, draw from the films discussed as a "lesson" in the poetics of space and its particular importance for women both politically and in the imagination. The chapters not only are around a central sea but also set in motion a journey that has a historical dimension attached to it: in a central and recurring figure, the concept of collective space returns, whether that of a nonurban community of women or through the public space of modernity. However, the journeys that crisscross the geographical space of the Mediterranean, those of particular directors, those of the chapters' ' authors who may or may not belong to the nation whose cinema they analyze, and those of the fictional or documentary protagonists, all draw attention to a spatial flexibility, a plurality of thought and the potential offered by cultural exchange. On the one hand, these journeys evoke the antiquity of the Mediterranean, always known as a sea that enabled exchanges of populations, ideas, trade, cultures, and so on. On the other hand, the book is itself a record of the journeys it traces and thus makes its own absolutely contemporary contribution to the specific phenomenon of the Mediterranean's historical geography. As an implicit direction, a layer, as it were, of aspiration hovering within the book's topographical complexities is the conceptual space of "nomadism," one of the oldest forms of human economic and social organization and one that has recently emerged as a figure for a decentralized space for communication and imagination, located in new forms of media and suggesting new possibilities of liberation and the reconfiguration of human relations.

It is not, unfortunately, possible within this foreword to draw out the richness of the topics and themes covered by the films included here or, indeed, the value of the individual chapters themselves. I would, however, like to make a few comments on some of the ways in which space recurs across the book and in some of the films discussed. Over and over again, the "home" emerges to epitomize the way in which a highly evocative space may simultaneously be literal and conceptual, real and lived while also deeply invested with ideology, myth, and politics. The collection begins with Yosefa Loshitzky's trenchant critique of two Israeli films (by Yulie Cohen-Gerstel), the only ones in the book that reproduce the ideology of the "home" to reinforce an aggressive myth of "homeland." Her poignant and perceptive analysis establishes, at the very beginning, the power of spatial imagery and its political and psychoanalytic implications. Approaching "the home" from a very different perspective, Florence Martin, discussing films made in the Maghreb, introduces and adapts Freud's idea of the *"Heimlich"* and the *"Unheimlich"* to demonstrate the way that the domestic space easily shifts away from the female sphere to house a dangerous and oppressive patriarchal power. The "familiar" is violently "defamiliarized" and many of the films discussed in the book as a whole follow their female protagonists' escape from this claustrophobic and constraining space into a female collectivity. This shift is vividly evoked in Yamina Bachir-Chouikh's *Rachida* in which the village women create a protective space for the young woman's traumatized body with their brightly colored scarves. With this image, the director uses the cinema and its language to create a metaphor for an alternative public sphere away from the private and oppressive space of the home. The home is, of course, also the privileged site of "the private" in which domestic violence is inflicted on women by their husbands. Mónica Cantero analyses the way that the ideology of the home, privacy, and violence is located within a legacy of fascism in Iciar Bollaín's *Take My Eyes*, and the films of Roberta Torre show a similar syndrome flourishing in the macho world of the Mafia. Once again, in *Take My Eyes*, escape is offered by the collective solidarity of women and through the protagonist's involvement with the public culture of her home town and its history. This critical opposition between the private and the public spheres, the woman in relation to her family in tension with her public role, both political and cultural, is the subject of both the Greek films analyzed by Maria Paradeisi. The two directors dramatize the dual spaces, materialized in *A Song Is Not Enough* by the political space of activism and prison as well as the cultural space of the theatre and professional self-realization, and suggest that analyzing these contradictions, narratively and cinematically, might allow women to challenge and transcend their opposition. From a very different but fascinating perspective, the protagonist of Yeşim Ustaoğlu's *Waiting for the Clouds* is able to overcome her isolation and recover her repressed ethnic identity through the care and solidarity of other peasant women of the Black Sea region in their strange, surreal annual migration to the mountains. The protagonist's journey takes the film out of a mythology of a unified nation-state into "transnational" or even "post-national" spaces that address the injustice involved in lost histories, but, in bringing these stories to the surface, they suggest the possibilities of more flexible, plural identities that transcend traditional boundaries.

In her contribution, the book's editor, Flavia Laviosa, discusses films that take on the difficult and painful topic of "honor killings." These ritual violations of women's, particularly young women's, human rights emerge out of a "familiar" space that includes but also extends beyond the space of the individual home to the wider networks of tribal societies and their customs and traditions. Within this spatial configuration, women function literally as property, to be exchanged between male groups, between father and husband, and the value of a woman's life is not only reduced to a basic sexual value, calculated by male relatives, but one may be bartered for the other. Women's powerlessness within this topography gives rise to the image, frequently referred to in the stories traced by these films, of "escape" and "running away." Young girls who have managed to achieve a level of education outside their traditional space are often the ones who rebel against its rules, and those threatened by its vengeance often try to find refuge within the alternative sphere of national and law. However, the chapter emphasizes the weakness of these alternatives as defenders of women's rights. In a paradoxical twist, male "ownership" of women's sexuality and its equation with the "honor" of the tribal or family group has a strange resonance with the Mediterranean cinema generated at its furthest cultural and social distance. In her discussion of the "extreme" cinema made by certain French women directors, Carrie Tarr points out that the violence that characterizes these films might be seen as a reaction against a society and economy in which the female body is relentlessly commodified and circulated as an erotic object of exchange. Allegories of female empowerment (*Baise-moi*), and satires of a sex-driven world (*Trouble Everyday* and *Anatomy of Hell*), these films depict marginal, fantasy spaces of retreat into violence and the abject. Here too, the female body circulates as a signifier of sexuality, but the films' cultural perspective is charged with the postmodern rather than the premodern, and self-referential narratives, questioning the adequacy of images to represent a social real, inhabit a parallel world in which the female body struggles to assert itself, literally in the case of *In My Skin*, through masochistic mutilation.

In her chapter on Karin Jurschick's film *The Peacekeepers and the Women*, Marguerite Waller analyses the porous nature of boundaries in Eastern Europe across which young women are "trafficked," literally bought and sold, as the space of the black market overwhelms its legal alternatives. The topography of this "non-space," occupied by international peacekeeping forces, ultimately echoes and mimics that of the Bush-era neoliberal economics and its flourishing market in policing and security.

Rasha Salti's chapter on the Syrian filmmaker Hala Alabdallah brings the collection to a full geographical circle while also raising two specific topographical issues. More, perhaps than any of the other films discussed, Alabdallah's cinema explores a poetic interior space, using the specificity of the film medium to reclaim a lost political experience and, most of all, to capture the invisible meshes of love, friendship, and emotion. Alabdallah also, however, brings back to the book the literal space of travel as she moves between semi-exile in Paris and the varied landscapes of her homeland.

The presence of Syrian cinema evokes the transnational nature of Arabic culture itself, stretching across the geographical space of the southern rim of the Mediterranean in a network of historic crisscrossings of influence and dialogue. These cultural links between the Middle East and the Maghreb also evoke the ghostly presence of France, as a colonizing power, of course, but also as a magnet for cinephilia, a source of training and finance for both North African and Middle Eastern filmmakers. Florence Martin's chapter specifically foregrounds the complexity of these cinematic cultural convolutions through the term the "wiles" of Maghrebi women's cinema, which works across on-screen and offscreen space, between acknowledged and implicit discourses. Ultimately this chapter points toward a topographical future from a borderless past. Her mastery of the virtual, global space of the computer enables the protagonist of Nadia El Fani's *Bedwin Hacker* to penetrate the official space of the television screen with her iconic emblem of the ancient symbol of nomadic society, the camel. As Martin points out, these images "no longer portray frustrated dreams of a fantasized elsewhere but recondition familiar spaces into new ones" blurring "the line hitherto drawn between the familiar/alien space for women [to] appropriate new spaces and finally invest old spaces with new values."

LAURA MULVEY

# Acknowledgments

I am first of all grateful to Chandra Talpade Mohanty, Series Editor of the Comparative Feminist Studies series, whose enthusiastic interest in the idea has strengthened my work throughout the completion of this volume. I also thank her for writing the *Series Editor's Foreword* for this book. I am particularly thankful to Lee Norton and Brigitte Shull at Palgrave Macmillan for their punctual and skillful assistance throughout the editorial process. I gratefully acknowledge the anonymous readers whose insightful reports offered critical advice on revisions.

This volume is the result of a two-year collaboration with the contributors who were rigorously committed to the project, and who appreciated the frequent reviews and numerous suggestions throughout the various stages of editorial revision. It has been a rewarding experience for me to work with such a remarkable group of women scholars from diverse cultures and different countries in the Mediterranean, Europe, and the United States, and I thank all of them for their extraordinary intellectual contributions to the book.

I am especially grateful to Laura Mulvey for offering to write the foreword and Chris Holmlund for agreeing to write the endorsement for this book. I also thank directors Karin Jurschick, Buthina C. Khoury, and Yeşim Ustaoğlu for granting permission to use the photo posters of their films *The Peacekeepers and the Women*, *Maria's Grotto*, and *Life on Their Shoulders* as illustrations in the book, respectively, in Marguerite Waller's, my, and S. Ruken Öztürk's chapters. Preparing this volume for publication involved precious advice, constant support, and generous mentoring from a number of inspiring people, including Laura Mulvey, Marguerite Waller, Áine O'Healy, Yosefa Loshitsky, Salem Mekuria, and Abele Longo, to whom I am indebted. My gratitude extends to my student Jenna Miller (Wellesley College Graduating Class of 2010) for her original cover artwork of this book, to Chris Souza and Sarah Gray for their editorial revisions, and special acknowledgment to Lisa Kleinholz for her assistance in indexing.

This book stems from an international symposium held at Wellesley College, Massachusetts on November 2–3, 2007, entitled *Visions of Struggle: Women's Filmmaking in the Mediterranean* (full program available at www.wellesley.edu/Italian/flaviosa/symposium.html), and organized by me. Gathering twelve women scholars and one film-maker from the Middle East, Europe, and the United States to engage in women's issues in the context of contemporary cinema produced by women directors in Mediterranean countries, the symposium attracted and inspired the faculty, students, journalists, and film critics who attended the two-day meeting. This event was made possible thanks to the help of a dedicated group of about forty students from my Fall 2007 courses of Italian Studies 101 and Italian Studies 201, who volunteered and contributed to its success with their talents, skills, countless hours, boundless energy, and inspiring enthusiasm. Institutional financial support for the symposium and for the invited guest speakers was generously provided by the Wellesley College Committee on Lectures and Cultural Events; the Davis Museum and Cultural Center, Kathryn Wasserman Davis (Wellesley College Graduating Class of 1928) Fund for World Cultures and Leadership, and Amy Sommer (Wellesley College Graduating Class of 1987) Treves Memorial Fund; the Departments and Programs of Italian Studies, History, Jewish Studies, Writing, Art, Political Science, German, Newhouse Center, Middle Eastern Studies, French, Religion, Media Arts and Sciences, Cinema and Media Studies, Women's Studies, Peace and Justice, Theatre and Wellesley Summer Theatre Company, Africana Studies, Spanish, Sociology; and the Italian Student Society. The symposium was also cosponsored by the Boston Palestine Film Festival. I am indebted to my colleagues and administrators at Wellesley College for their very generous support in funding the symposium, which has now led to the publication of this book.

Finally, and above all, I thank my parents in Italy, who have encouraged me and whose sacrifice, love, and patience have always sustained me. This book is dedicated to them.

# Contributors

**Mónica Cantero** is Associate Professor of Spanish and Chair of European Studies at Drew University, United States. She has written on Spanish film and Spanish linguistics. Her articles have appeared in *Film-Historia, Filología y Lingüística, Developmental Science, Morphé Ciencias del Lenguaje, Journal of Comparative Psychology,* and *The Virginia Review of Asian Studies,* among others. She is also author of essays in the edited collections *Research on Spanish in the US* (Cascadilla Press, 2002) and *Historia & Cinema* (Publicacions i Edicions Universitat de Barcelona, 2009). She is the editor of *Language, Identity, and Images in Chicana/Latina and Caribbean Literature* (Lincom, 2006). She is currently editing a book on migration and film in Spain, *Analyzing Discourses of Migration and Diversity in Spanish Films,* in collaboration with the Film-Historia research center at the University of Barcelona.

**Flavia Laviosa** is Senior Lecturer in the Department of Italian Studies at Wellesley College, United States. Her articles, in English and Italian, have appeared in *California Italian Studies, Journal of Mediterranean Studies, Studies in European Cinema, Italica, Rivista di Studi Italiani, Kinema, American Journal of Italian Studies, Italian Politics and Society, College Board-Special Focus,* and *Rivista Italiana di Linguistica Applicata.* Her publications include essays in the edited collections *Cinema and Culture in Twentieth Century Italy* (IBT Tauris Academic Publications, Forthcoming, 2011); *Zoom 'd'oltreoceano': istantanee sui registi italiani e sull'Italia* (Vecchiarelli, 2010); *(Ri)narrare il Meridione* (Metauro, 2010), *Watching Pages, Reading Pictures: Cinema and Modern Literature in Italy* (Cambridge Scholars Press, 2008), *Teaching Italian Culture: Case Studies for an International Perspective* (Cambridge Scholars Press, 2008), *Italian Cinema-New Directions* (Peter Lang, 2005), *La Scuola Italiana di Middlebury* (Metauro, 2005), and *Incontri con il Cinema Italiano* (Sciascia, 2003). She is also on the international editorial board of *Sine/Cine: The Journal of Cinema Research.*

**Yosefa Loshitzky** is Professor of Film, Media, and Cultural Studies at the University of East London, UK. She is the author of *The Radical Faces of Godard and Bertolucci* (Wayne State University Press, 1995),

*Identity Politics on the Israeli Screen* (University of Texas Press, 2001), and *Screening Strangers: Migration and Diaspora in Contemporary European Cinema* (Indiana University Press, 2010), the editor of *Spielberg's Holocaust: Critical Perspectives on Schindler's List* (Indiana University Press, 1997), and a guest editor of a special issue of *Third Text* on *Fortress Europe: Migration, Culture, Representation* (2006). She is currently writing a book, tentatively entitled, *Just Jews? Anti-Semitism and Islamophobia in Contemporary Culture and Beyond*. She has also written extensively on film, media, and culture for a variety of journals and book anthologies, and served on the editorial board of *Cinema Journal*.

**Florence Martin** is Professor of French and Francophone Studies and Chair of the Department of Modern Languages and Literatures at Goucher College, Baltimore, United States. She is also on the editorial board of *Studies in French Cinema* (UK), and the author of two books in French: *Bessie Smith* (Parenthèses, 1996) and *De la Guyane à la diaspora africaine* (coauthored with Isabelle Favre, Karthala, 2002). Her most recent publications include chapters and articles on Algerian director-writer Assia Djebar, Tunisian directors Raja Amari, Moufida Tlatli, and Nadia El Fani, as well as a chapter on the history and current state of Tunisian cinema. Her third book is *Veils and Screens: Maghrebi Women's Cinema* (Wallflower Press and Columbia University Press, 2009).

**Áine O'Healy** is Professor of Italian and Director of the Humanities Program at Loyola Marymount University, United States. She is the author of a monograph on Cesare Pavese (G.K. Hall, 1988) and of numerous essays in edited collections including *Feminine Feminists: Cultural Practices in Italy* (University of Minnesota Press, 1994), *A History of Women's Writing in Italy* (Cambridge University Press, 2000), *Federico Fellini: Contemporary Perspectives* (University of Toronto Press, 2002), *The Pleasure of Writing: Critical Essays on Dacia Maraini* (Purdue University Press, 2002), *The Cinema of Italy* (Wallflower, 2004), *Queer Italia: Same Sex Desire in Italian Literature and Film* (Palgrave, 2004), and *Sinergie narrative in letteratura e film nell'Italia contemporanea* (Cesati, 2007). Her articles on contemporary Italian cinema and cultural studies have appeared in *Screen, Cinefocus, Spectator, International Journal of the Humanities, Annali d'Italianistica, Women's Studies Review, Italian Culture, Controcorrente, Italian Studies, Italica, The Italianist; CIS,* and other journals. Additionally, she is coeditor of *Transnational Feminism in Film and Media* with Katarzyna Marciniak and Anikó Imre

(Palgrave, 2007). She is currently coediting a special issue of *Feminist Media Studies* entitled *Transcultural Mediations and Transnational Politics of Difference*, and her book on contemporary Italian cinema is forthcoming from Indiana University Press.

**S. Ruken Öztürk** is Associate Professor in the Radio, Television, and Film Department, The Faculty of Communication, Ankara University, Turkey. She has co-translated and coauthored (with Sabri Büyükdüvenci) several articles in English in *Postmodernizm ve Sinema* [*Postmodernism and Cinema*] (Ark, 1997). She is the author of two books in Turkish: *Sinemada Kadın Olmak* [Being a Woman in the Cinema] (Alan, 2000) and *Sinemanın Dişil Yüzü: Türkiye'de Kadın Yönetmenler* [Female Side of the Cinema: Women Filmmakers in Turkey] (Om, 2004). She has also written (with Nilgün Abisel, Tümay Arslan, Pembe Behçetoğulları, Ali Karadoğan, and Nejat Ulusay) a book on classical Turkish melodrama, *Çok Tuhaf Çok Tanıdık: 'Vesikalı Yarim' Üzerine* [The Strangely Familiar, The Familiar Estranged: On 'My Licenced Beloved'] (Metis, 2005), and edited a book on director *Zeki Demirkubuz* (Dost, 2006). Her article in English on Nuri Bilge Ceylan's *Uzak/Distant* appears in *The Cinema of North Africa and the Middle East* (Wallflower Press, 2007).

**Maria Paradeisi** is Assistant Professor in the Department of Communication, Media, and Culture at Panteion University of Athens, Greece. She participates in the research project Ge.M.I.C. (Gender, Migration, and Intercultural Interaction) financed by the European Union. Her numerous articles on Greek cinema and women's cinema have appeared in *O Politis* [Citizen], *To Vima ton Koinonikon Epistimon* [Social Sciences Forum], *Optikoakoustiki Koultoura* [Audiovisual Culture], and *Istorika* [Historica]. She is also the author of the book *Cinematic Narration and Delinquency in the Greek Cinema 1994–2004* (Typothito Press, 2006). She has worked for the Greek radio, television, and cinema and has directed the films *One-act play for a telephone*, *The neorealism in the work of Stelios Tatasopoulos, Vasilis Papavasiliou*, the third episode of the serial *Fashion and civilization in the Twentieth century*, and the short film *The blackmailing* for Greek television.

**Rasha Salti** is a curator, freelance writer, and Creative Director of ArteEast. She writes about artistic practice in the Arab world, film, and general social and political commentary. Her essays, articles, and chronicles, in Arabic and English, have appeared in *al-Ahram Weekly* (Egypt), *Zawaya* (Lebanon), *The Jerusalem Quarterly Report* (Palestine), *Naqd* (Algeria), *MERIP* (USA), *Bidoun* (USA), *Mizna*

(USA), *The London Review of Books* (UK), *The Purple Journal* (USA/France), *Afterall* (USA), in addition to contributions in catalogues for international festivals and artistic events. In 2006, she curated a retrospective of Syrian cinema, which opened at the Lincoln Center in New York City before touring the Arab world. On the occasion of this retrospective, she edited and translated a volume on Syrian cinema, *Insights into Syrian Cinema: Essays and Conversations with Filmmakers* (ArteEast and Rattapallax Press, 2006). Her most recent publication is the artistic book *Beirut Bereft, Architecture of the Forsaken and Map of the Derelict* (Sharjah Biennial, 2009).

**Carrie Tarr** is Professor of Film in the School of Performance and Screen Studies, Kingston University, UK. She has written widely on gender and ethnicity in French cinema. Her publications include: *Diane Kurys* (Manchester University Press, 1999), *Women, Immigration and Identities in France*, coedited with Jane Freedman (Berg, 2000), *Cinema and the Second Sex: Women's Filmmaking in France in the 1980s and 1990s*, with Brigitte Rollet (Continuum, 2001), *Reframing Difference:* beur *and* banlieue *cinema in France* (Manchester University Press, 2005), and *A 'Belle Epoque'? Women in French Society and Culture 1890–1914*, coedited with Diana Holmes (Berghahn, 2006). She has also coedited (with Gill Rye) a special issue of *Nottingham French Studies* on "Focalising the Body in Contemporary Women's Writing and Filmmaking" (2006), and guest-edited a special issue of *Modern & Contemporary France* on "French Cinema: Transnational Cinema?" (2007). She is currently researching the work of migrant and diasporic women filmmakers in Europe.

**Marguerite Waller** is Professor of Women's Studies and Comparative Literature at the University of California, Riverside, United States. Her articles in the areas of feminist theory, contemporary women's activism, Italian and Central European cinema, new media, border art, feminist performance, and European Renaissance literature have been widely published. She is the author of *Petrarch's Poetics and Literary History* (University of Massachusetts Press, 1980) and coeditor of several anthologies: *Frontline Feminisms: Women, War, and Resistance* (Routledge, 2001), *Federico Fellini: Contemporary Perspectives* (University of Toronto Press, 2002), *Dialogue and Difference: Feminisms Challenge Globalization* (Palgrave, 2005), and *The Wages of Empire: Neoliberal Policies, Repression, and Women's Poverty* (Paradigm Publisher, 2007). She has also coedited a special issue of *Social Identities on Emerging Subjects of Neoliberal Globalization* (September, 2006).

# Introduction

*Flavia Laviosa*

The date December 10, 2008 marks the sixtieth anniversary (1948–2008) of the Universal Declaration of Human Rights (UDHR). In 1946, the United Nations was established to weave the international legal fabric that protects fundamental human rights. Two years later, the governments of forty-eight nations crafted the documents that define international human rights standards, laws, and institutions, reflect global values of equality and justice, and set in motion an international movement that holds every government, organization, and individual accountable to the same universal standards of respect for human dignity and freedom. Born of the atrocities of the Second World War, the UDHR was developed by a commission chaired by Eleanor Roosevelt, who described it as "the Magna Carta of all mankind." Over time, international human rights treaties focusing on particular issues have been signed, such as the 1979 treaty protecting the rights of women. The year 2009 marks the thirtieth anniversary of the Convention on the Elimination of Discrimination Against Women (CEDAW).

The UDHR gave humanity a set of values ensconced in international law, proclaimed the promise to respect these rights, and invited people to protect them. "That promise has been broken repeatedly, for sixty years," but "that invitation still stands," comments Larry Cox, Executive Director of Amnesty International USA (2008, 1 and 5), who admits that human rights abuses continue across the world, and recognizes that there are still huge challenges in making that promise a reality for all. In 2004, Amnesty International embarked on a six-year global campaign to stop violence against women with the report "Making Rights a Reality: the Duty of States to Address Violence Against Women." The campaign frames violence against women as a human right abuse, and emphasizes that governments, communities, and individuals have a responsibility to take action to end it. These activities have been important and commendable, however, evidence shows that violence against women continues around the world at an alarming rate. This critical situation is the result of intercultural interpretations, and contemporary women's conditions are consistently determined by "the tension between a universalizing perspective of human rights and the protection of cultural practices that negate such claim" (Pepicelli 2007, 315).[1]

When in 1995 the European Union decided to establish a new framework for its relations with the countries of the Mediterranean basin, the Member States agreed on the Barcelona Declaration and Euro-Mediterranean Partnership (EMP),[2] which was followed by the Euro-Mediterranean Human Rights Network in 1997. The EMP establishes a multilateral framework bringing together economic and security aspects to strengthen political stability and democracy in a shared area of peace and security, to promote free trade and common economic prosperity between the Euro-Mediterranean partners, and to foster stronger relations among the peoples of these countries through cultural, social, and human partnerships. The treaties of the EMP establish that the development of democratic instruments and respect for human rights be the *conditio sine qua non* for commercial and cultural cooperation among the twenty-seven Member States (Rizzi 2004). Gender-specific and women's human rights were addressed and included in the document only in November 2001. Although the EMP does not specifically address women's rights, MEDA programs (the financial body of the Euro-Med Partnership) have funded organizations working on women's issues (Naciri and Nusair 2003).[3]

The dramatic transformations that have characterized Mediterranean countries since the end of the cold war make this redefined economic and political area, comprising the southern European Union, southwestern Balkans, North Africa, and the Middle East, a privileged site for a cultural inquiry focused on a national and supranational (Euro and Mediterranean regions) perspective on women's issues. In light of the major changes that have contributed to the reconfiguration of Mediterranean societies, this book explores the dynamic negotiations and formalizations of local, national, and cross-national women's identities and rights in relation to the many sites of cultural patterns, ritualized forms of behavior, and lifestyles.

Organized around distinct geographical areas and focusing on burning sociopolitical, legal, ethical, and psychological issues, the ten commissioned and selected chapters in this volume examine films directed by women filmmakers, produced around and since the year

2000. These films denounce violence, protest against abuse, expose hypocrisy, and address the consequences of cultural conflicts and changes for women's lives in the Mediterranean regions. More specifically, this book illustrates the hybrid expressions of modernity as manifested in the ways of being a woman in Mediterranean countries, paying special attention to women's cinema as an expression of counter-art and a form of reinterpretation of women's shifting roles. This book also situates feminist arguments on questions of women's psychology, sexual politics, and political militancy. The chapters in this volume address the violation of women's rights as infringement of human rights, and the topics discussed include: family relationships and gender roles, domestic violence and sexual abuse, women's bodies and physical mutilations , moral codes and cultural practices, prejudices and taboos versus rebellion and awareness, women victims/collaborators in organized crime, peacekeepers and women's safety, political militancy and resistance.

These issues are examined through the works of contemporary women filmmakers whose cinema is confrontational and relevant to a women's studies discourse. These artists are motivated by diverse cinematic forms of intervention, take on the responsibility as outspoken and leading advocates for women's problems, and purposefully use their cinematic art to document a new feminist realism. Furthermore, their films are expressions of cultural challenges, political advocacy, and artistic commitment for Mediterranean women's collective experience of struggle. Their cinematic feminism reproduces and structures the discourses of realism recreating prototypical characters and figurations and magnifying the complex and unambiguous truth about women's gender struggles.

Focusing on the neighboring countries around the Mediterranean basin as the general unifying geo-cultural location for a contemporary discussion on women's human, civil, and social rights, this book elaborates a transcultural definition of being a woman in struggle in the twenty-first century, transcending geo-ethnic boundaries and bringing together shared life experiences. The ten chapters, identified by country and related topics, follow a geographical progression starting from the Middle East with Israel, moving westward through the Maghreb, then proceeding northwest to Spain and France, reaching Italy followed by the Balkans in the East, and gradually moving southeast to Greece and across Turkey, to end back in the Middle East with Syria, Jordan, and Palestine. This Mediterranean circumnavigation intends to highlight the geo-thematic connectivity among the nations, to stress the intrinsic continuity among the issues explored in each chapter, and to create a pan-national short-circuit effect of causes and effects of women's struggle within the Mediterranean landscape.

Yosefa Loshitzky opens the collection with her chapter discussing two films that both veils and unveils exclusionist practices of Europeanization and Judaization, while trying to give voice and image to repressed nationalities and peoples. The author argues that Israel's struggle to acquire a Mediterranean identity typifies the contradictions prevalent to the formation of its national identity, deeply rooted in its continuing conflict with the Arab world in general, and with Palestine in particular. Loshitzky analyzes these ambiguities by examining two documentaries, *My Terrorist* (Israel, 2002) and *My Land Zion* (Israel, 2004), both by the Israeli woman director Yulie Cohen-Gerstel. Using the genre of a personal-subjective journey, these films elaborate the process of identity formation by reflecting and articulating arguments around Israeli national identity. Although the director challenges the dominant Zionist narrative and exposes its contradictions, her confessional performativity defines a narcissistic self that remythologizes the Israeli collective political self and its Zionist core.

Florence Martin writes about Maghrebi women directors' struggle to negotiate transcultural and often paradoxical identities as women, others, and individuals split between two cultures. Consequently, their films portray women's winding itineraries across various cultures and systems of cinematic expression. In order to project their own visions of women in a world that is both alien and familiar, these directors establish an interactive connection with their audiences on-screen and offscreen. These women filmmakers also rely on the shared subtext of cultural traditions and available cross-cultural scripts, while they reconfigure issues of class and ethnicity. One of their "wiles" lies in their art of (re)negotiating gendered spaces on screen, and on reframing cinematic narratives. The analysis of two exemplary films, Yamina Bachir-Chouikh's *Rachida* (Algeria, 2002) and Nadia El Fani's *Bedwin Hacker* (Tunisia, 2002) reveals that by shifting the traditional values of gendered spaces the directors construct female images of political and transcultural resistance.

Mónica Cantero explores the discourse of gender violence and abuse in the feature *Te doy mis ojos/Take my eyes* (2003) by Spanish director Iciar Bollaín. The chapter discusses the film's interactional dynamics and linguistic implications through a pragmatic and discourse analysis. Cantero highlights the ways in which gender-based violence is regulated and codified in male-female interaction and how language and images mirror brutality and social control. Mapped against forty years of fascist-national rhetoric on women's duties, relegated to the home and raising of children, the film foregrounds domestic abuse in contemporary Spain as still "normal."

Carrie Tarr's chapter addresses the contribution made by French women filmmakers to the phenomenon known as "extreme" French cinema through an analysis of four controversial films: *Baise-moi/ Fuck Me* (Virginie Despentes and Coralie Trinh Thi, 2000), *Dans ma peau/In My Skin* (Marina de Van, 2002), *Trouble Every Day* (Claire Denis, 2002), and *Anatomie de l'enfer/Anatomy of Hell* (Catherine Breillat, 2004). These films are representative of women directors' intention to explore the medium of cinema by approaching and reworking styles and genres (porn and horror) generally associated with male directors and male audiences. These filmmakers construct female protagonists who are instrumental either in the mutilation of others or the disfiguration of themselves, performed through the style of dark, postmodern fantasy rather than social realism. In their portrayal of women's corporeality, estrangement and violence, nevertheless, these directors offer an unsettling response to the ways in which the female body is controlled in contemporary postmodern but still patriarchal society.

The chapter by Áine O'Healy reviews the artistic achievements of Italian director Roberta Torre, a Milan native who, in 1991, moved to Palermo, where she directed three feature films about Sicilian culture. Torre has described her approach to filmmaking in Sicily as analogous to an ethnographic project, characterized by an uninvolved and objective exploration of a specific social environment. O'Healy, however, argues that Torre's filmic style is not detached and uncritical. The director's first two features, *Tano da morire* (1997) and *Sud side stori* (1999)—both musicals featuring nonprofessional casts— are actually marked by a satirical distance. In her third film, *Angela* (2002), Torre instead employs a more subjective, psychologically realistic register, thus suggesting an empathetic response to the protagonist, portrayed as both accomplice and victim of her husband's criminal activities. Inspired by the experiences of the alienated wife of a Mafia boss, *Angela* offers a perceptive insight into the complex involvement of women in Sicily's network of organized crime, expressing a strong critique of the gender dynamics defining and supporting the Mafia's code of honor.

Marguerite Waller focuses on the documentary, *The Peacekeepers and the Women* (2003), directed by German-based filmmaker Karin Jurschick. The director addresses the extensive admission of women to perform various forms of sex work in U.N. administered Bosnia and Kosovo(a). Waller explains that Jurschick's film avoids taking either the "anti-trafficking" or the "anti-anti-trafficking" position that at present limits most feminist debate on sex trafficking. Instead, through the investigation of the multifaceted violations of women's human rights, paradoxically allowed by human rights enforcement, the director deconstructs the nation-state-based binary oppositional logic that produces the categories of victim and perpetrator. In so doing, Karin Jurschick brings to the fore the gendered economic flows and political contradictions that make migration and sex work the best available option for an increasing number of women living in areas devastated by war and/or in communities undergoing economic restructuring.

Maria Paradeisi's chapter discusses two contemporary Greek directors who represent women's portraits using similarly innovative cinematic narrative styles. The feature films *You Will Regret It* (2002), by Katerina Evangelakou, and *A Song Is Not Enough* (2003), by Elissavet Chronopoulou, present dynamic female personalities who struggle to gain access to the public sphere, to assert their identities, and fulfill their dreams. Both films foreground women's private and individual struggle, subvert their traditional and domestic stereotypes, while following the evolution of women's roles in modern Greece from the late sixties to the beginning of the twenty-first century.

Ruken Öztürk analyzes Turkish director Yeşim Ustaoğlu's third feature film *Waiting for the Clouds* (2004), and her first documentary *Life on their Shoulders* (2004). The feature film is Ayşe/Eleni's private story enacted against a historical, political, and sociocultural background of major tragic events, death, memories, and loss of identity. The film is also an intense portrayal of the female protagonist's journey in search of her family ties and cultural roots. The documentary is a visually captivating film about the annual migration of the Laz villagers to the mountains for the summer months. In both films Ustaoğlu does not offer solutions to women's struggle, but she emphasizes the value of women's solidarity as a way to cope with the pain of a hard life.

Rasha Salti explores in her chapter the work of Hala Alabdallah Yakoub (born in Syria, living in France) and describes her as the boldest and most compelling of experimental women filmmakers in the contemporary Arab world. Salti explains that while Hala Alabdallah is considered a major contributor to a number of masterpieces of Syrian cinema directed by men since the 1980s, she started directing her own films only a few years ago. The director has become famous for creating a rare lyrical cinematic language that combines an extraordinary conceptual approach with forceful emotions, as demonstrated in her two nonfiction, nonnarrative feature-length films, *I Am the One Who Carries Flowers to her Grave* (2006) and *Hey!*

*Don't Forget the Cumin* (2008). Salti describes Hala Alabdallah's profoundly subjective voice as appealingly unadorned, while steering remarkably clear of any navel-gazing. Salti also clarifies that the director's work records the memory of lived experiences that the state claims are untrue and society dismisses as the oblivion of dementia.

The last chapter, by Flavia Laviosa, addresses women's daily fear for their lives in honor-centered societies in Mediterranean regions. The author elaborates on the multilayered reasons for crimes of honor, a practice intended to punish women accused of tarnishing their family's reputation. A review of the works of prominent human rights activists and journalists sheds light specifically on the pervasiveness of honor killings in countries where murder for honor-related cases is legitimized. The second part of the chapter is an in-depth analysis of the work of four women directors whose films denounce the practice of crimes of honor in Turkey, Jordan, and Palestine. These award-winning films, *Crimes of Honour* (Shelley Saywell, 1999), *In the Morning* (Danielle Lurie, 2004), *Vendetta Song* (Eylem Kaftan, 2005), and *Magharat Maria/Maria's Grotto* (Buthina Canaan Khoury, 2007), play a critical role in raising international public awareness of honor killings. Laviosa concludes her chapter explaining that men themselves are victims of social beliefs and cultural traditions as their families put the burden and pressure of committing the murder onto them.

The contributors to this book discuss experiences of abuse, trauma, death, and atrocities against women, through the works of women directors who foreground private accounts of suffering and articulate global manifestations of violence. This book is an open-ended text with multiple entry points and pathways, it also constitutes an unmediated "working through" women's collective testimony without providing answers, suggesting solutions, or attempting to give closure to the gender-based problems raised and the human rights violations discussed. The purpose of this collection is ultimately to engage with a multiplicity of unresolved forms of women's struggle through cinema, and to be immersed in an intersubjectivity of space and temporality, corporeity, and psychology, where the screening of the silenced traumatic experience is bound with a shifting cultural climate in women's *dramascape*.

# Notes

1. "*la tensione tra una prospettiva universalizzante dei diritti umani e la tutela di pratiche culturali che negano tale pretesa.*" (My translation).

2. Following on from the guidelines already drawn up by the European Councils in Lisbon (June 1992), Corfu (June 1994), and Essen (December 1994) and the Commission proposals. The Barcelona Declaration and Euro-Mediterranean Partnership, drafted at the Barcelona Conference of November 27 and 28, 1995, brought together the Ministers for Foreign Affairs of fifteen EU Member States and the following twelve Mediterranean countries: Algeria, Cyprus, Egypt, Israel, Jordan, Lebanon, Malta, Morocco, the Palestinian Authority, Syria, Tunisia, and Turkey. The League of Arab States and the Arab Maghreb Union were also invited, as was Mauritania.

3. This report illustrates the dynamics that hinder and promote women's rights in the Middle East and North Africa and within the Euro-Mediterranean Partnership (EMP). It also presents recommendations on how the EU and Partner States can better address women's rights in the framework of the EMP, and highlights the need (1) to eradicate all forms of discrimination against women within the framework of human rights and democratization; (2) to overcome any reservations to the CEDAW; and (3) to stop treating women's rights as an issue of religious norms and cultural traditions. The report finally suggests that gender mainstreaming should be integrated into all EU and EMP policies and programs, while at the same time affirmative action and specific programs targeted at women should be put in place. www.euromedrights.net.

# References


Cox, Larry. "Promised Broken and Kept." *The Magazine of Amnesty International USA* 32, 3 (Fall 2008): 1.

Cox, Larry. "Protect the Human." *The Magazine of Amnesty International USA* 32, 3 (Fall 2008): 5.

Naciri, Rabéa and Isis Nusair, eds. *The Integration of Women's Rights into the Euro-Mediterranean Partnership: Algeria, Egypt, Israel, Jordan, Lebanon, Morocco, Palestine, Syria and Tunisia*. Available on www.euromedrights.net, 2003.

Pepicelli, Renata. "Donne e diritti nello spazio mediterraneo." In *L'alternativa mediterranea*, ed. Franco Cassano and Danilo Zolo, 315–333. Milan: Feltrinelli, 2007.

———. *2010 un nuovo ordinamento mediterraneo?* Messina: Mesogea, 2004.

Rizzi, Franco. *Un Mediterraneo di conflitti. Storia di un dialogo mancato.* Rome: Meltemi, 2004.

*Israel: Orientalism and Europeanness*

# Chapter One

## Veiling and Unveiling the Israeli Mediterranean: Yulie Cohen-Gerstel's My Terrorist *and* My Land Zion

*Yosefa Loshitzky*

Although the Mediterranean, as a geopolitical entity and as an ideological concept, has rested on a historical process of absorbing, hybridizing, and assimilating different people from diverse ethnic, religious, and national groups, its hegemonic culture imagines, views, and represents itself as the origin and cradle of "Western Civilization" at the expense of excluding its rich and diverse Arab, Muslim, Jewish, Levantine, African, and Semitic cultures.[1] This article explores and reassesses how a particular example of women's cinema produced in Israel, one of the so called Mediterranean countries, both veils and unveils the exclusionist practices of "Europeanization" and "Judaization" by struggling to give a voice and an image to repressed nationalities and cultures. In this article, I argue that Israel's struggle to construct a "Mediterranean identity" epitomizes the contradictions endemic to the country's formation of a national identity and is intimately linked to its continuing conflict with the Arab world in general and the Palestinians in particular. I analyze these contradictions by closely studying two documentary films, *My Terrorist* (Yulie Cohen-Gerstel, Israel, 2002) and *My Land Zion* (Yulie Cohen-Gerstel, Israel, 2004), both made by a politically engaged female Israeli director. Using the device of a personal/subjective journey, these films articulate the process of forming an identity by reflecting, projecting, and constructing debates around Israeli national identity. In particular the films focus around three major foundational sites of struggle over Israeli identity: the Holocaust versus the *Nakba*,[2] the Orient, and the so-called (in an ironic historical twist of the "Jewish Question") Palestinian Question. The films raise fundamental questions about the identity of the "second and third generation" of Jewish Holocaust survivors, the traumatic encounters between Israeli Jews

and Palestinians, and the problems associated with conventional defi-
nitions and understandings of the notions of "Orientalism,"
"Europeanness," "indigenous Mediterranean nativism," and "terrorism." By raising and articulating these issues through a personal cinematic essay, these films challenge the dominant Zionist narrative
and expose its contradictions and cracks. However, I argue that the
films' confessional performativity ultimately constructs a narcissistic
self that, despite its critical aim, remythologizes the Israeli collective
political self and its Zionist core.

## Mediterranean Veils

Since its establishment in 1948, Israel has constructed its image as a
European country, closer to the Western world than to the Arab world
in whose midst it "unfortunately" "found" itself planted. Within this
self-perpetuating fantasy, the Mediterranean, signifying Europe only
by proxy, had no significant role.[3] Only since the mid-1990s has there
been a growing interest, expressed mainly by intellectuals, academics,
and artists, in the Mediterranean as a cultural sphere with which
Israel should affiliate itself. The advocates of the Mediterraneanization
of Israeli society and culture have argued that the Jewish state should
cultivate and celebrate its so called Mediterraneanism as a way of
integrating into the region and reclaiming its historical roots.[4] The
bustling scenes of steamy streets teeming with life, where the people
live their day-to-day lives on balconies, in cafes, and on the beach,
particularly in Tel Aviv, Israel's business and cultural capital and *Ha'ir
Ha'ivrit Ha'rishona* (the first modern Hebrew city) whose name literally means "Hill of Spring" and derives from Herzl's book *Altneuland*,
which envisions the Zionist utopia, are, according to the new "school
of Mediterraneanism," an authentic manifestation of Israel being and
becoming an organic part of the Mediterranean.

There are several explanations for the emergence of the
"Mediterranean" as a cultural and political trope in Israeli discourse.
First, since it coincided with the "return of the old Jew" to Israel's
social, political, and cultural life, it can be viewed as the attempt by
secular Zionism to counter and confront this return, which it (and
particularly its left-leaning part) viewed with suspicion if not with
open hostility. In addition, it can also be explained as a response to
growing Mizrahi critique of the political and cultural dominance of
the Ashkenazim.[5] The newly emergent cult of the Mediterranean, as
such, was an attempt to marginalize and naturalize this critique by

embracing the concept of the Mediterranean, a concept that has the power to appeal to both Ashkenazim and Mizrahim and even to the Ashkenazi elite, which has been traditionally anti-Mizrahi and anti-Arab and continues to see itself as essentially European. The Mediterranean, thus, can be seen as a displacement mechanism to replace the suppressed Oriental aspect of Israeli Jewish culture. Although seemingly deserting the "prestigious" European/Western image (connoting association with the first, developed world) by embracing the more "inferior" Mediterranean culture, Israel has not de-eurocentrized its self-perpetuated European image. On the contrary, it has reenforced its "Europeanness" while fusing it with the "exotic" face of Europe: the Mediterranean, a cultural and political entity, seemingly, less threatening than the Arab/Oriental. Embracing the Mediterranean, a region popular with European tourists and highly esteemed for its cultural heritage, enables Israel to present itself as "Europe-on-the-beach," combining the prestige of civilized Europeanness (after all, Herzl's utopia was a rebuilt Imperial Vienna in the Middle East) with the more informal and relaxed attractiveness of the continent's southern part.

The new Israeli cult of the Mediterranean is a suppression, denial, and veiling of the Arab. Rather than thinking about Israel as a state founded on Palestinian land, and planted within the Arab world, Israelis find it more convenient and less threatening to see the Jewish state as part of a thriving, fluid, open space (symbolized by the sea): the Mediterranean. Linked to this new identity is the suggestion that Israel is no longer a state under siege, a heavily militarized and fortified gated Jewish community in the midst of the Middle East and the Arab world, a "foreign body" as the Arabs commonly describe it, but a Mediterranean country, open to the sea and connected to the rest of the world through its affiliation and association with "the Mediterranean," an attractive part of the world known, among other things, for its rich cuisine, sunny weather, and relaxed way of life. This is undoubtedly an image that Israel would like to project to itself as well as to the outside world. After all, in today's world this is a more attractive image than that of Fortress Israel.[6]

The association of Israel with the Mediterranean Sea also negates the image of the desert, which is traditionally linked with the Arab. Israel, the new Mediterranean image implies, is not a desert land, but rather a sea country. This denial of the Arab, the "troubled Middle East" and the Orient, applies not only to the non-Jewish but also to the Arab element embedded in Jewish culture. It is a total disavowal of the Arab, a suppression of both the Orient within and the Orient "outside," though even the differentiation between inside and outside the Orient is ideologically constructed, as many critical scholars have noted.[7] This flight from the Arab, the wish to separate the Jew and the Arab, is literally and symbolically epitomized by the Apartheid Wall, or what Israel prefers to call, in sanitized language, the "separation wall" or the "security barrier."[8] The adoption of the Mediterranean as the expression of the new Israeli self, thus, attempts to harmonize and tame the irreconcilable schism between self and the other that Zionism created. But, above all, the newly emerging fascination with the Mediterranean is just another stage in the continuing struggle of Zionism (in its diverse forms from religious to secular Left) to create a cult of Israeli "nativism" in order to reclaim the desired status of the indigenous people of Palestine, its real "natives," and, therefore, the undisputed heirs (rather than conquerors or colonizers) of the land.[9]

# The Cruelty of Zionism According to Cohen-Gerstel

The two films by Yulie Cohen-Gerstel, *My Terrorist* and *My Land Zion*, demonstrate and perform the anxiety of the Israeli self in relation to its claim for "the land of Zion." The films have been both marketed and received as the progressive and courageous plea of an Israeli woman director for peace and reconciliation between Israelis and Palestinians. In this article, however, I would like to offer a less laudatory reading of the films (although I do not have any doubt about Cohen-Gerstel's sincerity and good intentions) by attempting to expose their underlying ideology, which is ultimately (though not consciously) another manifestation, consistent with Israel's hegemonic Zionist ideology, of a "mini theory" of Israeli/Jewish "nativism" articulated through the genre of an essayist's personal journey film.

*My Terrorist* tells the story of the special relationship that Cohen-Gerstel developed with Fahad Mihyi, who participated in an attack on crew members of *El Al* (Israel's official air line) in London in 1978 in which she, who was at the time an air stewardess, was injured and another air stewardess who was sitting next to her on the bus was killed. Twenty-two years later, Cohen-Gerstel begins a quest to trace "her terrorist" and, upon discovering that he is rotting in a British jail, decides to help get him released. The process of their evolving relationship is followed by Cohen-Gerstel's personal and introspective journey toward understanding and exploring the Israeli collective ideological myths on which she has been raised. Cohen-Gerstel continues this autobiographical journey in her following film, *My Land Zion*, where she further explores some of Israel's foundational myths and collective memories. The two films are journeys in search of the personal and collective self, and the point of departure of both is that the personal self is inseparable from the collective self.

In *My Terrorist* Cohen-Gerstel interweaves into her life story certain events that mark the official history of Israel, such as the euphoric celebrations following the victory of the 1967 War (known in Israel as "The Six Day War"), the Entebbe rescue operation, Egypt's President Anwar Sadat's historic visit to Jerusalem, Israel's invasion of Lebanon in 1982, and so on. By interweaving her biography with that of the state and blurring the boundaries between the private and the collective (even her voiceover narration frequently shifts from "I" to "we"), and by demonstrating how her personal biography is intimately connected with the biography of the nation, she introduces herself as both an active agent in the making of this history and as the passive, uncritical recipient of its official interpretation. This juxtaposition of the private and the collective constructs Cohen-Gerstel as the summation of the collective I, the ideal Israeli subject. The end of her journey culminates in the conclusion that life is more important than land, and yet she chooses to stay in this disputed and tormented land precisely because of what she defines as "the land," her physical sense of belonging to the tactile "earthiness" of the land with its peculiar Mediterranean smells and landscapes.

It is important to stress, however, that despite the fact that Cohen-Gerstel's self is presented as embodying the Israeli collective self and the body politic of the Israeli state, her experience of Israeliness in the land of Zion is a very particular one, representing not "the collective I" but "the privileged minority I" to which she belongs. Cohen-Gerstel is a contemporary "replica" of the mythological *Sabra* (the new Jew, born in Israel/Palestine and therefore perceived by Zionist ideology as indigenous and native, an antithesis to the despised "old Jew").[10] She comes from the crème de la crème of the Israeli elite, known in Hebrew as *"Melah Ha'aretz"* (salt of the earth). She is a sixth-generation descendant of the *"old yishuv"* (the pre-Zionist Jewish community in Palestine) and, furthermore, her grandfather, Aharon Chlusch, was a member of the old Yishuv Sephardi aristocracy and the founder of Neve Tzedek, the first Jewish neighborhood of Tel Aviv. Currently a gentrified area full of cafes, restaurants, and arty boutiques, Neve Tzedek, since the outbreak of the *al-Aqsa* Intifada, has for many Israelis replaced the "Oriental exoticism" of Jaffa, "bride of the sea" as the Palestinians called this Arab city, "long considered Tel Aviv's ancient and backward alter ego" (Levine 1999, 15).[11]

As a sixth-generation "native," Cohen-Gerstel implies that she has a stronger claim to Zion as her land than most Israelis, who are first-, second-, or third-generation immigrants. She is also a daughter of *Palmach* (pre-state Jewish militia) fighters who constituted the military and political elite class of Israel until the rise to power of the right-wing *Likud* party in 1977. She was raised in *Tzahala* (named after *Tzahal* the Hebrew name of the IDF, the Israeli Army), a famous and affluent Tel Aviv suburb inhabited by former generals, the military, and political elite of Israel. Among Cohen-Gerstel's neighbors in this gated community, this fortress within fortress Israel, were Yitzhak Rabin, Moshe Dayan, Ezer Weizman (who was also a relative), Ariel Sharon, and other prominent members of the intertwined Israeli political and military elites. Cohen-Gerstel is thus part of the privileged Israeli ruling class and while her questioning of Israel's myths and dominant beliefs is, to a certain degree, and certainly in the eyes of mainstream Israeli dominant ideology, critical and unusually courageous, it is not particularly radical.

Although Cohen-Gerstel's films problematize the morality of some of Israel's hegemonic ideologies, the overarching question that structures the narrative, as well as the moral dilemma posited at the core of the films, is intimately linked to the narcissistic self, introduced as the mother-self or the self of the m/other. Despite Cohen-Gerstel's awareness of the colonial aspect of Zionism and the brutality of the occupation and the fact that she, although not explicitly, even raises the idea of a single state for and of all its citizens, an idea embraced by some Palestinian and Israeli intellectuals, she is more concerned about endangering her daughters by continuing to stay in Israel. While on a journey to Masada with her friend, the Israeli left-Zionist historian Motti Golani, they begin to discuss Israeli and Jewish history. Confronted by Golani's desire to investigate deeper into the Zionist moral entitlement to the land, Cohen-Gerstel retreats to the traditional niche (the womb) reserved for women in Israeli nationalism and says: "I'm not interested in thorough political analysis. I come from the place of the mother." Occupying the traditional space of the mother in national discourse, she invokes the biological side of Israeli motherhood: "How can an animal raise its offspring in a dangerous environment, risking their lives?" she asks. Thus "biology" and "instincts" configure her narrative and structure the route of her journey. Her morality seems to be grounded in social Darwinism and the desire to preserve her Jewish offspring, rather than in a concern about the suffering caused to the Palestinians and the injustice inflicted on them. Although Cohen-Gerstel acknowledges the Palestinian tragedy (she even attends *Nakba* ceremonies for the first time in her life) and the atrocities committed by Israel against the Palestinian people—described by some Israeli critics as her courageous exposure of the "cruelty of Zionism"[12]—this cruelty is presented more as the cruelty of Zionism toward its own chosen members, the Israeli Jews. The prime victims of Zionism from the standpoint of Cohen-Gerstel are not the Palestinians or the Mizrahi Jews, about whom Ella Shohat wrote in her groundbreaking article "Sephardim in Israel: Zionism from the Standpoint of Its Jewish Victims" (whose title is a variation on Edward Said's famous article "Zionism from the Standpoint of Its Victims"), but, ironically, the children of the Zionist elite, people like herself and her daughters.

The question of whether the decision to raise a family in Israel is a sensible one runs throughout the two films, constituting the ideological core of Cohen-Gerstel's journey. Even her sympathy toward the so-called "Palestinian Question" is grounded in emotionalism traditionally attributed to women.[13] Inherent in the personal narrative voice used by Cohen-Gerstel is the entire absence of the terrorist Mihyi as a subject. As Gali Gold observes, the gaze on the Palestinian other is problematic and Cohen-Gerstel's look at herself is "only partially reflexive" (Gold 2007, 95). Mihyi, although he is the structuring absence of the narrative, is never to be seen, or heard. His letters are read by Cohen-Gerstel, subjected to her point of view, to her voice (both literally and metaphorically) and, fittingly, also to her voiceover narration and interpretation. We are granted only a brief glance of his face from an old photo published in a British newspaper. The scarce visibility accorded to "her terrorist" contradicts her declared view of her film as a journey, "an attempt to find out what made us, Israelis and Palestinians, into enemies." What, however, really counts for Cohen-Gerstel is herself, how the Palestinian other affects her and the Israeli self. The journey (unlike, for example, Michele Khleifi's and Eyal Sivan's journey film *Route 181* (France, 2004)) is not a journey taken by two partners, buddies, or even equally captivating protagonists, but by the colonizer alone who uses the other as a trigger for colonial anxiety. Mihyi is only a catalyst, a backdrop for the tormented Israeli self. He is not, as Gold observes, "constituted as a subject" (2007, 97). Furthermore, he is used merely as a mirror, a passive receptacle for the projection of Jewish Israeli fears and anxieties. Mihyi is left "without biography or history" (Gold 2007, 97), with neither his personal biography nor the history of his people. Even the fact that Mihyi is not a Palestinian but an Iraqi who was mobilized into the Palestinian cause is not sufficient to motivate her to further explain and explore his life. His absent presence is portrayed right from the beginning of the film as menacing and aggressive, and Cohen-Gerstel's most powerful traumatic memory of the attack is his hostile look at his potential "victims." This is counterbalanced by the more progressive ending of the film that uses a quote from her grandfather's book *Parashat Hayay* ("The Story of My Life"), which appealed, at the early stages of Zionist settlement in Palestine, not to ignore the people of this land, an appeal that went against the grain of the Zionist propaganda of the time, epitomized by the slogan "a land without people for a people without land."[14]

Whereas *My Terrorist* might be characterized as an unusual personal story that brings into relief the crisis of Cohen-Gerstel's questioning of her naïve belief in Zionism, *My Land Zion*'s emphasis is more on the relationships with the physical land, creating an interesting, though problematic, version of Israeli *Sumoud* (an Arabic word describing the Palestinian principle of stubborn and steadfast clinging to the land). Built as a personal essay, a subjective, yet ideological, journey into some of the foundations of the director's self and her collective's memories, *My Land Zion* constitutes an interesting sociocultural document on the Israeli politics of belonging, or, rather, the politics of constructing belonging. This politics is expressed mostly by the prominence of the theme of house/home in the film. The opening scene of *My Land Zion* establishes the film's ideological tone. Cohen-Gerstel is seen mowing the lawn in front of her house in *Tzahala*'s satellite suburb *Ramat Hachayal* (literally Soldier's Heights).[15] She is wearing shorts and sports shoes and holding on tightly to the heavy and noisy lawn mower. Despite her contemporary attire, her image recalls the mythical image of the Zionist woman pioneer, the new Jewish woman (who actually appears in some of the archive footage used in the film). It is the image of a physically very strong and active woman literally occupied with the occupation of the land.

This personal act of reclaiming the land, Cohen-Gerstel's variation on the Palestinian *Sumoud*, assumes the symbolism associated with possessing and conquering the land, so typical of Zionism from its early beginnings. The impression conveyed by the visual image of Cohen-Gerstel's act of "conquering the land," though described using lyrical and intimate language and supported by her soft feminine voiceover, is nevertheless one of aggression. The irony is that despite the voiceover narration, which explains that she likes to mow the grass on Saturday morning because it is the most quiet and peaceful time of the week when she likes to listen to this silence and enjoy the smell of the earth, there is nothing silent or tranquil about the scene; it is dominated by the aggressive and annoying noise of the motor, which merges with the image of the mythical Israeli bulldozer (that actually is both referred to and seen in some of the film's scenes), a Zionist icon of aggression.[16] Hence, what seems at first to be a fragment of peaceful suburban life becomes an emblematic symbol of aggressive nationalism, recalling continuing Zionist ambitions to turn the desert into a cultivated garden, an "empty" land into a green European Eden in a zealous pioneering spirit, which Cohen-Gerstel, unconscious of or undisturbed by the contradiction, herself mocks in one of the archive footage scenes of the film. The act of mowing also invokes the erotic symbolism assumed by the Zionist act of conquering and penetrating the land, which was usually reserved, in the rhetoric of early visual Zionism, to the male body of the "new Jew." Yet, Cohen-Gerstel's strong and muscular body is a postmodern variation on the old theme.[17]

In addition to its affiliation with the long tradition of Zionist imagery and rhetoric, the mowing of the lawn is also a classic suburban image associated with the Anglo-Saxon world in general, and America in particular. Perhaps this curious associative juxtaposition of Zionist imagery with mascots of American suburbia conveys, more than anything else in this thesis film, the true contemporary Israeli zeitgeist. Furthermore, the type of Israeli-style *Sumoud*, inspired by the rhetoric of early Zionism, is practiced in an affluent, Tel Aviv suburb, located only a few miles away from the Palestinian occupied territories, the "hollow land" in Eyal Weizman's imploded language (Weizman, 2007). The aggression of suburban Zionism is reinforced by the noisy reclamation enacted against the silence of the Sabbath. The image of the mowing, thus, becomes also an image of aggressive secularism because, according to Jewish law, Jews are not supposed to work on the Sabbath. Ultimately, the mowing of the lawn in suburban fortress *Ramat Ha'hayal* becomes emblematic of contemporary Israel combining eroticized military conquest of the land (a continuation of the original Zionist colonial project of *kibbush ha'adama* (the conquering of the land)) and the suburbanization and Americanization of fortress Israel. It is an image of a not-so-holy marriage of military colonialism and the capitalist globalization of the American dream, a merger of Anglo-Saxon style suburbia with military Zionism.

The theme of the house in fortress *Tzahala* and *Ramat Ha'hayal* echoes and reverberates in a number of other images of houses/homes in the film. In fact, the two documentaries together provide a cinematic

meditation on the meaning and significance of the big home (Palestine/
Zion as the Jewish homeland) and the small homes that comprise it.
There are several symbolic houses in *My Land Zion* and they all raise
issues of the politics and ethics associated with the notion of home in
the context of Jewish history and its tragic conflation with Palestinian
history. The complex web of connections, links, and associations
among the three other houses/homes that appear in the film become
a metonym, like in other significant Israeli documentaries, for example, in Amos Gitai's *Bayit* (House/Home, 1980), of the overlapping of
two historical tragedies: the Holocaust and the *Nakba*, which, in the
suggestive words of the Polish-born Israeli Jewish poet Avot Yeshurun
(1974), are distorted into "but one Holocaust of the Jewish people."
Another significant house/home that appears in the film is that of
Shula, Holocaust survivor from Hungary and the mother of Motti
Golani, whose book *Milhamot lo Korot Meatzman* (Wars Do Not
Just Happen)[18] is used as the historical and intellectual framing of the
film, in a fashion invoking Claude Lanzman's use of *The Destruction
of the European Jews* by Raul Hilberg in *Shoah* (1985).

The house, located in what is now the Jewish village *Kfar Daniel*,
faces a deserted and destroyed Arab house, a remnant of the Palestinian
village of Daniel. The village, which had numbered 2,784 inhabit-
ants, was destroyed and its population expelled in 1948 as part of the
Dani Operation to ethnically cleanse the Arab population of the
Palestinian towns of Ramla and Lydda (today, Lod).[19] Cohen-Gerstel
politely confronts Shula, asking her if she has ever seen, noticed, or
taken an interest in this house. Shula acknowledges that she has never
paid any attention to the ruined house, adding: "This is one of the
things we have ignored." The irony is, of course, that Shula, the
Holocaust survivor who was expelled from her own home in southern
Hungary, a house that ever since has been occupied by local Hungarian
people, built her new home upon the ruins of a Palestinian home,
completely oblivious to the tragedy inflicted on the Palestinians in the
name of her personal tragedy and the collective tragedy of her people,
the Jews. The blindness to the other's tragedy is enhanced by the
architecture of oblivion and erasure resurrected in front of her and
the viewer's gazes. While one tragedy is, seemingly, redeemed (Shula
has a new home), the other tragedy is not only physically and historically obliterated from memory but it, in the powerful words of Lila
Abu-Lughod, "continues into the present in every house demolished
by an Israeli bulldozer, with every firing from an Apache helicopter,
with every stillbirth at a military checkpoint, with every village
divided from its fields by the 'separation' wall, and with every

Palestinian who still longs to return to a home that is no more" (Abu-Lughod 2007, 103).

The journey to Golani's mother's home village in southern Hungary is deliberately inserted into the film, not only to explain why the Israelis are so oblivious to the Palestinian tragedy (as Golani's mother confesses, "when we arrived here we were too occupied with our own tragedy") but also in order to lessen the moral entitlement of the Palestinian right of return. During the journey, Golani is joined by his daughter (who is about to join the Israeli Army) and Cohen-Gerstel by her daughter (who is not sure yet if she will join the army for ideological reasons, in spite of the mandatory requirement for military service in Israel). The people who now live in Shula's home/house not only deny that the Jews have a right of return (and, indeed, the Jews have never claimed such a right) but even the right of visiting and looking at their occupied houses/homes. The Hungarian family who now lives in Shula's house refuses to show her former home to the visitors from Israel, and they leave. The political message of the film has thus been made: the Israelis are no worse than others (actually they are even better), and furthermore, the right of return is a historically and politically infeasible solution to the conflict. The Jews cannot return to Europe and the Palestinians cannot return to Palestine.[20] Thus, the three houses, Shula's lost home in Hungary, her new home in Israel, built in a destroyed Palestinian village, and the ruined Palestinian house, the only physical remnant of the *Nakba* and its involuntary memorial, become an allegory to a saga of lost and "gained" homes, old and new homes, and ultimately of homelessness.

## Conclusion: Collective Suicide, *Sumoud*, and Exile

One of the major scenes in *My Land Zion* revolves around the director's journey, guided by her friend, the historian Golani, to Masada, one of the significant sites in preexilic Jewish history, which still functions as an active *lieu du memoire* for Israelis raised on renewed mythologies constructed by Zionist interpretation of this site as one of Jewish collective suicide.[21] Much of the film subverts the Zionist ideological lesson derived from Masada, which suggests that the land is more important than human life. For Cohen-Gerstel, the ultimate message is the opposite: life is more important than the land. The cult of death and collective sacrifice advocated and perpetuated by the state of Israel and revitalized by the enduring power of the Masada myth does not suit her. On the contrary, Cohen-Gerstel attempts to revive the words of warning voiced by her grandfather, who in his book called for an acknowledgment of the Palestinian presence and peaceful coexistence between Arabs and Jews on the land.

Yet, the end of the film seems to contradict Cohen-Gerstel's newly gained understanding of the Palestinian-Israeli conflict. She states that, ultimately, her sensual and emotional connection to the land explains why she chooses to live in Israel despite risking her daughters' lives: "I look and I love what I see, the landscapes, the smell, the earth, the sea, it is my love of the landscape of Eretz Israel[22] that makes me stay here." What might seem to the spectator, particularly the one not familiar with the complexities of political positioning within Israel's public sphere, to be Cohen-Gerstel's spontaneous epiphany, a moment of revelation of "natural belonging" and "indigenous nativity," in fact constitutes a veiling and unveiling of the core ideology of the Israeli Zionist Left, which consistently denies the basic right of the Palestinian people to the land of Zion. In this respect, Cohen-Gerstel, much like her intellectual guru, the historian Motti Golani, is an authentic representative of "soft Zionism," a political stance typical of the positioning of the Israeli Left (currently defined as left of the Labor party) in relation to the Palestinians.

It is common among scholars of Israeli cinema to argue that Israeli documentary cinema, in contrast to Israeli fictional feature films, is more attuned and sensitive to Israeli society at large and to the Palestinian-Israeli conflict in particular. Many of these documentaries, much like Cohen-Gerstel's film, are domestic ethnographies, which engage with the Palestinian-Israeli conflict through the construction and deconstruction of the trope of the private home and its ambivalent relationships with the public homeland. Some of these films, for example, Simone Bitton's *Wall* (France, 2004), even succeed in crossing boundaries and borders, in breaking down the wall, and challenging the idea of an exclusively Jewish national homeland in Palestine. They implicitly or explicitly call for a real integration, rather than domination, of the "new Jews" in the Arab Mediterranean. In contrast, contemporary Israeli fictional cinema, despite having recently infiltrated the international market and having enjoyed some commercial and critical success, is escapist and evasive. Films such as *Late Marriage* (Dover Kashshvili, Israel, 2001), *Broken Wings* (Nir Bergman, Israel, 2002) and others were applauded by international critics for "humanizing" Israel by transcending the obsessive and "tiresome" preoccupation with the occupation, showing that there is "an-other" Israel, one untouched by the Palestinian-Israeli conflict. Yet, however naïvely appealing "an-other" Israel may be, I obviously cannot and do not want to join the international critics in praising filmmakers who deny reality and injustice in the name of "human" stories. Moreover, I agree that the critical voices of Israeli cinema are best articulated by documentaries, many of them made by women directors, who until the 1990s played only a very marginal role in the Israeli film production scene. However, Cohen-Gerstel's work, as I have demonstrated in my brief discussion, cannot be counted among the documentaries that have succeeded in crossing boundaries and making real demands, as they are still situated under the shadow of the Apartheid Wall.

# Notes

1. For an interesting discussion of this issue, see Alcalay (1993).
2. The *Nakba* (catastrophe) is the word the Palestinians use to describe the tragic events following the 1948 War that ended with the establishment of the State of Israel and the forced exodus of the majority of Palestinians who lived in historical Palestine. The Nakba, in the words of Lila Abu-Lughod, "has thus become, both in Palestinian memory and history, the demarcation line between two qualitatively opposing periods. After 1948, the lives of the Palestinians at the individual, community and national level were dramatically and irreversibly changed." (Sa'di and Abu-Lughod 2007, 3)
3. Israel is the only non-European country that participates in the Eurovision Song Contest. It also enjoys a preferential status in the EU and participates in European football leagues.
4. One of the most common criticisms leveled at the Eurocentric (Central and/or Eastern European) attitude of the founders of Tel Aviv is that they completely ignored the Mediterranean Sea, creating a line of buildings near the shore that blocked the sea breeze from cooling the city during the long, hot summer. Literally and symbolically Tel Aviv, the first Zionist city, turned its back to the Mediterranean Sea.
5. Although they had long been the majority, the Mizrahim continued to be treated in Israel as a minority, yet their culture and presence had come to fully transform the official parameters of Israeli society. Originally, as Amiel Alcalay suggests, a component of the pejorative label used to institutionally categorize non-European Jews (*benei `edot ha-mizrah* / "the offspring of the Oriental communities"), the word *mizrah* ("East") and *mizrahi* ("Easterner") "gradually took on qualities of pride and defiance as the *mizrahim* (plural: "Easterners") came to describe themselves." See Alcalay (1994). For the first major Mizrahi critique in the realm of Israeli cinema, see Shohat (1989). There is a latent association between the notion of Israeli identity and Ashkenazi origin. This association causes difficulties

in the application of this identity to Orientals (and definitely to Arabs) as well as, to a certain extent, to women. In Israeli collective identity the Orientals are categorized as occupying a (constant) transitional phase from Oriental identity to an Israeli-Western one. The Orientals thus live in a paradoxical situation: their countries of origin constitute for the non-Orientals an obstacle in their attempt to acquire an Israeli identity. So, despite the fact that most of them try hard to achieve an Israeli identity and are officially identified as Israelis, they are not perceived as such by either the Ashkenazim or by the members of their own ethnic groups who internalized the Ashkenazi-dominated conception of Israeli identity.

6. For an excellent analysis of the import of Fortress Israel to the new post 9/11 global space, see Naomi Klein, "How War Was Turned into a Brand" in *The Guardian*, and "Losing the Peace Incentive: Israel as Warning," in her new book *The Shock Doctrine: The Rise of Disaster Capitalism*. French President Nicolas Sarkozy's launch of a new Mediterranean Union in Paris on July 13, 2008, in which Israel, alongside several Arab countries and the Palestinian leader Mahmoud Abbas, participated, represents the political agenda behind the cultural trope.

7. See Shohat (1989) and Shohat (2006, 201–232, 330–358).

8. For a further discussion of the Wall, see Loshitzky (2006, 327–335) and Weizman (2007, 161–184).

9. It is beyond the scope of this article to even outline the history of Zionist attempts to cultivate theories and practices of "nativism" and "indigenization," in both the political and cultural realms, in order to reclaim "Zion." It should be mentioned, however, that one of the prominent examples is the Canaanite movement, a literary and artistic movement active in Israel during the years following the 1948 War, led by the poet and intellectual Yonatan Ratosh. Many of the members of this group were former members of the *Etzel* and *Lehi* underground organizations. Canaanite ideology was based on the belief that a new Hebrew nation, culture, and identity, separate and distinct from the historical Jewish people and the Jewish Diaspora, had come into being in the Land of Israel (*Eretz Israel*). The Canaanites rejected the cultural heritage of Diaspora Jewry. For an interesting critique (very similar to my own) of the emergence of Mediterraneanism as a strategy to do away with the "Palestinian problem" altogether and to exclude Arabs and Muslims from this vision, see Gil Z. Hochberg (2007). See, in particular, "Mediterranean Israel or The Levant without Its Arabs": 69–72.

10. The word *Sabra* means cactus fruit, which is tough and thorny on the outside and sweet and tender on the inside.

11. For an interesting self-reflexive account of the memory of Jaffa, see Lila Abu-Lughod, Lila, "Return to Half-Ruins: Memory, Postmemory, and Living History in Palestine," in Sa'di and Abu-Lughod (2007, 77–108).

12. Cited on the back of the cassette of the Hebrew version of the film and attributed to Yaron London (an Israeli writer and broadcaster), in London and Kirshenbaum, Israeli Television Channel 10 (September 6, 2004).
13. Her ability to cross over to the "enemy" side and to take an interest in "her terrorist" invokes the prominent motif of "forbidden love" narratives in Israeli cinema. For a discussion of this trope, see Loshitzky (2001).
14. For an interesting discussion of this myth, see chapters five and six in Rose (2004, 80–116).
15. *Ramat Hachayal* is a suburb near *Tzahala*. Whereas *Tzahala* is a suburb that was built for generals, *Ramat Hachayal* is a suburb for low-ranking officers.
16. For a further discussion of the factual and symbolic place of the bulldozer in Israeli and Palestinian life and ideology, see Loshitzky (2001, 119–121; 2002, 134–151).
17. For a further discussion of the erotic and libidinal dimensions of *Kibbush Ha'adama* and the Zionist body (the new Jew) versus the diasporic body (the old Jew), see, among others, Boyarin, Gilman (1991), Biale (1992), particularly chapter 8, "Zionism as an Erotic Revolution," Doneson (1997, 140–152). For a comparison between the construction of the Sabra image and the New American Adam, see Shohat (1997, 88–105) and Shohat (1998). For a discussion of the male body in Israeli cinema, see Loshitzky (2002).
18. The most prominent and controversial argument that Golani presents seems to be that peace has not always headed Israel's list of priorities and war has not always headed its neighbors' list of priorities.
19. For a further discussion of this operation, see Pappe (2006).
20. The irony is that when Golani is rushing his daughter and Cohen-Gerstel to go and see the house in the Hungarian village, he says "*nikanes yallah!*" (Let's go inside). Neither Golani nor Cohen-Gerstel are conscious of the irony of Golani using the Arabic word "*Yallah!*" which, like many other words, has been assimilated into Hebrew slang.
21. An example of a much more radical and critical treatment of the enduring myth of Masada (and also of Samson) by Israeli Zionist ideology is Avi Mograbi's essayist documentary, *Avenge but One of My Two Eyes* (Israel/France, 2005). For a discussion of the ideological significance of Masada in the Zionist national narrative, see Zerubavel (1995).
22. The use of the notion of "Eretz Israel" is ideologically and politically loaded. It is a biblical notion that can be literally translated as "the land of Israel." Within the framework of Israeli political discourse it has become associated with the Right and the settlers' movement. Cohen-Gerstel must have been aware of the resonance of her linguistic choice. It should also be noted that Golani, despite his "soft Zionism," is the head of the department of "Limudey Eretz Israel" (Studies of the Land of Israel) at Haifa University.

# References

Alcalay, Amiel. *After Jews and Arabs: Remaking Levantine Culture.* Minneapolis and London: University of Minnesota Press, 1993.

————. "The Keys to the Garden: An Introduction." *The Literary Review* 37, 2 (Winter 1994), A special issue, "The Key to the Garden: Israeli Writing in the Middle East": 153–155.

Biale, David. *Eros and the Jews: From Biblical Israel to Contemporary America.* New York: Basic Books, 1992.

Boyarin, Daniel. "The Colonial Drag: Zionism, Gender, and Mimicry." Unpublished paper.

Doneson, Judith. "The Image Lingers: The Feminization of the Jew in *Schindler's List.*" In *Spielberg's Holocaust: Critical Perspectives on Schindler's List,* ed. Yosefa Loshitzky, 140–152. Bloomington and Indianapolis: Indiana University Press, 1997.

Gilman, Sander. *The Jew's Body.* London: Routledge, 1991.

Gold, Gali. "Israeli Women's Documentaries 1988–2004." PhD dissertation, University of East London, 2007.

Hilberg, Raul. *The Destruction of the European Jews.* New York and London: Holmes and Meier, 1985.

Hochberg, Gil Z. *In Spite of Partition: Jews, Arabs, and the Limits of Separatist Imagination.* Princeton and Oxford: Princeton University Press, 2007.

Klein, Naomi. "Losing the Peace Incentive: Israel as Warning." In *The Shock Doctrine: The Rise of Disaster Capitalism,* by Naomi Klein, 423–442. London: Allen Lane, 2007.

————. "How War Was Turned into a Brand." *The Guardian,* June 16, 2007, 34.

Levine, Mark. "A Nation from the Sands." *National Identities* 1, 1 (1999).

Loshitzky, Yosefa. *Identity Politics on the Israeli Screen.* Austin, Texas: University of Texas Press, 2001.

————. "A Tale of Three Cities: Amos Gitai's Urban Trilogy." *Framework* 43, 1 (Spring 2002): 134–151.

————. "Pathologising Memory: From the Holocaust to the *Intifada.*" *Third Text* 20, 3–4 (May/July 2006): 327–335.

Pappe, Ilan. *The Ethnic Cleansing of Palestine.* Oxford: Oneworld, 2006.

Rose, John. *The Myths of Zionism.* London and Ann Arbor: Pluto Press, 2004.

Sa'di, Ahmad H. and Abu-Lughod, Lila, eds. *Nakba: Palestine, 1948 and the Claims of Memory.* New York and Chichester: Columbia University Press, 2007.

Shohat, Ella. "Sephardim in Israel: Zionism from the Standpoint of Its Jewish Victims." *Social Text* 19/20 (Fall 1988).

————. *Israeli Cinema: East/West and the Politics of Representation.* Austin, Texas: University of Texas Press, 1989.

————. "Columbus, Palestine and Arab-Jews: Toward a Relational Approach to Community Identity." In *Cultural Readings of Imperialism: Edward Said and the Gravity of History*, ed. Keith Ansell Pearson, Benita Parry, and Judith Squires, 88–105. London: Lawrence and Wichart, 1997.

————. "Taboo Memories and Diasporic Visions: Columbus, Palestine and Arab-Jews." In *Performing Hybridity*, ed. Jennifer Fink and May Joseph. Minnesota and London: University of Minnesota Press, 1998.

————. "Taboo Memories, Diasporic Visions: Columbus, Palestine, and Arab-Jews," and "Rupture and Return: Zionist Discourse and the Study of Arab-Jews." In, *Taboo Memories, Diasporic Voices*, ed. Ella Shohat, 201–232 and 330–358. Durham and London: Duke University Press, 2006.

Weizman, Eyal. "The Wall: Barrier Archipelagos and the Impossible Politics of Separation." In *Hollow Land: Israel's Architecture of Occupation*, ed. Eyal Weizman, 161–184. London and New York: Verso, 2007.

Yeshurun, Avot. *HaShever HaSuri Afrikani* (The Syrian-African Rift: Poems). Tel Aviv: Siman Kria, 1974 (in Hebrew, translation mine).

Zerubavel, Yael. *Recovered Roots: Collective Memory and the Making of an Israeli National Tradition*. Chicago: University of Chicago Press, 1995.

*Maghreb: Political and Transcultural Resistance*

# Chapter Two

# The Wiles of Maghrebi
# Women's Cinema

*Florence Martin*


## Introduction

Maghrebi women's cinema is a dynamic, fascinating paradox: while solidly anchored for over forty years in the history of Maghrebi cinema,[1] it has nonetheless manufactured and sustained an uncommon form of resistance that goes against the grain of at least two superimposed patriarchal systems: the global system of film production, and the regional configuration of culture, society, and politics particular to Algeria, Morocco, and Tunisia.

Often trained in Europe, Maghrebi women directors, who are at least bicultural, find themselves negotiating transcultural, often paradoxical identities in their filmmaking practices. As a result, their cinema often portrays women's winding itineraries across various cultures set against a complex and ever changing Mediterranean landscape. Sometimes their female protagonists travel from one space to the next; at other times they are filmed in fixed locations, the meanings of which "travel" and resonate above and beyond the cultural script underpinning the filmic narratives. By shifting the values of traditional gendered physical spaces, the directors efficiently create and project images of political and transcultural resistance.

In order to describe female Maghrebi directors' distinct cinematic language of resistance, I propose to analyze two films, both released in 2002—Yamina Bachir-Chouikh's *Rachida* (Algeria and France) and Nadia El Fani's *Bedwin Hacker* (Tunisia and France)—in which each director expresses several levels of empowering resistance in her treatment of space. In both films the director, by manipulating both the intricacies of the cinematographic language and a plural referential reality offscreen, creates a filmic narrative that addresses several audiences at once. Thanks to the deft manipulation of the familiar and the unfamiliar, or, in Freudian terms, the *Heimlich* and the *Unheimlich*, each renegotiates traditionally gendered notions of spaces and "home" and reconfigures—at times even erases—the patriarchal boundaries that used to define them.

## Maghrebi Women Directors are Transcultural Agents...

Maghrebi directors are transcultural: conversant in at least two cultures (if not three: French, Arabic, and Amazigh or Berber), they are able to interpret one culture with the tools of another and vice versa. Some have trained at film schools in France (e.g., both Moufida Tlatli and Farida Benlyazid attended FEMIS in Paris), while others trained at home (e.g., Yamina Bachir-Chouikh studied to become a film editor in Algiers; Nadia El Fani started her career in Tunisia). They have all traveled between France and the Maghreb and know the codes of both cultures. Beyond this original dual connection, they can also claim some affiliation with a variety of other discrete groups, for example, a specific social class, a specific ethnicity, speakers of Arabic, of French, of Tamazight/Berber. Their films often reflect this plural context superimposed on the already complex landscape of the Maghreb.

The very term "Maghreb" also has a transcultural history. From its original Arabic meaning, *al maghrib*, "where the sun sets," "the West," or "Morocco," it has come to name a geopolitical alliance (the "Union of the Arab Maghreb," i.e., Libya, Tunisia, Algeria, Morocco, and Mauritania). In today's Arabic and French parlance, it replaces the former colonizer's term *Afrique du Nord* (North Africa) to designate three independent countries currently governed by strong regimes: Morocco, Algeria, and Tunisia. In the end, the name "Maghreb" has two functions: it both spells out the region's Arabic cultural affiliation and signals a will to deny or transcend its recent past under colonization.[2]

This first duality is only the tip of the iceberg, for the Maghreb does not erase the multiple traces of its Mediterranean history: it leaves them exposed (like the Roman amphitheater and the mosaics of Cherchell in Algeria) or recycles them, using the old stones to erect new dwellings. The Maghreb is so haunted by both the histories of its wars and occupiers and the imported narratives performed and adapted on its shores that it is impossible to ignore—in what Braudel (1998) called the *"longue durée"* (long duration)—its entanglements with the wider Mediterranean region. The latter, with its interweaving of cultures and tale-tellers (the Phoenicians, the Carthaginians, the

Romans, the Arabs from the Peninsula, the Andalusians and later the Italians, the Spanish, the French), forms a fertile multi-accented open space for the trade and recycling of multiple narratives. It is against this nurturing backdrop that these directors create their own films.

This, however, is but one transcultural aspect of the Maghrebi filmmaking process, as the latter quickly becomes enmeshed with the transnational phenomenon of global film production. Algeria and Tunisia, for instance, produce films via a complex system of international coproductions: the funding gathered at home, issued by a government agency and/or a private or semiprivate production company, is insufficient. Filmmakers therefore set up their own production companies (e.g., Nadia El Fani's *Z'yeux Noirs*) and search for funds in Europe, such as *Fonds Sud*,[3] *Canal+* (a private French TV channel that coproduced Bachir-Chouikh's *Rachida*), or the Hubert Balls Fund in Holland. However, these few funding sources are also open to directors outside the Maghreb, from sub-Saharan Africa, Asia, Eastern Europe, or South America. This competitive search for money, on the basis of the film script, immediately raises the question: to whom must the film speak? The funding agency first and foremost? The art house moviegoers? The festival juries in the North? The Maghrebi population? The latter, who, in the 1960s and 1970s, at least in Algeria and Tunisia, enthusiastically attended regular film screenings at various cinemas throughout the two countries, seems to now steer away from the poorly kept theaters that mostly show American, Egyptian, and Bollywood films. Film distribution in the Maghreb is highly problematic: faced with (a) the insurmountable global competition of the Hollywood machine that is strongly implanted in the local film theaters; (b) little or no advertising at home (due to lack of budget); (c) rampant DVD piracy: people prefer to watch DVDs in the comfort of their own home or at a café, while the general state of movie theaters grows more and more derelict by the day (Martin 2007, 213–228). Under these conditions old-fashioned cinephilia is fast dwindling across the Maghreb.

So how does a woman director from the Maghreb address the various parties involved in her filmmaking process? How does she manage to tell a story that the local population will heed but that will be funded by a foreign source? How does she convey various stories at the same time? Something else is always afoot in her film: in order to jump through the first hoop of film production (and in order to secure a minimal distribution at the very least), she has to circumvent various restrictions at home. The censorship she faces there is at first political (and enforced by her nation's overbearing leader) and cultural (Martin

2007, 213–228), only to gradually become self-imposed. Tunisian producer Dora Bouchoucha eloquently summarizes the tensions inherent in the various layers of local censorship that, in turn, affect the making and the global production and distribution of a film:

> How can we create, innovate, astonish...? It should be pointed out that it is culturally difficult for us to bare all, and to deal with current issues without first going through a didactic discourse. Apart from worries about censorship, which can most often be circumvented, there is a resistance to "letting ourselves go completely." (Fallaux and Halasa 2003, 40)

Juggling with these competing forces, the filmmaker becomes wily and full of tricks, as her cinematic discourse has to escape the censor's vigilant radar while still sharing secrets with the local viewers and telling a story whose interest transcends the frontiers of her nation. It is in the creative ways in which she develops her own discourse and system of representation around these prohibitions that she designs a new cinema. For, as we know, cinema produces meaning through a semantic montage of offscreen (mentally constructed) images and on-screen shots. As Tunisian filmmaker Nouri Bouzid explained in his "Cinema Lesson" in Rome:

> The essence of cinematic language resides in the offscreen space, for the latter must be constituted in the viewer's mind without him seeing it; it also excludes a few moments...Students need to learn to place one detail on-screen and relegate the rest off-screen. The power of cinema lies in its ability to convey at once what is on-screen and what is off-screen. (Bouzid and Barlet 2005)[4]

The only way such a semantic approach can function successfully is if the viewer recognizes, at the faintest hint, the offscreen reference to which the on-screen narrative is referring. The immediate construction of meaning based on a subtle on-screen clue functions only if the viewer shares the cultural referent (for which he or she needs no explanation, no description). Thus one could argue that the offscreen/on-screen production of meaning plays with the Freudian two-pronged notion of *Unheimlichkeit* (with its sometimes opposite, *Heimlichkeit*), and its adjectival form *Unheimlich* (as opposed to *Heimlich*).

In his essay "The Uncanny," Freud defines both notions as follows: *Heimlichkeit* designates that which is from the home (*Heim*)—the homely, known, familiar, comfortable, cozy, intimate—and, in an extension of this: the secret or clandestine (e.g., "a secret affair") and the mysterious (e.g., the arts of magic, shared only by a few initiates).

Its opposite, *Unheimlichkeit*, is the uncanny, "that species of the frightening that goes back to what was once well known and had long been familiar" (Freud 2003, 124), and designates what we should (no longer) know, the repressed (as indicated by its *Un-* prefix, 151). In the first part of his essay, which focuses on linguistics, Freud also states: "In Arabic and Hebrew the 'uncanny' merges with the 'demonic' and the 'gruesome'" (125). Under its spell, an eye can morph into an "evil eye" while luck turns into misfortune.

Maghrebi women directors use offscreen/on-screen spaces to configure two values of the *(Un)Heimlich*: first, what is kept offscreen is a secret partly or largely shared with an audience in the know; second, the sudden appearance of elements of the offscreen narrative in the on-screen space creates an *Unheimlich* effect, which occurs "when the boundary between fantasy and reality is blurred, when we are faced with the reality of something that we have until now considered imaginary, when a symbol takes on the full function and significance of what it symbolizes, and so forth" (Freud 2003, 150–151).

In the filmic narrative, the offscreen space represents the locus of the imaginary, the fantasized narrative that each viewer needs to construct (based on the clues given on-screen, and within his or her own participation in the director's referential world), while the on-screen space provides a locus for the fictitious yet "familiar" microcosm of the film narrative. Hence, when a character "returns" from the shadows offscreen, in other words when the offscreen narrative suddenly intervenes on the screen, the (extra-diegetic) viewer is subjected to a shock that might be both alienating (frightening) and affirming (as the interplay between on-screen and offscreen signs is recognized). Filming in a sort of call and response fashion between these two spaces reminds us of what Stone McNeece called "a tendency to exploit the ambiguity of connotation systems by putting on hold what the images and words refer to" (2004, 69). Although the reference seems "on hold," each image launches a connotation system that is always ready to be activated.

Hamid Naficy's notion of "accented cinema" (2001) points to the same type of cultural sharing and movements between the "here" and "there" that are at work in Maghrebi women directors' cinematic language and styles around the very notion of "home." Paradoxically (and revealingly) enough, the themes of dislocation, of nostalgia for the home left behind, as well as the feeling of uneasiness verging on claustrophobia in the new cultures that Naficy describes as staples of accented cinema of exile, are the negatives (in the photographic sense of the term) of those found in Maghrebi women's films of the 1980s and 1990s. In the latter, characters often feel claustrophobic at home, dream of a space elsewhere, while simultaneously feeling nostalgic for a lost paradise, a lost mother figure, or previous abandoned dreams. This difference echoes the one Carrie Tarr describes when she compares "*beur* cinema" (i.e., made by French people of Maghrebi descent) and Algerian immigrant cinema in the 1990s and 2000s (2005, 189). In both cases, cinema projects the dream of a space elsewhere, filtered by either a parental idealized nostalgia or a painful personal memory.

However, in Maghrebi women's films, the longing for elsewhere that previously existed has changed over the past few years and today has a different configuration. Chamkhi's close study of the New Tunisian Cinema of the 1980s and 1990s analyzed how protagonists under the societal pressures of the *Heim*—feeling trapped at home in the smothering family house, in the narrow gossip-filled streets of the medina—had turned the familiar into a space of oppression that stifled the subject's desire to reach his or her own fulfillment. Chamkhi described the latter as "a desire that is thwarted, contradictory, and never satisfied"[5] (Chamkhi 2002, 13) because that very communal space contained all the tensions that society (the family, the neighborhood, the town, the nation) imposed on the subject. In such films, then, the familiar had come to equate to that which alienates the individual subject who aspires to be free from the mostly patriarchal strictures of home: in other words, an unbearably alien space, harmful to self-realization. Since 2000, however, even though the interplay between familiar and uncanny is still central to film discourse, Maghrebi women directors no longer seem to portray frustrated dreams of a fantasized elsewhere, but instead recondition familiar spaces into new ones.

In the two films analyzed below, the semantic play on the *Heimlich* and the *Unheimlich* is twofold, as the on-screen/offscreen montage further illustrates a reconfiguration of what has traditionally constituted a familiar, gendered space. In their films, Bachir-Chouikh and El Fani first start to blur the line hitherto drawn between the familiar/alien spaces for women, then appropriate new spaces, and finally invest old spaces with new values.

## … Who Displace the Notion of the Familiar in the Traditionally Gendered Values of Space …

The reframing of gendered values within space is most readily visible on the screen. As the camera scrutinizes the village, the home, the traditional Arabic house with its enclosed patio, the director shows how what used to be familiar and safe has become a dangerous place, possibly lethal to women. This first degree of estrangement unfolds and takes on several dimensions as the political mingles with the personal in Yamina Bachir-Chouikh's *Rachida* (2002). In this film, as the *Heimlich* and the *Unheimlich* play with the on-screen and off-screen organization of meaning, what is known (and recognizable) is shown on-screen, yet it becomes also entwined with elements of the unknown and the frightening. The art of the author in this fiction is to make the extra-diegetic viewer fully identify with the fictitious "reality," thus augmenting the effect of the uncanny:

> ...The writer can intensify and multiply this effect far beyond what is feasible in normal experience; in his stories he can make things happen that one would never, or only rarely, experience in real life. In a sense, then, he betrays us to a superstition we thought we had "surmounted"; he tricks us by promising us everyday reality and then going beyond it. We react to his fictions as if they had been our own experiences. By the time we become aware of the trickery, it is too late: the writer has already done what he set out to do. (Freud 2002, 157)

This last quote by Freud resonates ominously as we watch *Rachida*, whose narrative was inspired by the true story of a young teacher named Zakia Guessab who was killed at the hands of terrorists in the 1990s (the fact that the fictitious, on-screen Rachida survives simply highlights that, in the history of human violence, fiction is not as cruel as life). As Bachir-Chouikh revealed in an interview, the film is dedicated both to Zakia and to her own brother, Mohamed, who also died during the years of terror in Algeria.

Yamina Bachir-Chouikh, who now lives in France, wanted her film to show the overwhelming violence and its effects on the psyche of women during the 1990s, when Algeria was ravaged by a terror campaign and a bloody civil war, its population caught between the Islamists and the government's army.[6] Her film focuses on women and children, that is, the most vulnerable and, traditionally, the most protected in society. The eponymous film tells the story of Rachida, a young teacher in Algiers, who is accosted on her way to work by Sofiane, a former student of hers who has turned Islamist. He hands her a bag carrying a bomb, asking her to simply take it to her school. Rachida refuses and Sofiane's accomplice shoots her. She survives, however, and, traumatized, moves out of the city with her mother to a village in the country. But the violence spills over the city walls and spreads to the countryside as well. The old *Heimlich* here is shot in such a way as to show extreme vulnerability, a sense of entrapment, of no hope for an exit or possible freedom from the threat of violence.

Bachir-Chouikh shows the interior of houses, apartments, schools, and villages, all various shades of the *Heimlich*, the former familiar, feminine protective cocoon of home. But the boundaries of the village have now become porous and a subgroup of the GIA (*Groupe Islamique Armé*—Armed Islamic Group), the armed wing of the FIS (*Front Islamique du Salut*—Islamic Salvation Front), located outside the home, the village, literally "in the wild," raids the village, kidnaps women, pillages, and destroys the village. When a woman returns from a terrible ordeal with the FIS men (who, under a devious, self-serving interpretation of the Qur'an, marry, rape, and repudiate their victims), she is shunned by her father and denied entry to what used to be her home. The former cocoon of the family has now become a place of alienation and of rejection, as we see in the sequence of Zohra's return to the village. The *Heimlich* has become *Unheimlich*.

## Zohra's Veiling Sequence

Zohra's return is filmed in two parts: first she is shown running through the forest by herself, followed by her entrance to the village.

### *Out of the Unheimlich*

In the first part of the sequence, the camera is unsteady as it follows the young woman trying to find a path through the woods. The sequence opens with a close-up of Zohra's head turning from side to side, as the character tries to find her way: first we see her haggard-looking face, then the nape of her neck. The only sounds we hear are "natural" ones: the sound of her panting, the sound of dead leaves being crushed under her feet. Cut to a frontal medium shot: Zohra moves across the screen diagonally. Close-up: she stops, rests her hand on the trunk of an old tree and looks upward as she pauses to catch her breath. Her bewildered look expresses both an attempt to find her bearings and a deep-rooted, overwhelming fear of the enemies she has just left behind. Her sense of alertness is further conveyed by the extra-diegetic discordant chord now heard, superimposed over the noises of the forest.

Cut to a full shot of Zohra from behind as she runs ahead, barefoot. Another cut: the camera now moves alongside the running woman. The extra-diegetic music has now developed into a somewhat lyrical, sweeping orchestral piece in a decidedly Western classical style: she has found her way to the village. The first sequence ends in a quick-paced montage of medium to full shots of Zohra, her arm occasionally pressing the rags of her torn dress to her body. Throughout this montage, the extra-diegetic viewer is given access to her feelings in the close-ups (on her panting face and swaying hair, illustrating feelings of loss and of chaos), her spatial whereabouts in the full shots (in the forest, alone, running away from hell), and her rhythm in the medium shots (filmed using a portable camera) as she runs to safety. The initial multiple cuts reinforce the sense of chaos and of utter disorientation. Zohra returns to the *Heim* from the realm of the untamed, the violent, the perilous that lies outside the boundaries of the familiar, marked aurally by the sustained discordant chord. The core of that space (the hiding place where she was confined, raped, tortured) remains off-screen; her own erratic race out of it, still bearing traces of her trauma, is vividly illustrated by the seemingly erratic way in which it is shot.

## *Into the Heimlich*

The camera precedes her as she enters the village, and pans over those watching her: the children and teachers behind the railings of the school where Rachida teaches. Zohra's race is not over. Her nephew's repeated call, "Auntie Zohra," is heard over the sweeping music, as he runs in a parallel line to her on the other side of the school enclosure. Cut to a medium, slightly low angle, fixed shot of the teachers holding the bars of the railings, with Rachida in the center.

The camera now follows Zohra, still running, as she bangs on the various closed doors of her family's house or compound, crying "let me in!" No door is opened. Exhausted, Zohra finally drops down onto the street, out in the open public space of the village. Two men immediately approach her: "Don't touch me!" she cries. "Don't be afraid!" one of them replies repeatedly. Cut to a medium shot and then to a close up on Zohra's face with the men's hands in midair, trying to allay her fears. The remainder of the sequence splices fixed camera frontal (slightly low angle) shots of the onlookers, their gaze steadily on Zohra (seated below). No longer unsteady, the camera now focuses on distinct, highly composed stills. The construction of these portraits and the poses of their subjects evoke those of a journalistic report featuring a string of motionless (powerless?) witnesses of the event: three veiled women and one boy (What is he doing there? We know it is a school day). An older woman, protective of Zohra, shoos the men away. Cut to a medium shot of three veiled women: one of them starts to remove her yellow veil. Cut to a fourth, veiled young woman: she is occupying the right side of the screen, leaving the other half empty, the camera slightly tilted in a low angle shot. She is taking off her red head-scarf in a graceful arching gesture. Cut to the three women again: the one on the left, as if in visual response to the preceding shot, is in the last stage of removing her red veil. All the women approach Zohra to cover her with their colorful, translucent veils: Zohra's legs and arms, her torn dress, and her hair are now covered in yellow, red, and indigo. Finally a fifth woman drops a pale blue scarf over her feet.

The women have thus stepped out of beautiful photographic stills and out of their roles as silent witnesses in order to envelop the victim with their own protection. Here, on-screen, we are given a silent representation of women's compassion. After the veiling, they all stay where they are, surrounding Zohra. The final shot of them together is a carefully constructed tableau: Zohra is sitting on the ground at the center, her legs stretched straight out in front of her, framed by two crouching older women, while the younger ones have supplicant positions, as if paying homage. No one is placed in the foreground: Zohra remains the focal point of the shot.

This sequence illustrates at least two phenomena: the first one is the estrangement of women by men, illustrated by the kidnapping and rape by the FIS thugs (the offscreen *Unheimlich*) and by the foreshadowing of Zohra's banishment from home by her own father (suggested by the closed, unwelcoming doors of her house). Now the young woman, who used to be found within the house, invisible to the outside, no longer has access to the customary "invisibility" and shelter provided by either the walls of a house or a veil. The protection from the desiring or envious "evil eye" of the other (men from outside her family, the FIS, malevolent spirits) has vanished. Or, in Freudian terms, she has become vulnerable to the malevolent looks of others:

> Anyone who possesses something precious, but fragile, is always the envy of others, to the extent that he projects on to them the envy he would have felt in their place. Such emotions are betrayed by looks, even if they are denied verbal expression, and [...] people are ready to believe that his envy will reach a particular intensity and then convert this intensity into action. What is feared is thus a covert intention to harm. (Freud 2003, 146–147)

The communal presentation of veils could be seen as a feminine attempt to restore Zohra's traditional defense against the harmful eye of the

*Unheimlich* to which she was subjugated in the offscreen sequence of her kidnapping. The second phenomenon is the ensuing feminine solidarity in the face of violence against one of the women. It is a gesture that, even if fairly ambiguous to a Northern audience, might signal the return of the *Heimlich*, the return to the rules of home and the protection of home that only women can perform for Zohra now. Here, although the offscreen male violence against Zohra is still perceptible in the on-screen space (e.g., the torn dress on Zohra's body), the women's solidarity evicts all male protagonists from the public space of the village and relegates them to a peripheral position (none of them is seen from the front: there is no adult male face in this sequence), hence the women-only final tableau of the sequence. The space traditionally occupied by women (the home, *Heim*) has spilled into the street to succor Zohra, for whom the safety of the *Heim* no longer exists anywhere. Hence the possible reading of the film as a likely model of female resistance: women conquer the space of their agency by reconfiguring the traditional gendered space. Since the male order is failing to protect them (against the FIS masculine wave of flagrant violence that has brutally dismantled the traditional, patriarchal dichotomy between interior and exterior space), women start to (re)occupy the space of the village. Their traditional personal space having been "politically" invaded by outside male forces, women now start appropriating and sharing the outer political space within the city ("polis"), and within society. Meanwhile the FIS is relegated to its murky actions and existence in the realm of the uncivilized, offscreen.

On-screen, the gendering of space has been reversed: by the end of the film, the women are prominently visible outside the home, reconstructing the village, and eventually, hopefully, Algerian society, as they start to teach the young again. In the film's last sequence, Rachida is in the classroom again. Bachir-Chouikh's treatment of *Heimlich* space thus points to a crucial political renegotiation of space that clearly denounces the outdated, inefficient, dangerous patriarchal boundaries of old Algeria. Our next director, El Fani, goes one step further, moving beyond the national or regional to redefine or erase traditional boundaries.

## …and Peacefully Occupy New Spaces

*Bedwin Hacker* (2002) is Nadia El Fani's first feature film, and it negotiates various spaces that bridge and/or divide cultures and languages, as we follow Kalt, a Tunisian hacker, who travels between Paris (France) and Midès (Tunisia), and proposes a cultural detour to a third—and global—site: the at once familiar and unfamiliar virtual world of computer hackers. It can be read as a reflective piece on the state of Tunisian cinema—and perhaps even culture—as it travels back and forth between France and Tunisia, the national and the transnational, the tangible and the virtual. Here the notion of the *Unheimlich* reverberates in several ways, as we can see in the opening sequence: the uncanny can be something alien, something familiar that contains something alien, or something difficult to know. Yet *Bedwin Hacker* also turns this concept on its head, inverts its values: the unfamiliar world of hackers becomes a safe, familiar space open to nomadic travels.

The narrative starts simply: Kalt, also called "Pirate Mirage" (Mirage Hacker) manages to hack into TV transmission systems in order to superimpose the funny cartoon of a little camel onto the screen of all European TV programs. The camel simply states "we exist" in Tunisian Arabic, and promotes messages of peace. There is no "terrorist" demand, but the French secret service is up in arms, as is the Tunisian government. Julia, a French secret service agent who has known Kalt in the past, devises all sorts of tricks to try to corner her.

This main narrative offers flashes of various subplots (e.g., a flashback to Julia and Kalt's past relationship, to Kalt as a brilliant student at *École Polytechnique*; a quick incursion into the plight of the illegal immigrants in France; the lack of imagination on the part of the police when confronted by the hacker), all against the back drop of a broader narrative: neither Tunisia nor France are what they pretend to be.

Throughout the film, Kalt travels back and forth between France and Tunisia, and keeps returning to her house in the desert, where she continues hacking. A nomadic film in the true sense of the term (it always comes back to its original point of departure), it blurs national borders (indeed, it potentially erases them as irrelevant on the World Wide Web) and boundaries between the political, the virtual, and, in the final analysis, the digital (this was the first Tunisian film to be shot digitally). On several levels, then, the film tells more than one story, as it pushes the limits of what can be said on the airwaves, via satellite, and on-screen.

## The Opening Sequence of *Bedwin Hacker*

The film's emblematic opening sequence shows most of the resistance tools Nadia El Fani plans to use during her film, as well as the three spaces of her narrative: TV and the web, the Tunisian desert, and Paris. The overture is structured in three sections.

In the first section, the inaugural shots show a juxtaposition of images reflecting a montage of various narratives, a hip-hop style mix of aesthetics and politics, as the hacker imprints the colorful image of her little camel over the black and white film of the well-known, historical speech, delivered by U.S. president Harry Truman, in 1945, when he inaugurated the Tennessee Valley Authority dam. The TV screen already shows two stories: the archive footage of the speech, spliced with shots of the atomic mushroom. The whole program looks like a television documentary on the atomic age, with the French subtitles of Truman's speech aiming to reassure (*"we now have this tremendous responsibility instead of our enemies..."*) belied by the image of the ominous mushroom.

In this sequence, the sound track features a mute TV, extra-diegetic music (a sample of synthesized music evocative of a modern-day Maghreb), the intra-diegetic tapping sounds of someone typing on a computer keyboard, and a French-speaking female voice offscreen announcing "enemy on the right" as another camel leapfrogs up onto the TV screen. The subtitles now read: *"We have just now discovered the source of the power of the sun..."* as the feminine voice says "enemy on the left" in synch with the sudden appearance of the same camel on the left. *"Nuclear power. This incredible source of energy ushers us into the greatest era of all times,"* the subtitles now predict, as the French-speaking voice warns: "Careful: there is one in the back." Now, both previous camels are gone, but one emerges in the center of the screen, seemingly from the back, zooming all the way to the forefront, invading the screen. It is wearing blue jeans, a green shirt, and has bare, human-looking feet. The historical documentary, already reduced to a mere background framing the invasive, enormous camel, now fades to black; the camel is the only visible figure left on-screen.

Thus an unknown animated figure, emblematic of nomads, of the South, has invaded the European TV screens. Interestingly enough, its appearance succeeds in: (a) coinciding with a program on the nuclear hegemony of the North; (b) diminishing the impact of the latter and proposing a friendly, nonthreatening alien presence in contrast to the nuclear mushroom, thus suggesting that aliens (whether legal immigrants or not) might be much less hazardous to the world's health than the Northern/Western leaders' foreign policies.

In the second section, cut to a canyon in the desert near Midès (Tunisia), with a smooth aural transition: the same extra-diegetic music accompanies the second sequence, this time with cries of children superimposed on it (as opposed to the computer clicks and disembodied female voice). The camera is still fixed, this time filming a canyon in the desert. Credits appear on the left side of the screen in the same fashion the cartoon appeared on the TV screen beforehand. The information (in the Arabic alphabet above the Roman alphabet) seems to be springing from the depths of the canyon. The viewer finally distinguishes a group of joyous children coming up a trail to the right. Cut to the heads of a band of children with a close-up on a little girl, Qmar, leading a donkey. Cut to Qmar's father, Mehdi (medium shot) bent over what looks like a barrel, outside a house. The camera follows him as he calls to Kalt (in French): "Kalt, it is already plugged in." Kalt is seen through the window. She comes to the threshold of the house and puts on her military-style cap before she joins Mehdi at the barrel. "Go ahead! After you!" he tells her (still in French), as he hands her a remote control.

Qmar, still in her pink schoolgirl's smock, reaches Kalt and her father and exclaims in Tunisian Arabic: "I knew you'd do it. You're the best, Auntie." Kalt (in Arabic): "Please don't call me that! . . . You'll keep your promise, right? School comes before everything else." Cut to an antenna coming out of the barrel, with the last inscription of the Arabic credits over the French ones, a dedication to Nadia El Fani's grandmother: "To my grandmother, 'Bibi,' who still inspires in me the courage to resist." The ending frame is a close-up on the antenna, now fully extended out of the barrel.

Here we see, literally, the origins of the cartoon camel: a tiny house in Midès, in the Tunisian South. We also see that its appearance on European TV screens is again, literally, *un jeu d'enfants* (i.e., as easy as "child's play," a piece of cake) for Kalt and her "tribe" of hackers, that even includes a child (Qmar), in a low-tech environment, symbolized by the old barrel concealing the hacker's antenna (like one of Ali Baba's jars concealing a thief).

In the third section, cut to an indoor space hosting a meeting of illegal immigrants in Paris. A cross on the wall signals to the viewer the rest of the space (offscreen): it is most probably a church. This sign alone echoes the factual narrative of the three-hundred illegal immigrants from Africa who occupied St Ambroise Church in Paris on March 18, 1996, and were forced out of their sanctuary by the police four days later. They then moved to St Bernard Church on June 28, to be, yet again, evicted by the police.[7] The media are here: Chams (one of the main characters) is one of the reporters interviewing immigrants. He is shot at the same level as they are (a visual clue to his egalitarian views as well as to his own status as an immigrant). Cut to a pan over the demonstrators' faces (medium shots to close-ups) and of signs that read "Legal Status For All" and "No to Exclusion." Close-up on Frida clasping her *'ud* (Arabic lute): she is sitting next to a woman who looks French, wearing a Palestinian *kafiya* and clapping to the rhythm of the drums that others are playing. Whistles are heard. The police come in and invade the place. Mayhem ensues.

Here the offscreen narrative is complex: it refers to historical events (in 1996, for instance) and to the various peaceful marches by illegal immigrants in Paris that turned into musical performances in the streets. It also foreshadows the role of Kalt, on-screen and offscreen; the role of Chad, the reporter who tries to know the truth and ends up being manipulated throughout the narrative; and, finally and perhaps most importantly, the semantic polyvalence of "screens" in *Bedwin Hacker*.

Nadia El Fani's *Bedwin Hacker* pushes the limits of what can be said over the airwaves, via satellite, and on screen. First of all, it shows that screens are frames, in every sense of the term: the initial TV screen frames a second screen: that of the camel/Kalt's hacking. One computer screen in Midès can show the command to a local relay that will affect screens far away (in Europe). Conversely, the TV screen in Midès can also reveal to Qmar that her mother, Frida, is in trouble in Paris, as the police take her away "live" on television. From the very first sequence, then, we are shown, through a *mise en abyme* of screens, that space is moveable, dynamic: the film opens with a screen onto the virtual, before it even starts to move from Tunisia to France. The space we see is embedded in another one; a screen contains another screen; one locus points to another, constantly, along a line of flight. A hacker needs an emitting point (which we are shown immediately) but it is a portable one (as we shall understand later in the narrative). Here, what is left silent and invisible is also what is most significant, for it assumes that the viewer is going to fill in the blanks of the narrative: how do all these screens fit in with one another? Interestingly, there are two types of observers in this film: the intra-diegetic ones (e.g., the French police and secret services, Chams the reporter), and us, the extra-diegetic viewers. Although we have a slight advantage over our intra-diegetic colleagues (e.g., we know who is doing the hacking) when faced with this feat, we experience the same bafflement as the intra-diegetic television viewers. We can no more understand than they how, and to begin with, why, Kalt's exploits are achieved, than they can. Both the extra-diegetic and intra-diegetic viewers witness an invasion of the unfamiliar into the familiar as we watch the hacker's *Unheimlich* virtual space disturb the familiar TV screen at home.

The image of a camel and its evocation of the nomadic way of life might provide a telling metaphorical clue to the way the semantics of the film are structured. The camel appears here and then there, its presence is always ephemeral, almost fluid. In that, it symbolizes Kalt, who can outdo both the French police and secret services and Ben Ali's dictatorship, thus beating two sets of authorities at their own game: the French DST (*Défense Secrète du Territoire*) and the Tunisian police state. She thus transcends either identity, literally hacks them both, and refuses to be from one nation or the other. She is a citizen of the world, "bi" both sexually and "nationally." Issues of proper legal status are irrelevant to Kalt because the very notion of nation no longer applies to transcultural agents like her, equally at ease on the Northern and Southern shores of the Mediterranean. Better yet, Kalt is literally "at home" in the desert, in her father's house in Tunis, in a friend's apartment in Paris. She carries her own brand of *Heimlichkeit* with her. However, she never stays long in one spot, living in a state of dissidence she alone designs, away from both the French and the Tunisian regimes. In this film, then, El Fani offers the picture of a woman negotiating her own freedom along spaces both geographical and virtual. In this way, her film takes the next step after Bachir-Chouikh's appropriation by women in *Rachida*: it fashions and projects the image of a female subject empowered to achieve her own fulfillment anywhere she chooses.

The protagonist's power to bypass all police barrages (both virtual and literal) points to a formidable freedom of movement, identity, and thought. Nadia El Fani wanted to represent a hero in an Arab film, and a woman to boot! Both Bachir-Chouikh and El Fani project images of women resisting the various establishments that have had the arrogance to decide upon women's fate and place in the city. Kalt clearly says: I am home wherever I wish to plant my tent or wonder, thus giving *Heimlichkeit* a novel global spin.

## Conclusion

In Maghrebi women directors' cinema, the elements kept offscreen are the ones that, literally, "make sense," and the viewers' construction of meaning often relies on shared references and patterns of communication. This points to an astute and effective way of representing that which you are not supposed to film or say in a society ruled by a strong regime with powerful political and cultural censorship. However, wily as they are, Maghrebi women directors seem to have a reserve of filmic detours at the ready to resist male diktats, whether political or cultural, and whether decreed in the Maghreb (the West in the Arabic sense), or in the North (France, Europe). Their films, these days, seem to not only claim ownership of a public space that was once beyond their reach, but also, and most formidably, to empower women (and children, and, ultimately, men too) to fearlessly venture out of their homes and old habits into an exhilarating, liberating zone.

# Notes

1. Its founding films, Selma Baccar's *Fatma 75* (Tunisia, 1976) and Assia Djebar's *The Nuba of the Women of Mount Chenoua* (Algeria, 1978), led the way in telling women's stories during the period in which Maghrebi countries attained independence.
2. "In reality, the Maghreb is constructed on the denial of the colonial expression 'Northern Africa.' The North (of Africa) became the West (of the Arab world), and, i. n a *soft* form of retaliation on the part of history, what had hitherto belonged to the Third World now became part of the South. This semantic puzzle tells a lot about the situation. The frenetic force of the Arab identity claim highlights, *a contrario*, the influence of the French and, more generally speaking Western culture. It does not erase it" (Chikhaoui 2004, 25). (My translation).
3. *Fonds Sud* is a French governmental agency that has coproduced films from developing countries, often African, although not exclusively so (it also coproduces films in Latin America, Asia, and Eastern Europe). Its average financial contribution has been 110,000. Euros (about US$170,000.00) per film.
4. "*L'essence du langage cinématographique est le hors-champ car il doit être constitué dans la tête du spectateur sans le voir mais c'est aussi l'exclusion de certains moments. (…) Les étudiants doivent apprendre à mettre un détail dans le champ et le reste hors-champ. La force du cinéma est d'exprimer l'ensemble champ et hors-champ.*"
5. "*un désir contrarié, contradictoire et jamais abouti. Se manifestant dans le désordre et le débordement, il bute sur la tension entre la réalisation du Moi et le contentement du Nous.*"
6. The FIS was founded in 1989, and won 55 percent of the votes in the 1990 election. The government reacted by reforming the electoral system, limiting, for instance, political campaigning in the mosques. The "dirty war" between the FIS and the army was sparked by the dissolution of the National Assembly by the president in January 1992, after the FIS had won 188 seats at the first round of local elections in December 1991. The government, afraid of the FIS winning a majority of the votes, declared a state of emergency. The army was in power. The number of deaths due to this "dirty war" in the 1990s is estimated at 150,000.
7. See "La saga des sans-papiers." In *Libération* (August 23, 2006).

# References

Accad, Evelyne. *Sexuality and War: Literary Masks of the Middle East*. New York: New York University Press, 1992.

Armes, Roy. *African Filmmaking North and South of the Sahara*. Bloomington: Indiana University Press, 2006.

Bachir-Chouikh, Yamina, interview. http://www.diplomatie.france.gouv.fr/fr/actions-france_830/cinema_886 (Accessed on December 27, 2008).

Bouzid, Nouri and Barlet, Olivier. "La Leçon de cinéma de Nouri Bouzid." In *Postcolonial Images. Studies in North African Film*. Bloomington: Indiana University Press, 2005, http://www.africultures.com/index.asp?menu.affiche_article&no=4385 (Accessed on December 27, 2008).

Braudel, Fernand. *Les Mémoires de la Méditerranée*. Paris: Editions de Fallois, 1998.

Chamkhi, Sonia. *Cinéma tunisien nouveau—Parcours autres*. Tunis: Sud Éditions, 2002.

Chikhaoui, Tahar. "Maghreb: de l'épopée au regard intime." In *Au Sud du cinéma: Films d'Afrique, d'Asie et d'Amérique Latine*, ed. Jean-Michel Frodon, 22–29. Paris: Cahiers du Cinéma/Arte Editions, 2004.

———. "Une Affaire de Femmes / Stories of Women." *Africultures* 8, Second Quarter (1994). http://www.africultures.com/revue_africultures/articles/ecrans_afrique/8/8_08.pdf (Accessed on December 27, 2008).

Dönmez-Colin, Gönül. *Women, Islam and Cinema*. London: Reaktion Books, 2004.

Emile Fallaux, Malu Halasa, eds. *Funding the Art of World Cinema. True Variety*. Rotterdam, International Film Festival Rotterdam: 2003.

Freud, Sigmund. "The Uncanny." In *The Uncanny*, translated by David McClintock, 121–162. London and New York: Penguin, 2003.

Khannous, Touria. "Strategies of representation and postcolonial identity in North African Women's Cinema." *Journal x: A Journal of Culture and Criticism* 1, 6 (2004): 49–61.

Khelil, Hédi. *Le Parcours et la trace: Témoignages et documents sur le cinéma tunisien*. Tunis: Médiacom, 2002.

Martin, Florence. "Tunisia." In *Small National Cinemas*, ed. Duncan Petrie and Mette Hjort, 213–228. Edinburgh: Edinburgh University Press, 2007.

———. "Transvergence and cultural detours: Nadia El Fani's *Bedwin Hacker* (2002)." *Studies in French Cinema* 7, 2 (2007): 119–129.

Mernissi, Fatima. *Dreams of Trespass: Tales of a Harem Girlhood*. New York and Ontario: Addison-Wesley Inc., 1994.

Naficy, Hamid. *An Accented Cinema: Exilic and Diasporic FilmMaking*. Princeton: Princeton University Press, 2001.

Serceau, Michel, ed. *Cinémas du Maghreb*. Cinémaction 111 (2004).

Shafik, Viola. *Arab Cinema. History and Cultural Identity*. Cairo: American University in Cairo Press, 1998.

Shohat, Ella. "Framing Post-Third-Worldist Culture: Gender and Nation in Middle Eastern North African Film and Video." *Jouvert* (1997). http://152.1.96.5/jouvert/v1i1/shohat.htm (Accessed on December 27, 2008).

Stone McNeece, Lucy. "La lettre envolée: l'image écrite dans le cinéma tunisien." In *Cinémas du Maghreb*, ed. Michel Serceau, 67–76. *Cinémaction* 111 (2004).

Tarr, Carrie. *Reframing Difference:* Beur *and* Banlieue *Filmmaking in France*. Manchester and New York: Manchester University Press, 2005.

*Spain: Domestic Violence*

# Chapter Three

## Visions and Voices of the Self in Take My Eyes

*Mónica Cantero*

Many memorable and original films have emerged from Spain in the past twenty-five years, giving the country a commanding and enviable position in the world of filmmaking. With noticeable frequency these films address issues of gender roles—a topic with which audiences almost everywhere struggle, as social practices and customs change and adapt to contemporary pressures and new knowledge. Influenced by the literary discourse of women's liberation and the political discourse of civil rights, Spaniards have begun to question and scrutinize the deeply ingrained stereotypes of traditional roles. Eventually, gender roles may cease to be understood as essentialist and fixed, and gender identities may be seen as flexible and fluid, thus legitimizing what in the past might have been unthinkable or certainly unacceptable. Spanish directors have sought to startle, to excite, and to break with the stifling traditions that had shackled creative freedom and impeded progress, social change, and experimentation under the repressive regime of Francisco Franco (1936–1975).

One of contemporary Spain's most accomplished and versatile film personalities is Iciar Bollaín, a Madrid native (born 1967) who has been active in all aspects of the motion picture industry, as a performer, producer, director, and screen writer. She came to prominence at an early age, appearing in Víctor Erice's *El Sur/The South* (1983). Later, her debut as a director in *Hola, ¿estás sola?/Hi, are you alone?* (1995) earned her a Goya award nomination for Best New Director. Bollaín is credited with initiating and strongly promoting the film genre of social realism. Her films focus primarily on the plight of women abused by male violence. Her interest in the sources of both the victim's and perpetrator's behavior infuses her films with a dark and harrowing edge. The film *Flores de otro mundo/Flowers From Another World* (1999), which she wrote and directed, depicted the social and personal difficulties facing immigrant women who marry Spanish nationals, and their bitter quest for a better life in rural Spain. With *Te doy mis ojos/Take My Eyes* (2003), her third film as director, Bollaín became the second woman[1] to win the coveted Goya award for Best Director from the Spanish Academy of Film, in 2004.[2] Although her films do not preach, they often show moral and psychological redemption. The director herself has spoken of the power of film to portray brutality: "seen violence is not the same as suggested violence."[3]

This chapter examines the "authorized," explicit, sexist, and violent discourse found in Spanish society, as reflected in *Take My Eyes*. Centered on gender violence, the film depicts the mechanisms and linguistic implications of an entrenched national discourse in which gender violence is encoded within male-female interaction, and by extension within society. This discourse and its images are ultimately indicative of a brutality and social control intrinsically connected to, and often perpetuated by, established political forces. Beneath the film's fictional plot lies a political correlative: the last years of right-wing Popular Party's rule in Spain (1996–2004) and the strong desire among filmmakers and artists to react against the right-wing policies that had further legitimized particular discourses, especially in relation to gender and gender roles. Films like *Take My Eyes* represent a form of rebellion within the system (Losilla 2005), with the purpose of openly displaying existing social structures on the screen and causing them to be debunked or modernized.

*Take My Eyes* tells the story of Pilar and Antonio, a middle-class Spanish couple living in Toledo with their young son. They find themselves caught up in the dreadful web of the husband's continual violence toward his long-suffering and submissive wife. The film depicts familiar and stereotypical images of gender behavior by intensifying and magnifying the assumptions that accompany these traditional roles. Through the film's unambiguous portrayal, audiences realize they are going to watch what seems to be a real-life story of spousal abuse—a story that echoes similar ones that were beginning to appear in the Spanish news media at the time of the film's release. Repelled by male violence and sickened by the victimization of the female, the audience is able to place Pilar and Antonio within the larger framework of gender behavior legitimized by the political right, the church, and an entrenched system of social traditions. In so doing, viewers are challenged to rethink, reframe, and reform the national way of thinking, expectations, and customs regarding gender, gender roles, and gender behavior.

On a larger scale, the United Nations General Assembly has also addressed this issue. Its resolution 48/104 of December 20, 1993 recognizes in the *Declaration on the Elimination of Violence Against Women* the vital urgency with which gender violence must be addressed. More specifically, it defines "violence against women" as "any act of gender-based violence that results in, or is likely to result in, physical, sexual or psychological harm or suffering to women, including threats of such acts, coercion or arbitrary deprivation of liberty, whether occurring in public or in private life" (Article 1). This Declaration represents the first narrative to focus on the global phenomenon of gender-based abuse, and to address and recognize "the urgent need for the universal application to women of the rights and principles with regard to equality, security, liberty, integrity and dignity of all human beings." Furthermore, the U.N. resolution promotes the education and awareness of future generations as fundamental mechanisms to help eradicate violence and abuse toward women, regardless of where it might take place.

In 1997, Spanish citizens were given an abrupt wake-up call and were forced to face the "never before publicly discussed" issue of gender-based violence when the case of Ana Orantes was televised one December afternoon. In the comfort of their living rooms, Spaniards learned of the forty years of tragic physical abuse endured by sixty-year-old Ana at the hands of her husband, and the official indifference to her plight. During her interview on the Spanish *Canal Sur* program *De tarde en tarde*, Mrs. Orantes detailed her beatings and related her fear, whilst pointing out that denouncing her husband's behavior to the police had been useless, because this was not an established practice during the years of Franco's dictatorship. During *aquella época* (that time)—a euphemism used by the older generations to refer to the 1936–1975 period—political and legal forces framed gender-abuse in terms of "normalcy within the family," thus completely undermining a woman's right to seek justice and protection.

Ana Orantes stated in her interview: "At the beginning I did not report him, because at that time it wasn't something usually done, nobody did. Then, finally I did it, in the end, yes, but in all honesty it did not help much. What I have been told is that those are normal fights within the family. And the only thing he does is to threaten me by saying that one day he will have to kill me"[4] (*El País*, 1997). This interview aired on December 4, 1997. Thirteen days later, Spaniards learned of the tragic and horrifying death of Mrs. Orantes, who had been attacked, doused with gasoline, and set on fire by her husband in the yard of the family home. This case represented a shocking turning point for a newly sensitized Spanish society, and it helped to lift the heavy curtain of silence regarding gender-based abuse. The media started reporting other cases of physical violence and abuse on a regular basis, thus opening up the debate in the public sphere and reflecting the cultural change that was gradually taking place. According to data provided by the Spanish newspaper *El País* (2005), in 2003 seventy women were murdered in cases of domestic violence and 50,000 cases of abuse and charges of violence were reported.

Elections were imminent and most of the political debate focused on structuring the commitment of the State to crack down on gender-based abuse—or male violence exercised upon women. This change was linguistically codified as the *"promesa de tolerancia cero"* (promise of zero tolerance) by Mariano Rajoy, the general secretary of the right-wing *Partido Popular.* Therefore, it came as no surprise that, under the newly elected socialist government of José Luis Rodrigo Zapatero in 2004, the State had begun its first attempts to raise public awareness on these issues through education and information. These efforts resulted in the unanimous approval of the *Ley la protección integral contra la violencia de género* (Integral Law of Protection against Gender-Based Violence) by the Spanish parliament, in December 2004. The State had finally officially recognized the reality of gender violence as a human rights issue.

*Take My Eyes*, released in 2003, resonated with the ongoing political debate and embodied this moment of social awareness. The film also expressed a relevant filmic narrative for an audience that was becoming an active participant in the fight against gender-based violence, and was recognizing this problem as a national reality for the first time. The Spanish title of the film, *Te doy mis ojos*, literally translated, *"I give you my eyes,"* represents one of the protagonist Pilar's most important utterances. It also encapsulates the essential nature of the ties that bind the couple: by giving Antonio her eyes, one of the most important parts of her body, she also gives up the ability to perceive and examine her own reality. Of course, the implication is that she is rendered helpless, blind, and dependent on another person. At first, Pilar accepts and assumes her submissive role in the marital relationship. She has lost any trace of individuality, as she confesses to her sister: "I don't know who I am anymore." She has relinquished control of her life to Antonio by offering him her eyes and consequently her own connection with her immediate reality, while her husband completely dominates and manipulates her.

Furthermore, the metaphor *"I give you my eyes"* exemplifies the nature of the archetypical abuse as seen from the sufferer's viewpoint. The title serves as an entry point for the viewer who is about to watch the film for the first time; the intentionality of the title becomes a means through which to approach viewers and involve them in the film's plot. The eyeball-cutting scene in Luis Buñuel's *Un Chien Andalou* (1929) can be associated with *Take My Eyes'* idea of giving one's eyes, the implication being that the act of exchanging or offering one's eyes is both a horrifying gesture and an act of kindness. Thus, the audience is given the opportunity to witness, through the eyes of the female protagonist, what it means to be in a situation of gender-abuse. Syntactically, the Spanish second-person indirect pronoun "*te*," contained in the sentence "*te doy mis ojos*," speaks individually to the viewer as the recipient of the action. He or she is given a specific way to perceive a reality that, although fictional, correlates with problematic social circumstances. This is particularly relevant given the media treatment and portrayal of gender-based violence during the early years of the twenty-first century.

Bollaín's film *Take My Eyes* represents a problem usually addressed by social and political institutions, which are often the only source of information for the public. The characters on the screen represent every man and woman who lives the power struggle of an abusive marriage. The dominance of the authorities and their spokesmen as the only source of information (which is consequently limited and one-sided) is shown in the research conducted by Vives-Cases et al. (2005). This study consists in a quantitative analysis of the press coverage of violence against women. Based on the results, the authors argue that the main sources of information for news coverage are politicians of both sexes—men from legal institutions, and women from health institutions and associations. Also, men are the main source of information used in the news when reporting punishment measures. The authors also state that "It is evident that the tendency of the media is to not recognize the opinions of the affected persons and their surroundings…This journalistic focus is not impartial and could have important repercussions…the media may well be reflecting a simplified version of the problem and its possible solutions" (Vives-Cases et al. 2005, 27).[5] In short, media coverage does not recognize the opinions of the victims, even though they are obviously the real authorities on their circumstances and the nature of their problems.

Thus, *Take My Eyes* presents the audience with an extraordinary insight into Pilar's struggle. By giving the viewer her eyes, he or she becomes part of an engaged, responsible audience while profoundly identifying with Pilar herself. It is fundamental to note that the idea of "giving" is semantically lost in translation, since in English "to take" and "to give" are two opposing verbs. Moreover, in terms of syntax, while the Spanish title uses a declarative sentence "*I give you my eyes,*" the English one takes the form of a command: "Take my eyes." The English title therefore has the connotations of an imperative request rather than being the simple statement of the fact that functions as the linguistic device summarizing Pilar's submission to Antonio's manipulation. The sentence *"I give you my eyes"* becomes, in the filmic narrative, the mechanism that marks the unbalance of power within the asymmetrical discourse that constructs abuse.

The film opens with a background sequence of the well-preserved medieval city of Toledo, where the action takes place. The viewer is immediately shown a scene of a typical modern apartment building on the outskirts of the city, where middle-class families live. It is late at night as the camera takes us inside one of these apartments. Pilar, in a state of trepidation, rushes to wake her sleeping child, while simultaneously packing essential personal items to take with her as she flees from home. The atmosphere of fear and anxiety is apparent to the viewer, who intuitively recognizes that Pilar's chaotic and erratic actions are not the consequence of a simple spat, but reflect a desperate panic beyond her control. The immediate and ominous threat to Pilar is palpable to the viewer who recognizes that the horror from which she is fleeing emanates from within the domestic microcosm of her own home.

After an evening spent traveling by bus, Pilar and her son arrive at her sister Ana's house, located in the most traditional neighborhood of Toledo, a town protected by its medieval walls. Toledo[6] is a deliberate choice by Bollaín for the location to play out this plot of spousal abuse and disdain along with female submission and victimization. The city is also a place of strength and vision that will overcome the limitations of its ultraconservative traditions and offer power and a hint of freedom to Pilar. Selecting Toledo as the site of the confrontation between the old, traditional attitude toward women and the female journey toward freedom and independence is an appropriate choice since the city itself contains the old and the new in harmonious coexistence. Toledo, as an organic entity, becomes a silent participant in the film and serves as witness to Pilar's ordeal. While she is trapped between threat and shelter, her own domestic horror—where she has lost any ability to function—and during her subsequent therapeutic discovery of the culturally rich universe of the city, Toledo will allow her to regain control of her own life.

Ana, the sister, abruptly finds out about the abusive situation when she goes to Pilar's home to finish packing some necessary items for her. Buried beneath some clothing, Ana discovers Pilar's medical reports relating to the physical abuse she has suffered. The mise-en-scène places

Ana in Pilar's bedroom, directly in front of the drawers where she has found these hospital records. On top of the chest of drawers is a picture from Pilar's wedding day, showing her standing next to her husband. The filmic intentionality of this scene is crucial to our understanding of the relationship between Pilar's husband and the medical reports, as it constructs a visual triangle between Ana holding the reports, Pilar, and Antonio. Unexpectedly, Antonio arrives back at the apartment and, thinking that Pilar had returned home, he mistakenly calls out to her: "Pilar, are you there? Listen, Shorty,[7] this place is a mess. Wanna go out…get something to eat, Okay, Shorty?" When Antonio opens the door and sees Ana instead of Pilar, his voice fills with rage as he shouts, "What the hell do you want?" At that moment, Antonio realizes that Pilar is staying with Ana and that she is not coming back home. Without acknowledging any personal responsibility or blame for the terrible situation, he instead screams obscenities at the innocent Ana, "Staying with you? Bullshit! Tell Pilar to cut the crap and come home."[8] The viewer is now aware of the existence of a situation of gender-abuse violence as well as of the construction of the gender-based ideology of abuse that structures this heterosexual asymmetrical discourse, prototypically in the form of marriage (Cameron and Kulick 2003).

*Canija*—badly translated into English as "Shorty"—conveys in Spanish the semantic features of "puny," "weak," and "sickly." *Canija*, used in Antonio's speech as a vocative device or term of endearment, aims to maintain or emphasize his control over the verbal interaction with his wife. Antonio's speech underlies a linguistic intention of persuasiveness as well as a pattern of dominance through the overt assertion of his own position of power in the dialogue, determined by his own conceptualization of the female counterpart as "weak." Adams et al. (1995) carried out a rhetorical analysis of the discourse produced by men who have been recently violent toward women. Their work identifies a range of rhetorical devices and explores how these mechanisms are utilized in the discourse of male dominance and entitlement to power. The results of their analysis indicate that "metaphor reinforces the correctness and reasonableness of discourses of male dominance. Synecdoche and metonymy are added incrementally to the connotations and associations which resource these discourses" (403–404). Antonio's verbal interaction with Pilar signals synecdochic correlations with the specific sense of "weakness." This connotation articulates his linguistic behavior in terms of dominance: the subtle use of "*Canija*" as the opposite of the "masculine" enables Antonio's perspective of reality to dominate his wife.

This linguistic pattern of dominance and entitlement to power becomes even more obvious when Antonio character agrees to join a therapy group for men responsible for similar situations of domestic violence. Bollaín frames Antonio character within this culture of verbal and physical violence toward women. During Antonio's first visit to group therapy, he learns from the other members' remarks how this abuse is rooted, accepted, and understood as normal behavior within many sectors of Spanish society. Antonio agrees to participate in therapy to show Pilar that he can change. In an apparent attempt to understand his own excesses, he eagerly takes part in the men's circle as they describe their feelings of violence that systematically culminate in acts of abuse perpetrated on their partners and wives. The therapy session is particularly important at this juncture because it reveals the men's mental processes as they explain or attempt to justify their acts of violence: women are "hysterical," "never do the right thing," and "resist sexual intercourse," they contend. In their view, men should not have to be bothered by their recalcitrant wives who provoke these violent reactions. They are entitled, perhaps by tradition, to employ any means in order to maintain control and, moreover, physical abuse is in fact very effective: "Witness the calmer wife after a beating!"[9]

The tone that these men adopt when discussing their relationships with the female "other" during therapy sessions validates the use of violence in their marriages, which also supports the male entitlement to positions of power. The assumptions that inform this dialogue are based on the rationalization of the man's role as the authoritarian figure within the relationship, defended by his role as "breadwinner." Consequently, men beating their spouses is considered a substantiated action, as well as a mechanism to put them in control of the family structure. Discipline, sexual practices, and causes of violence are the premises that run through the masculine verbal violence during the sequences of discussions at the therapy sessions throughout the film. Antonio is also immersed in this culture of domination. By attending these therapy sessions, he aims to demonstrate control over his hostility and anger toward Pilar, as well as to prove his desire to change. He fails to realize, however, that beating her is just one of the many layers of his violent behavior.

Throughout the film, Antonio uses ambiguity with the strategic purpose of control. For instance, after Pilar's escape to Ana's home, he leaves presents for his wife at work. What might seem, from the outside, to be a loving gesture is in fact an act that will frighten the person suffering the abuse, since she is attempting to distance herself from the relationship. This targeted ambiguity generates disconnection and anxiety for the woman, as well as a confusing message of redemption. The viewer realizes Antonio's intentional ambiguity in the sequence showing Pilar's first day at work in Santo Tomé Church (which houses El Greco's famous *Burial of the Count of Orgaz*, a highly emblematic painting of male aristocracy and patriarchy). There she finds a pair of earrings on her desk that Antonio had left for her. Pilar's coworker infers a generous action from a man who is in love with his wife. However, Pilar's face shows an enigmatic mix of fear and hope; there is still an inkling of hope in Pilar that Antonio will change his behavior.

Nevertheless, Antonio is doomed never to overcome his own inflicted sense of inferiority. His insecurities regarding his job at the family's household appliance business, the teasing by his own family (his brother), and his questioned role as breadwinner, are channeled through domestic violence in an attempt to control his wife as a means to make him feel that he is in a position of authority in his home. The idea of the home as his own territory serves as a catalyst for Antonio's behavior because there he is able to affirm the control that the outside world will not allow. He is unable to function, and for him dealing with the outside world only exacerbates his angst. His fragmented masculinity deteriorates into a chaos of control and paranoia, and his emotions lead him to further nullify Pilar's personality, especially when she decides to define herself by starting a job at the museum and studying to give guided tours of classical paintings.

Through her work, Pilar discovers friendship and personal accomplishments outside her domestic realm of fear. For her, escaping the domestic walls and encountering the opportunities offered to her by the city shape her newly achieved individuality. However, Antonio's disturbed actions culminate in another act of domestic brutality when he learns that Pilar is going ahead with her plan to work (later, he makes a clumsy suicide attempt, as a way of coercing Pilar to stay). The morning of Pilar's job interview illustrates the cruel nature of the physical and psychological abuse to which Pilar has been subjected, and shows the basis of Antonio's sense of entitlement to control. Antonio feels betrayed and powerless as he watches an excited and hopeful Pilar prepare for an interview for a teaching position. He antagonizes her and tries to diminish her self-worth by criticizing her ambition, her clothes, and her appearance: "walking around while they follow you," "That's what turns you on," "That's some get up…And you want people to look at you, letting them look at your legs and ass." Moreover, he orders her about, attempting to diminish her authority, subjectivity, and recent empowerment: "Turn around. Look at me when I talk to you. Show me how you do it."[10]

As he tears out the pages of an art book, Antonio's obsession with other people looking at Pilar becomes the main compulsive utterance in his speech: "Your ass, your tits, everything, right? It turns you on when they look at you." Then Antonio—furious—pushes her down to the floor, strips her clothes off, and locks her out on the apartment's balcony while shouting, "That's what you like. Let's everyone see you."[11] Stripping Pilar of her clothes and locking her out on the balcony so that everyone can see her is an act of violation of human life that further debases the female. He takes her by her throat and is about to hit her when Pilar, unable to control her fear for her life, wets herself. At this moment, Antonio realizes what was about to happen and coldly orders her, "Go clean yourself."

The phrase *"I give you my eyes"* acquires strategic relevance in these scenes. Antonio is fixated on how others look at Pilar, and as a tool of control over his wife, he must legitimize his own singular unmediated gaze. Antonio's isolation becomes apparent at the end of the film, when Pilar and her friends return to the apartment to pick up the rest of Pilar's belongings. While looking at each other, neither of them can say anything; Antonio follows her around with his eyes while Pilar goes through her and her son's personal items, taking essential mementos for her soon-to-be new life. As Pilar and her friends leave the apartment the camera focuses on Antonio, sitting at the dining table, eating alone, and contemplating the view of the apartment complex and streets below, typical of a neighborhood on the outskirts of a city. He then looks onto the outside world where Pilar has found her new individuality.

As for Pilar, she finds herself at the crossroads of two very distinct generations. Her mother represents the women who grew up during Franco's dictatorship (1939–1975) and were subject to the patriarchal structures of State and Church. Her sister, Ana, an independent working woman exposed to other cultures,[12] embodies the new and pluralistic Spain within the ideological parameters of the contemporary European Union. Placed at the intersection between the past and the present, Pilar represents a defining moment for Spanish women to reconceptualize the power structure within heterosexual relationships, and by extension within society at large. In an earlier scene, soon after Pilar's escape, the sisters prepare for Ana's wedding as their mother arrives at Ana's home. She brings Ana wedding dress, the same one that Pilar wore on her wedding day. In this sequence, the image of the white wedding dress is used as a symbol for the "women's ethos" of the culturally perpetuated idea of the romantic, eternal love as a factor defining one of the most important days in a woman's life—her marriage.

The impossible reconciliation between the adherence to a traditional definition of women in society and the acceptance of more progressive views is shown vividly in the group comprised of Ana, Pilar, and their mother. Bollaín equates the suffering woman's role to that of the female martyr, the woman who wins sanctity through self-sacrifice and pain. Subsequently, the mother appears oblivious of her daughter's unhappiness, downgrades the importance of spousal violence, and unimaginably urges her daughter to return to her husband in order to sustain the all-important social order and maintain the appearance of normality at all costs. The young Ana recoils at the thought of Pilar's return to her husband and tells their mother the full details of Pilar's suffering at the hands of her husband: the cases of tendonitis, the torn muscles, and the loss of vision in one eye, "That bastard even kicked her in the kidney!"[13]

Pilar's physical and emotional damage has thus been articulated through Ana's voice. Pilar's secret is now acknowledged by the female members of her immediate family. Her mother, surprised by Ana's sudden revelation, approaches her daughter Pilar and wants to hug her. However, now that her pain has been exposed, Pilar refuses to be hugged. Instead, she expresses her awareness of her situation by throwing the wedding dress over the terrace and shouting to Ana in desperation, "You are right! You are right!" thus refusing to follow her mother's ill-fated path. The camera focuses on the long, white wedding dress absurdly suspended in the midst of the electrical cables above the old neighborhood of Toledo. By looking at the bridal gown, bodiless, now meaningless, Pilar psychologically terminates the traditional women's conception of the wedding day.

Immediately after this episode, the viewer indirectly learns that Pilar's deceased father was in the military. Being part of the State machinery under the dictatorship meant fully embracing the social, religious, and ideological discourse of the fascist regime. In line with this discourse, a woman's value in Spanish society of the 1940s, 1950s, and 1960s was judged on the basis of her dedication to home and husband.[14] Pilar's mother, like many others of that time, has rooted her values in the collective memory of those decades, and therefore her acceptance of this intricate ideology is understandable. She, however unwillingly, perpetuates within her discourse of femininity the moral values of submission and sacrifice. Conversely, Pilar represents women who will transform, but not without difficulty, the transitional generation.

Pilar's character is defined through the metaphorical sense of seeing—seeing or finding herself as a woman—and through the understanding of images in the art she encounters in her work as healing expressions of empowerment. Her connection to the visual arts constitutes the turning point that liberates Pilar from the violent past once her secret is revealed. Yet she is unable to articulate the circumstances of her abuse in words. Instead, she finds in the visual narratives of the paintings her own inner wordless discourse, thus giving an outlet to her struggle to find herself (after the initial unsuccessful abandonment of her home). Finally, Pilar is able to develop into a self-sufficient woman. The narratives and the tools of knowledge and education give her the courage to leave her husband and to understand that his abusive character will never change; only she can change.

The old and artistic city of Toledo presents Pilar with the opportunity to search for her inner soul. Her first encounter with Luis Morales' painting[15] *La Dolorosa* in Toledo's Church of Santo Tomé, where she is offered a job as a ticket-seller, and later her discovery of Rubens's *Orpheus and Eurydice* and Titian's *Danaë* are crucial moments of awakening and awareness. The painting *La Dolorosa* mirrors Pilar's grief in her difficult situation after her first escape from her husband (Beltrán 2007). Its dark colors and the submissive posture of resignation in the figure of the Virgin Mary visually parallel Pilar's thoughts and pain. Similarly, the mythology of Orpheus and Eurydice and Danaë tells stories of women subjected to punishment as a consequence of a man's behavior. Eurydice is condemned to remain in the underworld and Danaë is locked in a tower of bronze. These visual and artistic narratives echo Pilar's own personal experience as a woman who has been trapped like Eurydice in an inferno of marital abuse, and who, like Danaë, was caged in the realm of the domestic (where nobody could see her) and under Antonio's controlling gaze.

Toward the end of the film Pilar admits to her sister Ana: "I have to see myself, I don't know who I am." For this reason, the phrase "*I give you my eyes*" becomes for Pilar a declaration of resistance that documents her struggle to survive the situation of gender-abuse within which she has been trapped. This utterance clearly defines Pilar in opposition to Antonio's statements, "That's what turns you on. Let everyone see you." Pilar now sees herself inwardly, in a quest for her identity, while Antonio only sees what is not there. Pilar's past and present existence has been reconstructed by the paintings she sees at the museum, which offer a visual narrative of her experiences.

Iciar Bollaín portrays Pilar as a female character confined in a world created by men and their vision of women. Ironically, those voluptuous, naked female bodies in the paintings that Pilar explains to visitors—this erotic pictorial universe—will transfigure her voice and personal story. These art works will also transform Pilar into a woman on a quest to find her individuality, a woman who refuses to be self-sacrificing, repudiates patriarchal control, and transcends a situation of gender-based abuse. Thus, her catharsis reaches its apex when she admits her need to "see herself" to her sister. In this instance, in Pilar's mind *"I give you my eyes"* connects the idea of the empowerment of the visual to the idea of memory, since she is abandoning her own past (represented by Antonio's entitlement to express his fears through physical and verbal abuse) as well as a historical past embedded in Francoist ideas of a submissive patriarchal Spain (as represented by her mother's collective memory and past experiences).

To conclude, Antonio's actions and his perception of his wife within the family structure are framed in and ingrained with the more than forty years of fascist-nationalist discourse, where the role of women was reduced to the microcosm of the home and the raising of children. The regime was successful in silencing the female voice and controlling women's roles in society, thus making silence the predominant discourse during Franco's dictatorship.

In a study of the film industry and its practitioners in Spain, sociologist Fátima Arranz (2007) concluded, not unexpectedly, that the number of men in the industry far outweighed the number of women, especially in the positions and roles that could influence points of view and behaviors. For example, between the years 2000 and 2006 only 7.3 percent of directors working in Spain were women, and the total percentage of female producers, actors, and directors barely reached 20 percent. Cinema not only constructs identity, but it is often used as a vehicle to convey sociocultural beliefs and influence attitudes while mirroring society. Such a small number of professional women in the industry suggests that women are marginalized in the culture of the film industry and therefore their voices and narratives are underrepresented. By default, Spanish cinema thus promotes and perpetuates patriarchal representations of male identity. By asserting a vision shaped by female experience, as Bollaín does in *Take My Eyes*, the male-dominant perspective is both challenged and tempered.

Cinema, like language, conveys not just manifest meaning (what is explicitly stated), but also latent messages about social reality. Film directors, like language users, define men and women differently. Arranz's empirical study also pointed out that, amongst films directed by men, 30 percent depict violence against women and, of that number, 75 percent justify it or present it sympathetically. However, a mere 20 percent of films directed by women depict male violence toward women, and this violence is never condoned, it is always condemned.

*Take My Eyes*, a metaphor for this male-dominated discourse, narrates the story of gender violence and abuse in contemporary Spain, thus expressing a need to show situations that had been kept silent for so many years: a silence that for decades has meant complicity and acceptance of the gender imbalance. The film represents a journey deep into the heart of the dark issues surrounding gender-based violence. It also challenges traditional patriarchal values by making visible the microcosms of domestic violence in which men are agents and women, without agency, represent the abject Other.

# Notes

I wish to thank Elaine Bunn and Raúl Rosales.

1. Only Pilar Miró (1940–1997) had previously won the award, in 1996 for her film *El perro del hortelano*.
2. The Academy also showered the film with five more recognitions in "best" categories: film, leading actors (both male and female), female secondary role, and sound. The film's success outside Spain was acknowledged by the many international awards it won.
3. Director's statement in an interview after the release of the film *Take My Eyes*. English translations of interviews, articles, and/or other texts in Spanish are mine. Translations of film dialogues are taken from the subtitles of the DVD *Take My Eyes*.
4. *"Al principio yo no le denunciaba, porque en aquella época no se hacía. Luego, al final, sí, pero la verdad es que no me servía de mucho. Lo que me dicen es que ésas son peleas normales en la familia. Y él lo único que hace es amenazarme con que un día me tiene que matar."*
5. *"Se evidencia la tendencia de los medios a no reconocer las opiniones de las personas afectadas y su entorno que, en definitiva, son las 'expertas' en las características de su problema. Por el contrario, los medios de comunicación utilizan más a las instituciones oficiales como principalesfuentes informativas. Este enfoque periodístico no es imparcial y puede tener importantes repercusiones relacionadas con la capacidad de los medios de transformar situaciones indeseables en problemas sociales. Así, dado que la autoridad tiende a evitar la imagen de que tratan con problemas imposibles de abordar y a expresar consenso, los medios de comunicación, al centrarse en las instituciones oficiales y no dar un enfoque más multidimensional, podrían estar reflejando una decisión simplificada del problema y de sus posibles soluciones."*
6. In the imperial city of Toledo the cathedral looms over the city of seminaries, priests, and cloistered nuns. It is the place where the famous swords of the noble crusaders were forged and the forces of the right were positioned in the Alcázar bravely protecting the city from the infidel that

was the República (1936: Franco's coup d'état against the democrati-
cally elected government).

7. The Spanish word is "Canija" which is translated as "Shorty" in the
DVD English subtitles.

8. *Take My Eyes*, DVD Chapter 2.

9. Ibid., Chapter 9.

10. Ibid., Chapter 35.

11. Ibid.

12. Ana is about to marry her boyfriend, a Scottish man whom she met
when studying in the UK.

13. *Take My Eyes*, DVD Chapter 8.

14. Franco's dictatorship promoted the role "spouse-mother" for women, abol-
ishing civil marriage and divorce, reestablishing the Spanish Civil Code of
1898, and therefore reinforcing paternal and marital authority (*El paper de
les dones durant la república, la guerra civil i el franquisme*, 2001). Franco's
regime also created a social ideology of women's submission and repression
in which the rights obtained by women during the República (1931–1939)
were lost. Moreover, to ensure that the education of women followed such
ideology, Franco entrusted women's education to the "*Sección Femenina*"
(1934–1977) that declared as its fundamental mission to be "*la formación
de la mujer*" within parameters of home economics and of the care of children and the sick (Kromayer 1967). The "*Sección Femenina*" was an integral part of Falange, the ideological background to Franco's regime. Falange
recognized Christian families' role within its political project, in which
women were key members. The *Sección Femenina* defined the role of
women within paternalistic guiding principles that determined a subordi-
nate relationship with men. Thus, the *Sección Femenina* found its role
models in the figures of Santa Teresa and Queen Isabel La Católica.

15. Luis Morales: sixteenth-century painter. He was also known as El
Divino.

# References


Adams, Peter J., Alison Towns, and Nicola Gavey. "Dominance and
Entitlement: The Rhetoric Men Use to Discuss their Violence towards
Women." *Discourse and Society* 403–404, 6 (1995), http://das.sagepub.
com/ (Accessed on May 15, 2008).

Arranz, Fatima. Asociación de mujeres cineastas y de medios audiovisuales.
"Primeros apuntes del primer encuentro internacional de CIMA." CIMA
2007. http://www.cimamujerescineastas.es/Paneles.pdf (Accessed on
January 10, 2009).

Asociación de cultura popular Estrella Roja. "Entrevista a Iciar Bollaín."
ACP Estrella Roja, http://www.mujerpalabra.net/forum/viewthread.
php?tid=275&page=1#pid598 (Accessed on January 10, 2009).

Beltrán Brotons, María Jesús. "Universos pictóricos y el arte cinematográfico de Iciar Bollaín en *Te doy mis ojos* (2003)." In *Miradas Glocales. Cine español en el cambio de milenio*, ed. Burkhard Pohl and Jörg Türschmann, 323–335. Madrid: Iberoamericana, 2007.

Cameron, Deborah, and Don Kulick. *Language and Sexuality*. Cambridge: Cambridge University Press, 2003.

Eckert, Penelope, and Sally McConnoll-Ginet. *Language and Gender*. Cambridge: Cambridge University Press, 2003.

"El observatorio contra la Violencia Doméstica alerta sobre la "desoladora" cifra de 169 mujeres muertas desde 2001." *La Vanguardia*, November 25, 2003, Spain section, Spanish Edition. http://www.lavanguardia.es/premium/publica/publica?COMPID=51262784769&ID_PAGINA=22088&ID_FORMATO=9 (Accessed on May 16, 2008).

*El paper de les dones durant la República, la guerra civil i el franquisme.* (2001) http://centros5.pntic.mec.es/ies.parque.de.lisboa/alumnos2001/21.htm (Accessed on May 10, 2008).

"Entrevista a Ana Orantes." *El País*. December 19, 1997. Domestic section, Spanish Edition. http://www.gobiernodecanarias.org/educacion/3/Usr/pasillo/12/pagina_n2.htm (Accessed on May 12, 2008).

Kromayer, Astrid. "The 'Sección Femenina' of Spain." *Hispania* 50 (1967): 342–345.

*La Falange.* http://www.infonegocio.com/xeron/viva_la_falange.pdf (Accessed on May 21, 2008).

Losilla, Carlos. "Contra el cine español. Panorama general al inicio de un nuevo siglo." *Archivos de la filmoteca* 49 (2005): 125–145.

Spanish Parliament." Ley de protección integral contra la violencia de género." Boletín Oficial del Estado, December 2004. http://www.boe.es/g/es/bases_datos/doc.php?coleccion=iberlex&id=2004/21760 (Accessed on May 10, 2008).

*Take My Eyes.* Directed by Iciar Bollaín. Spain: Sogepaq, 2003.

United Nations. "Declaration on the Elimination of Violence against Women." U.N. December 20, 1993. http://www.un.org/documents/ga/res/48/a48r104.htm (Accessed on March 12, 2008).

"Violencia contra las mujeres" ELPAIS.com/Gráficos, November 25, 2005. http://www.elpais.com/graficos/sociedad/Violencia/mujeres/elpgrasoc/20051125elpepusoc_1/Ges/ (Accessed on May 8, 2008).

Vives-Cases, Carmen, María Teresa Ruiz, Carlos Álvarez-Dardet, and Marta Martí. "Historia reciente de la cobertura periodística de la violencia de género contra las mujeres en el contexto español (1997–2001)." *Gac Sanit.* 19(1), (2005): 27. Scielo Online Digital Library. http://www.scielo.br/pdf/gs/v19n1/original3.pdf (Accessed on May 8, 2008).

*France: Body Mutilation*

# Chapter Four

## Mutilating and Mutilated Bodies: Women's Takes on "Extreme" French Cinema

### Carrie Tarr

Of all the countries bordering the Mediterranean, France has not only the biggest film industry but also the highest number and proportion of women filmmakers (Tarr with Rollet 2001, Audé 2002). However, since the 1990s, few of these filmmakers have explicitly claimed to make films from a feminist perspective or opted for an alternative feminist counter-cinema, feminist discourses having been effectively marginalized in a postfeminist France.[1] Rather, they have elected to develop and consolidate their relatively strong position within the French film industry where they have been able to mainstream representations of female subjectivity and issues affecting women's lives, not only through auteur films but also through the appropriation of popular genres such as comedy, costume drama, crime fiction, and the road movie, evident in box office successes such as Nicole Garcia's *Place Vendôme* (1998), Tonie Marshall's *Venus Beauty* (1999), and Agnès Jaoui's *Look at Me* (2004).

Recent years have seen the development of a relatively new strand in French filmmaking that has become known as "extreme" French cinema. The phenomenon can be traced back to Gaspar Noé's *I Stand Alone* (1997) and refers to a body of mostly male auteur films that have shocked audiences with their taboo-breaking appropriation of elements of horror, gore, and porn, including stylized but graphic imagery of bodies (mostly, but not only, female) being raped, tortured, and murdered.[2] This "cinema of transgression," to use Martine Beugnet's term (Beugnet 2007), might seem alien terrain for women's filmmaking, yet it has attracted a number of French women filmmakers. This chapter focuses on women's contribution to such a cinema, with a view to assessing the extent to which they have been able to inflect it with women's and/or feminist concerns.

For critic James Quandt (2004), the hybrid nature of "extreme" French cinema is the sign of a cultural crisis whereby French filmmakers have responded to "the death of…French identity, language, ideology, [and] aesthetic forms…with desperate measures." Thus, for Quandt, as for many other critics, "extreme" French cinema is best understood as a calculatedly violent, porno-chic reconfiguration of French film aesthetics that is attempting to beat Hollywood and Asian cinemas at their own game in the transnational marketplace.[3] Consequently, it is not to be seen as a form of "authentic liberating outrage" (Quandt 2004). Rather, like the postmodern American blockbuster or what Paul Gormley calls the "new-brutality" film, it is a knowing, sadomasochistic mode of filmmaking that assaults the viewer via visceral imagery focusing on the physicality and vulnerability of the body in a way that, Gormley suggests (2005, 5), causes "a reaction based on immediacy and bodily affect which subordinates critical consciousness and awareness of the world or knowledge outside the image to its initial impact." These films, then, or particular moments in these films, require a different kind of analysis than that posited by classic feminist gaze theory, one based on embodied spectatorship and the masochistic pleasures of self-abnegation and abjection (Kristeva 1980, Studlar 1988, Clover 1992) rather than the sadistic power dynamics of "the male gaze" (Mulvey 1975).

At the same time, as feminist scholars have argued (Boyle 2005, Neroni 2005), violence erupts in film when ideology fails and strictly defined gender roles break down; and it is notable that the appearance of "extreme" French cinema coincided with a period of gay and feminist activism in France.[4] Furthermore, while the spectator may momentarily experience the simultaneous fascination and repulsion of abjection and loss of ego in their viewing of such films, extreme cinematic violence is nevertheless embedded in, and retrospectively made readable by, some sort of contextualizing narrative, which, arguably, might return the viewer to "critical consciousness of the world," not to mention "liberating outrage." And, arguably, such outrage may well be related to their representation of sexual difference. Thus, if "extreme" French cinema borrows from popular genres that have conventionally shored up masculine identities by addressing the desires, fears, and anxieties of male-identified spectators—porn by portraying women as instruments of male pleasure, horror by constructing women as either monsters to be destroyed or victims to be protected—women filmmakers' embedding of visceral imagery within narratives relating to female desire and female violence may still have the potential to disrupt and destabilize normative constructions of sexual difference, including the taken-for-granted understanding of violence as "normal" when associated with masculinity but traumatic and perverse when associated with femininity.

In her work on transgressive contemporary French cinema, Beugnet (2007) addresses not just films considered to be "extreme," but also films that foreground the materiality of film as a way of provoking affect. It is clear that numerous French women filmmakers are interested in exploring film's ability through synaesthesia to evoke touch, texture, taste, and other sensations.[5] Recent examples include Patricia Mazuy's costume drama *Saint-Cyr* (2000), whose vivid evocation of the clamminess of the eponymous seventeenth-century chateau amid the stagnant marshes is an apt corollary to the corruption of the court of Louis XIV, Emmanuelle Bercot's *Clément* (2001), whose dizzying camerawork invokes the intensity of an older woman's fascination with a schoolboy, or Isild Le Besco's *Demi-tarif* (2003), which explores in close-up, tactile fashion the everyday lives of three young children abandoned by their parents.[6] However, the films by women that have received international distribution, despite limited success at the French box office, are those that combine a concern with sensation and affect with borrowings from (and/or deconstructions of) porn and horror. Prominent among them are *Baise-moi/Fuck Me* (2000) by Virginie Despentes and Coralie Trinh Thi, *Dans ma peau/In My Skin* (2002) by Marina de Van, *Trouble Every Day* (2002) by Claire Denis, and *Anatomie de l'enfer/Anatomy of Hell* (2004) by Catherine Breillat.

All four of these films have proved controversial. *Baise-moi*, made by filmmakers and actresses with backgrounds in the sex industry, received vitriolic press reviews and was banned in response to protests from a right-wing French pro-family group, before being awarded first an X, then an 18 certificate. *In My Skin*, though well-received critically, and awarded the 2003 prize for most disturbing, iconoclastic film of the year by journalists, was only released on two screens in Paris (and very few elsewhere), and relegated to middle-of-the-night screenings on the French pay TV channel *Canal+*, with warnings that it contained scenes that would disturb some viewers (warnings also applied to *Baise-moi*). *Trouble Every Day* led to a critics' walkout at the Cannes film festival, despite Denis's auteur status. And *Anatomy of Hell*, the tenth in a series of films by Breillat to address female sexuality and sexual difference, was dismissed by many critics as self-parody. What the four films have in common is a troubling emphasis on women's corporeality and women's violence, constructing female protagonists who are instrumental in the mutilation either of others or of themselves. However, this violence is enacted through the mode of dark, postmodern fantasy, borrowing from porn and/or horror genres rather than social realism. The films thus raise the question as to how women's violence should be read in such a context. To what extent do they challenge the conventional disposition of gender roles and images and so deny the pleasures usually associated with these genres? To what extent can their takes on porn and/or horror be linked to visions of women's struggle in the "real world"? The chapter discusses the films in chronological order, assessing the invigorating work of first-time filmmakers Despentes, Thi, and de Van before comparing and contrasting films by veteran directors Denis and Breillat.

## *Baise-moi*

*Baise-moi* has divided feminists because of its shocking violence and use of imagery associated with hardcore porn. Like *Thelma and Louise* (1991) before it (see Tasker 1993, 134), it has been welcomed, on one hand, as a feminist reworking of male genres, here not just the buddy road movie but also the action thriller and porn film, and also as an admirable commentary on rape and sexual violence; but, on the other hand, it has been criticized for the construction of symbolically male, phallic, women-with-guns, and for the exploitation of its actresses, former hardcore porn stars Raphaëlla Anderson and Karen Bach. As Yvonne Tasker points out in relation to *Thelma and Louise*, however, feminist criticism of images of violent women is problematic, even ironic, given that it coincides with a more conventional sense of "feminine decorum, a sense of knowing one's place within a gendered hierarchy" (Tasker 1993, 136). The argument could also be extended to criticisms of images of sexually predatory women.

*Baise-moi* centers on two women, Manu (Anderson), a sometime hardcore porn actress of Maghrebi descent, and Nadine (Bach), a prostitute, who meet in a Parisian *banlieue* (suburb) after each has been driven to murder. The duo take to the road on a liberating fucking, stealing, and killing spree that involves extended scenes of sadistic carnage, and predatory sex involving "real" penetration and oral sex. Shot on a low budget with a handheld digital camera, the film gleefully makes its female protagonists the agents of a narrative in which they treat men as casual instruments of female pleasure, and obliterate those who antagonize them, in scenes of ritualized violence, often accompanied by a pounding techno soundtrack. A knowing postmodern film, its multiple intertexts include an extract from *I Stand Alone* (Nadine watches a scene from it on the television while she is servicing a client, one in which a phallic sausage is being brutally sliced in extreme close-up), and its protagonists self-consciously act out their genre roles, endowing themselves with post Tarantino-esque cool by commenting self-reflexively on the need for witty dialogue to accompany a killing, posing with a gun, or planning an appropriate headline-provoking ending to their odyssey (i.e., jumping from a bridge without a bungee).

Nevertheless, the film's brutal imagery of female-instigated sex and violence is clearly linked by the narrative to the two women's rebellion against their disenfranchised backgrounds and the way they are dehumanized by others. The opening sequences crosscut between them as Nadine returns from doing a trick as a prostitute and takes out her suppressed anger on her nagging bourgeois flatmate, strangling her to death, while Manu, having maintained a stoic stillness while being raped along with her junkie girlfriend (whose rape is visualized in a particularly gruesome manner), later reacts by killing her violent brother, who cares more about his honor than her feelings. The film thus focuses on two women who are different from—and therefore can be dissociated from—"ordinary" women, both because of their links to the sex industry and because of their extreme violence; but it also represents their decision to take action as positive in comparison with the passivity of other women who choose to remain victims of male brutality, be it Manu's girlfriend or the sad, servile blonde Nadine sees being treated like dirt by her boyfriend in the film's opening sequence. To some extent, then, their rebellion stands in for a wider protest against the treatment of women in a violent, patriarchal society. The duo's subsequent taking of control, the growing intensity of their female friendship, a relatively rare phenomenon in French cinema, even in women's films, evident here in their instant complicity, their shared pleasures (dance, drink, drugs, and music as well as sex, stealing, and killing) and their impeccable teamwork, and—if only because it reverses the taken-for-granted violence of so many films about women—their manipulation, mockery, and elimination of men who make certain types of sexist assumptions about women, all contribute to an allegory of female struggle and empowerment in a violent male-ordered world, which offers a variety of pleasures for many female, or female-identified viewers.

For male-identified viewers, however, the film might be something of a trap. Its widely publicized foregrounding of "authentic" hardcore sex scenes, the heroines dressed "to kill," seemingly invites conventional pornographic pleasures in the spectacle of the female body on display and open to penetration. Yet the camera does not probe the female body in the way one might expect from a porn film, rather, in contrast with the dispiriting opening sequences, it focuses on the women as active agents of their own sexual pleasure, picking up the men of their choice and having sex with them on their own terms.

Furthermore, viewers are aware that the two women are toting guns and likely to react to abusive treatment in a trigger-happy fashion, thus subverting the structures of the gaze and endowing the sex scenes with a sense of unease likely to inhibit pleasure in sex as purely porno-graphic spectacle. At the same time, these scenes also lead to occa-sional moments of tenderness, not just between the two women but also with their selected sexual partners, as long as the men simply accept them as they are. Tellingly, most of the male characters in the film treat Manu and Nadine as they treat other women, that is, to be laid, disdained, patronized or abused; and they are punished for their arrogance and contempt when the duo turn their guns on them, from the man making lewd remarks in the street to the manager of the joy-less "Fuck Club." Thus, Maximilian Le Cain's description of the film as an "electrifying, swaggeringly punkish, defiantly amoral tale of sex and mass murder" in which a "blankly indifferent world" is "suffused with unshakable [...] nihilism" (Le Cain 2002, 1), is just not ade-quate. Rather, apart from the initial, apparently indiscriminate killing of the middle-class woman whose bank card they steal, *Baise-moi* can be read as a moral tale, which attacks the loveless sexual violence and contempt that permeates and informs many women's everyday experi-ences, and offers in its place not just a jubilant woman-centered revenge fantasy but also a deconstruction of the performance of "femininity" and a vision of female solidarity, self-assertion and sexual reciprocity.

Unfortunately, however, this vision is largely recuperated by the film's disappointingly conventional ending, which brings about narra-tive closure and the restoration of order through the surprise shooting of Manu by a suspicious shopkeeper, followed by the capturing of grief-stricken Nadine by the police. Though the images spectators may retain from the film cannot necessarily be reduced to those of its narrative resolution, Despentes and Thi seem to have succumbed to the need to punish their otherwise admirably transgressive heroines by making them ultimately vulnerable to the patriarchal forces of law and order.

## *In My Skin*

*In My Skin* has also divided critics, in this case between those who con-demn its exhibitionism (the central protagonist is played by de Van her-self) and those who admire its accomplished exploration of the nature of corporeal existence. However, it has received little attention as a woman's film, even though it centers on a woman, Esther, an elegant, ambitious young Parisian, who discovers by accident the pains and pleasures of cutting herself. Since self-harming is a widespread contemporary social phenomenon often associated with women, the topic invites treatment along social realist lines. Rather than offering an insight into the psychological explanations for Esther's gruesome and not very typical behavior, however, de Van's stylized "art" film, accompanied by the eerie music of the Esbjorn Svensson Trio, borrows heavily from the horror genre, including the vampire film, in its fascination with the resulting abject female body and its foregrounding of the iconography attached to the cutting into and feeding on flesh: knives and other cutters, teeth, wounds, stitches, scabs, scars, and, above all, blood. A low-budget self-reflexive film, like *Baise-moi*, it uses techniques that draw attention to the film as film—split screen imagery, judicious cutting and framing devices, the incorporation of a camera within the film, panning shots over the final still image that lingers on the screen after Esther's exit—and it is informed by the fact that Esther, who eventually documents her self-harming with her own camera within the diegesis, can be read as a projection of de Van herself, controversial body shock actress, screenwriter, and director. Thus, as I have argued elsewhere, the film's representation of self-harming is on one level simply a shocking metaphor for, or expression of, de Van's experimental creative impulses and aesthetic values as an artist (Tarr 2006).

Nevertheless, the film is not for the squeamish, drawing its horror from its graphic visualization, in long often real-time sequences, of the spiraling intensity of Esther's perverse relationship with her body, from an apparent numbness—she does not feel the initial wound to her leg, which is the catalyst for her fascination with penetrating beneath the skin—to a delight in further mutilations. Hiding away from the world in dark spaces and secret hotel rooms, she cuts progressively into her legs and arms, gnaws at and nibbles morsels of flesh, smears herself with blood, cuts out and preserves a relatively large piece of skin from her leg, and eventually gouges holes in her face, the latter, according to David Le Breton (2003, 17), a sign in real life that self-harming has become really life-threatening. Furthermore, and perhaps more shockingly still, this self-harming is unambiguously eroticized. As Rob Horning (2003, 1) points out, "the film locks in on Esther's face, which registers, by turns, drugged stupor, deranged horror, and orgasmic frenzy." In a sense, then, Esther's solipsistic preoccupation with her body offers the spectator, male and female, a compelling vision of sadomasochistic abjection that blurs oppositions "between mind and body, subject and object, monster and victim, male and female, pain and pleasure" (Horning 2003, 1).

On the other hand, this solipsism can also be read as extremely transgressive in gender terms, since it is clear even from the elliptical,

**Figure 4.1**   Self-mutilation and *jouissance* in Marina de Van's *In My Skin*.

fragmented narrative of *In My Skin* that Esther finds *jouissance* in her relationship with herself rather than with her boyfriend Vincent (Laurent Lucas). And the film offers a series of indications suggesting that Esther's behavior, however perverse, can be read as a woman's response to the patriarchal world around her, be it the globalized corporate world of the public relations firm she works for, embodied by her uncomprehending male boss, or the increasingly oppressive world of the bourgeois couple she forms with the equally uncomprehending Vincent. Thus, in the early party sequence in which she accidentally gashes her leg, Esther is forced reluctantly to flirt with a (male) company executive in order to solicit a permanent job, a mode of behavior she derides as a form of prostitution. Later, her alienation from this world is brilliantly evoked in a surreal business dinner scene when her disconnection from her boss and clients is figured through her vision of her left forearm out of control, palpating the food on her plate, then completely detached from her body and only brought back to life by being surreptitiously jabbed with a knife. Similarly, her reaction to Vincent's increasing inability to talk to her about her situation, and refusal to accept that there are aspects of her life that might remain unknowable to him, is to withdraw into silence and further self-harming. This self-mutilation, however self-destructive, serves to give her back some sort of control over her life, if momentarily, as well as, paradoxically, energizing her into resuming work successfully. It can be understood in feminist terms, then, as a woman's visceral reaction against what Judith Butler (1993, x) describes as "normative constraints that not only produce but also regulate various bodily beings."

At the same time, the film undermines the potential political impact of such a reading, that is, women's self-harming as a form of rebellion against the constraints of a postindustrial but still patriarchal society, by also offering a construction of Esther as mentally unstable rather than an "ordinary" woman. The opening split screen sequence that evokes in disjunctive fashion the places where she works, from the high rise corporate offices of La Défense to the home computer in her flat, suggests not only a strong sense of detachment but also some form of split, damaged subjectivity, themes reprised in the final self-harming session. Furthermore, Esther's increasingly mutilated body is compared throughout with the unblemished body of her jealous and uncomprehending but more "normal" friend, Sandrine. And, at the end, after her final extreme self-mutilation, she is still apparently driven to set out for the office, even though she is hiding an unwashed blood-soaked bra and a piece of tanned skin beneath her new shirt, and the visible wounds on her face testify to her pathological mental state. The ending, then, is inconclusive and ambiguous, allowing Esther's self-mutilation to be read as a bold and necessary act of female defiance, a reaction to the way her body is regulated by the culture of corporate capitalism, and/or a sign that she has lost her grasp on reality and needs help.

## *Trouble Every Day*

*Baise-moi* and *In My Skin* are both troubling women-centered films whose shockingly violent imagery nevertheless allows for feminist readings and potentially offers more pleasures to female than to male-identified spectators. In contrast, *Trouble Every Day*, Claire Denis's pastiche of the horror film, is not specifically woman-centered—it braids together the horrific stories of both a male and a female victim of a mysterious disease—and is less obviously readable from a feminist perspective. Nevertheless, it is of interest to female viewers as a woman's representation of the way sexual desire taken to violent extremes posits a threat to the existence of the contemporary heterosexual couple. Cowritten by Denis with Jean-Pol Fargeau, and drawing on expressive cinematography by Agnès Godard and haunting music by Tindersticks, the film's languorous, elliptical narrative centers on individuals who literally devour their sexual partners with their desire, and contains a number of key scenes in which the camera lingers at length on landscapes of bodies, bloody, devouring and devoured. Even more than *Baise-moi*, the film revels in its playful reworking of elements of popular genres, here ranging from vampire and werewolf films, to Jekyll and Hyde, Hitchcock, and 1950s science fiction thrillers. However, its elusive, fragmented narrative does not offer a straightforward deconstruction of the way sexual difference tends to be constructed in such films. Rather, it plays with the idea that men and woman are both potentially monstrous (in their capacity for destroying others) and potentially victims (of their desire for others, or for their self-annihilation in others). At the same time, the film makes tenuous links between this state of affairs and the contemporary postcolonial, patriarchal, capitalist economy.

The two "monsters," Coré (Béatrice Dalle) and Shane (Vincent Gallo), are portrayed at different stages in the disease, with partners who face different degrees of risk. Coré is at an advanced stage, and is kept locked up in a lonely villa on the outskirts of Paris by her disgraced but loving research scientist husband Léo (Alex Descas), who appears to be seeking a treatment for her. Shane, an American arriving in Paris on honeymoon, is seeking former colleague Léo for help with his own less advanced condition in order to protect his pretty, ignorant, innocent wife, June (Tricia Vessey). To some degree, then, the film plays along with the conventional division of roles in classic cinema: the male figures have more active narrative roles, protecting dependent females and searching for solutions to the horror threatening to engulf them, whereas the female figures are more obviously linked to the visual spectacle of female abjection and what Barbara Creed (1993) calls "the monstrous-feminine," the product of male anxieties and fears about sexual difference. As monster, the mesmerizing, feral, vampiric Coré escapes her bonds and stalks, kisses, then consumes her prey, her body and her surroundings drenched in blood; later a young man is lured to his death at her hands when he follows his desire to free her from her imprisonment in the villa. As victim, June's barely recognizable blood-soaked body is the stuff of Shane's nightmare vision, replaced later by the spectacle of the hotel chambermaid's writhing body, dying from his no longer controllable, cannibalistic desires.

Yet when Shane arises from his victim's body, he, too, is represented as monstrous and abject, his body covered in blood. Whereas his previous killing of Coré in the blood-spattered villa could be seen as an attempt to eradicate the monster (and to protect his own life, since she tries to take him with her in the fire she has started), his role in the death of the chambermaid has no such justification. It is also clear that his role as agent of the narrative is unsatisfactory, as is that of Léo. Both men, it is suggested, are in some way responsible for the disease, thanks to a viral experiment that went wrong (and which is connected to the use of plants from French Guyana, previously a French colony). And both are paying for their scientific hubris, unable to achieve their goals (Shane does not find Léo, Léo does not find a cure for Coré), and sexually impotent (neither is able to make love to the woman he loves). Indeed, Shane is doubly punished since he is also a victim of the disease, his love for June forcing him to control his sexual desire for her either by masturbating or by breaking off from having sex (leading to a graphic cum shot, Denis's contribution to the breaking of cinematic taboos). At the same time, arguably, it is blood-drenched, world-weary Coré who takes on the most active narrative role since, aware as she is of the horror of her condition, she sets fire to the villa in order to bring about her own extinction. Her action underlines the fact that her monstrosity is not "natural" but "man-made," the result of human (male) scientific malpractice. To some extent, then, the film gestures toward a deconstruction of the myth of the monstrous feminine, replacing it with a vision of the monstrous male.

The film's ambiguity is evident in its final sequence. Shane is surprised in the shower by the return of his wife as he is washing off the blood from his killing of the chambermaid. The sequence cuts from shots of blood trickling down the screen, to Shane's view on it as he hugs June, to a close-up of June's wide open eyes, leaving spectators to speculate as to whether June has at last realized the threat hanging over her, and if so, if she is to be Shane's next victim, as predicted in his early nightmare vision, or if she might be able to take on the role of what Carol Clover (1992) terms the Final Girl and exact revenge (a possibility suggested perhaps by the contrast between her innocent face and her extraordinary bright red gloves). If *Trouble Every Day* has anything to offer female spectators, however, it is not through the construction of female agency, as in *Baise-moi* and *In My Skin*, but, rather, in complete contrast, through its blurring of gender roles and sexual difference. This blurring occurs not just at a narrative level but also at a visual level, as dramatic close-ups and panning shots focus on the materiality of the world, and, particularly, the corporeality of the human body, making the skin, hair, and blood of one body indistinguishable from that of another, including that of Coré and Shane. The film, then, from the opening kiss of two anonymous lovers, ultimately blurs the difference between killer and victim, male and female, and in this way deconstructs the conventional disposition of gender roles, suggesting that the capacity for monstrous behavior is human and context-specific rather than natural and gendered. At the same time, it presents a dark world in which the formation of the conventional hetero-normative couple proves fatally troubled and there is little prospect of a restoration of order.

## *Anatomy of Hell*

There is a certain similarity between *Trouble Every Day* and *Anatomy of Hell* in that both films feature mysterious, isolated, Gothic houses inhabited by a woman whose disturbed sexuality spells trouble for the men who frequent her; and both films graphically explore the shock value of the sexual encounters they portray, which in each case lead to death. However, whereas Denis's playful use of the genre draws on and questions its codes in ways that produce an ambivalent perspective on sexual difference, Breillat's borrowing from the classic horror tale uses the encounter between a man and woman to test out her thesis of the "absolute difference" between the sexes (Breillat 2004), an encounter that she intends to be of universal, allegorical significance.

The title *Anatomy of Hell* refers explicitly both to the patriarchal construction of femininity and the female body as a type of "hell," a reference to the damnation of the sexualized female body in Judeo-Christian theology and other discourses, and to the "hell" of inhabiting a female body in a society that continues to shore up such beliefs. It would thus seem to be aiming to deconstruct the notion of the "monstrous feminine." The woman in Breillat's hell is a nameless, suicidal young woman (played by Chanel model Amira Casar) who has strong feminist views on the way women are abused, misunderstood or ignored by men, and wishes to overcome the self-loathing she experiences at being a woman. Her savior is a nameless homosexual (played by Italian porn star Rocco Siffredi, costar of Breillat's earlier, controversial 1999 film, *Romance*), who, as a gay man, is apparently deemed to represent the ultimate in the culture's loathing and exclusion of women (a perspective set up by the explicit gay porn-inspired opening scene of a man giving another, possibly the woman's boyfriend, a blow job). Their initial encounter takes place in a gay nightclub where the man rescues the woman after she has cut open her wrist in the toilet, her bright red blood splattering over her very feminine pale pink skirt. After giving the man a blow job ("the only thing men want," she tells him, provoking him to anger), the woman then persuades him to help her overcome her shame and self-loathing by visiting her nightly in her cliff-top abode and watching her "where she is unwatchable," in return for payment (in itself an interesting gender role reversal).

The bulk of the film is taken up with the events of the next four nights, during which Breillat's voice-over commentary accompanies the dialogue between the man and the woman as they work through the "problems" of sexual difference. The woman's contract with the man (and the spectator) to gaze at length at the female body is an instance of Breillat's mission to counter the values of what she calls "the pornocracy," to attempt to "really see" (and see the beauty of) the naked female body in an openly self-conscious way, rather than accepting (and being disgusted by) the way it has been socially and religiously constructed. (Ironically, as signaled in the pre-credit sequence, Casar insisted on the use of a body double for the film's more intimate sequences, a device that confirms the artifice of Breillat's own cinematic construction of the body.) Breillat's trademark use of long takes, fixed frames, and shocking, tactile close-ups—including Siffredi's erect penis, the body double's extraordinarily hairy vagina and anus, and various bodily secretions—aims to counteract the way the female body is filmed in pornography and provoke not only spectatorial unease but also acceptance of "the truth" (Breillat 2004). We watch the man watching, as well as gazing ourselves at Casar's incredibly white body, displayed hieratically on the bed like a reclining model (and hence not at all like an "ordinary" woman); but the woman subsequently gazes back. And we see the man first behave aggressively toward her, daubing her genitals and mouth with lipstick one night, penetrating her anally with a garden fork another night; but subsequently he penetrates her anatomically in a way that produces orgasm, tears, and affection, as well as bringing her to orgasm through the use of a dildo. His agreement to drink the water in which she has dipped her blood-soaked tampon seals some sort of pact between them, and illustrates Breillat's desire to rescue from abjection the topic (and image) of women's menstrual blood (though the seriousness of these scenes unfortunately provokes as much mirth as it does shock or horror). Finally, however, in an unusually brief, unexpected, elliptical sequence, after the man has been paid off, we witness him angrily pushing the woman over the cliff in her virginal white nightdress, her body falling down to the powerful waves below. (The film gives no earlier intimation of its violent ending, apart from repeated imagery of the pounding sea.)

What is the significance of this final act of violence? David Durnell (2006, 1) argues, rather convincingly, that the murder occurs after the man, to his own astonishment, achieves a moment of genuine intimacy with the woman, the knowledge of which he chooses to repress when his fellow drinker in the local bar reproduces conventionally hateful attitudes toward women. The man's violence is thus a punishment of the woman for allowing him momentarily to experience tenderness toward her, before dismissing him without even letting him know her name. His reaction provides an extreme illustration of the deadly nature of socially constructed masculine attitudes toward women and the female body. At the same time, his earlier shift of positioning also points more optimistically to the possibility of change, had he been strong enough to resist the return of patriarchal conditioning.

However, this reading of the film is somewhat undercut by the problematic role of the woman. Breillat's obsessive but limited exploration of female sexuality in her films repeatedly constructs women who live out their hetero-normative sexuality in the shadow of social and religious taboos that they challenge but are unable or unwilling to transcend. Her female protagonists tend to connive in and flaunt their own abasement rather than questioning or resisting the terms in which they experience their bodies and their lives. They thus seem to be stuck at a stage of feminism that has long been left behind, if it ever existed, based on a presumed war between the sexes that ignores the postmodern world of fluid, performative identities and desires posited by feminists such as Judith Butler (1990, 1993). The impossibility of the couple in Breillat's world is thus due not just to the patriarchal attitudes of the male, but also to the passive aggressive attitudes of the female, who punishes the male by rejecting him (as in *36 Fillette* (1988) and *Une vraie jeune fille* (1999)), suppressing him (as in *Romance*) or goading him toward acts of murderous violence that will result in his damnation (as in *Sale comme un ange* (1991) and *Parfait amour!* (1996)). In *Anatomy of Hell*, the woman's contract with the man confirms as well as challenges her participation in her own abjection and propels him toward his final act of violence. Her annihilation in the closing sequence merely brings about what she appears to have sought at the beginning of the film; and if the intervening action makes explicit the murderous role of the man (as representative of the male sex), it also suggests that the woman is an active agent in provoking, traumatizing, and, ultimately, humiliating and punishing him.

This philosophical, apparently feminist take on horror and porn takes place in a world that is even more removed from the everyday social world than the other films discussed here. It is performed mostly in the *huis clos* of a once ornate, Portuguese villa, decorated (significantly) by a crucifix, amid stylized costumes and patterns of colors (grey-green walls and furnishings, virginal white sheets and clothing, red menstrual blood), between a couple who have no previous knowledge of each other. The only clue to their past histories is supplied by two sequences detailing their childhood memories: his of feeding and cradling a baby bird in its nest, then stamping on its body when he finds it dead after bringing it down from the tree; and hers of agreeing to play doctors with three young boys, her lower body then being exposed naked under a bush as they laugh at her. These memories point to the ways in which anxieties about feelings of tenderness and concerns about sexual difference and the female body are constructed in the male from an early age. But the woman's memory also shows her conspiring in the way she is treated. Thus, whereas Breillat undoubtedly sets out to deconstruct the "horror" that the female body inspires in a patriarchal culture, there is a danger that her treatment of hostility between the sexes can be read as the result of "natural" differences, the woman's responsibility as much as the man's.

## Conclusion

These "extreme" French women's films in their various ways all mobilize the unruly, sensory impact of sensational elements drawn from porn or horror genres to produce a cinema of affect that invites multiple spectator responses, including the pre-oedipal masochistic pleasures offered by the spectacle of abjection, and that has enabled their directors to carve out a place for themselves in a male-dominated transnational cinema that has increasingly foregrounded an aesthetics of extreme sex and violence. Nevertheless, their shocking images are embedded in self-reflexive, at times parodic, narratives that more generally challenge the objectification and submission of women and worry over the relationship between the sexes and the feasibility of the hetero-normative couple in today's postmodern but still patriarchal society. In particular, they address the issue of women's violence in relation to violence against women in contemporary European society, though the degree to which they draw on social reality and specific sociohistorical contexts varies from film to film.

*Baise-moi* and *In My Skin* both make some attempt to examine violence against women within a specific social context, the effects of the banalization of the sex industry and of deprivation in the run-down, working-class *banlieue* in *Baise-moi*, the impact of global corporate capitalism in *In My Skin*; and the women's violence in killing others or in self-harming can thus be seen as a fantasized reaction to such a situation that enables them to enjoy agency and control over their lives, even if it is ultimately self-destructive. The representation of violence against women in *Trouble Every Day* and *Anatomy of Hell* is somewhat more problematic. *Trouble Every Day*'s references to the social context of postcolonial, global capitalism are relatively oblique and construct both men and women as its victims, while the stylized, pared down mise-en-scène of *Anatomy of Hell* attributes violence against women to Western Judeo-Christian traditions in general rather than to specific contemporary circumstances. Nevertheless, all four films employ disaffected heroines who actively (and violently) reject the male-ordered social world and sexual submissiveness, and so point to the contingent nature of various fantasies about femininity. In so doing, arguably, they undermine the authority and stability of masculinity and male cultural and cinematic identities, and so provide visions of struggle.

# Notes

1. An exception to this was the debate stimulated by the wearing of the veil in France, when so-called feminists aligned themselves against the freedom of young Muslim women to wear the veil in the name of Republican values and equal rights, a debate brilliantly analyzed by Guénif-Souilamas (2004).
2. The corpus includes work by Léos Carax, Philippe Grandrieux, and Olivier Assayas.
3. Tartan Video uses the term "Extreme Cinema" to refer to Southeast Asian horror films.
4. This activism resulted in an acceptance of the need for parity in party political lists, and in the regularization of hitherto unacknowledged same sex relationships (the PaCS). Both measures covertly acknowledged a breakdown of French universalism and of the sense of complementarity between the sexes, which has traditionally underpinned the Gallic approach to sexual difference.
5. Beugnet draws on Siegrid Alnoy's *Elle est des nôtres* (2003), Catherine Breillat's *Romance* (1999) and *À ma soeur* (2000), Claire Denis's *Beau travail* (1999) and *Vendredi soir* (2002), Pascale Ferran's *Lady Chatterley* (2006), and Agnès Varda's *The Gleaners and I* (2000), as well as the films addressed in this chapter.
6. See also Emma Wilson's work on the tactile quality of women's films about children (Wilson 2006).

# References

Audé, Françoise. *Cinéma d'elles 1981–2001: situation des cinéastes femmes dans le cinéma français*. Geneva: L'Âge d'Homme, 2002.

Beugnet, Martine. *Cinema and Sensation: French Film and the Art of Transgression*. Edinburgh: Edinburgh University Press, 2007.

Boyle, Karen. *Media and Violence: Gendering the Debates*. Thousand Oaks, CA: Sage, 2005.

Breillat, Catherine. *Anatomy of Hell*, Tartan Video, 2004.

Butler, Judith. *Gender Trouble. Feminism and the Subversion of Identity*. London: Routledge, 1990.

———. *Bodies that Matter: On the Discursive Limits of 'Sex'*. New York and London: Routledge, 1993.

Clover, Carol J. *Men, Women and Chainsaws: Gender in the Modern Horror Film*. London: BFI, 1992.

Creed, Barbara. *The Monstrous-Feminine: Film, Feminism, Psychoanalysis*. London and New York: Routledge, 1993.

Durnell, David. "Woman's Body as an Anatomy of Hell: Nihilism, Recursion and Tragedy in Breillat's *Anatomy of Hell*." *Offscreen* 10, 7 (July 31, 2006), http://www.offscreen.com/biblio/phile/essays/anatomy_of_hell/ (Accessed on September 19, 2008).

Gormley, Paul. *The New-Brutality Film: Race and Affect in Contemporary Hollywood Cinema*. Bristol: Intellect, 2005.

Guénif-Souilamas, Nacira, and Macé, Eric. *Les Féministes et le garçon arabe*. Paris: Editions de l'Aube, 2004.

Horning, Rob. "In My Skin (Dans Ma Peau): Cutting." November 20, 2003, http://www.popmatters.com/pm/film/reviews/36164/in-my-skin/ (Accessed on September 19, 2008).

Kristeva, Julia. *Pouvoirs de l'horreur: essai sur l'abjection*. Paris: Éditions du Seuil, 1980.

Le Breton, David. *La Peau et la trace: sur les blessures de soi*. Paris: Métailié, 2003.

Le Cain, Maximilian. "Fresh Blood: Baise-moi." *Senses of cinema*, September 2002, http://www.sensesofcinema.com/contents/02/22/baise-moi_mx. html (Accessed on September 19, 2008).

Mulvey, Laura. "Visual Pleasure and Narrative Cinema." *Screen* 16, 3 (1975): 6–18.

Neroni, Hilary. *The Violent Woman: Femininity, Narrative, and Violence in Contemporary American Cinema*. Albany: State University of New York Press, 2005.

Quandt, James. "Flesh & blood: Sex and Violence in Recent French Cinema." *Artforum International Magazine, Inc.* 2004, http://findarticles.com/p/ articles/mi_m0268/is_6_42/ai_113389507 (Accessed on September 19, 2008).

Smelik, Anneke. "Feminist Film Theory." http://www.let.uu.nl/womens_
    studies/anneke/filmtheory.html (Accessed on September 19, 2008).
Studlar, Gaylyn. *In the Realm of Pleasure: Von Sternberg, Dietrich, and the
    Masochistic Aesthetic.* Urbana and Chicago: University of Illinois Press,
    1988.
Tarr, Carrie. "Director's Cuts: The Aesthetics of Self-Harming in Marina de
    Van's *Dans ma peau.*" In Special Issue: *Focalizing the Body in
    Contemporary Women's Writing and Filmmaking in France*, ed. Gill Rye
    and Carrie Tarr, 78–91. *Nottingham French Studies* 45, 3, 2006.
Tarr, Carrie with Rollet, Brigitte. *Cinema and the Second Sex: Women's
    Filmmaking in the 1980s and 1990s.* New York and London: Continuum,
    2001.
Tasker, Yvonne. *Spectacular Bodies: Gender, Genre and the Action Cinema.*
    London: Routledge, 1993.
Wilson, Emma. "Women Filming Children." In Special Issue: *Focalizing the
    Body in Contemporary Women's Writing and Filmmaking in France*, ed.
    Gill Rye and Carrie Tarr, 104–118. *Nottingham French Studies* 45, 3,
    2006.

*Italy: Women of the Mafia*

# Chapter Five

# Anthropological Anxieties: Roberta Torre's Critique of Mafia Violence[1]

Áine O'Healy

Throughout most of the 1980s and 1990s, film critics in Italy repeatedly declared Italian cinema to be dead or dying. Lamenting the passing of an era in which the national cinema had enjoyed worldwide prestige, these commentators offered a scathing dismissal of "*il cinema carino*," the blandly appealing yet ultimately shallow films that they identified as the dominant trend among an emerging generation of Italian directors. In a cinematic environment perceived as deficient in innovation and artistic vision, it is hardly surprising that the bracing originality of Roberta Torre's *Tano da morire* (1997), an exuberant, stylistically complex musical about the Mafia, attracted immediate critical attention upon its release. Set in the crime-ridden streets of Palermo and performed by a nonprofessional cast, this vibrant production was the first feature directed by Torre, a young Milanese filmmaker currently living in Sicily, whose previous experience was in documentaries and short subjects. While the film's flamboyant aesthetics and grotesque humor won rave reviews, a small number of dissenting voices took objection to its lighthearted approach to Mafia violence. *Tano da morire* thus marked the director's emergence as an innovative if potentially controversial presence on the Italian filmmaking scene.

Torre went on to make two additional feature films, *Sud side stori* (1999) and *Angela* (2002), which are similarly set in the dilapidated neighborhoods of the Sicilian capital. Considered together, the three films may be described as the director's "Sicilian cycle," as they are each inspired by actual events that occurred in Palermo, and offer a unique cinematic construction of the city's lawless subculture.[2] Thematically, these films are loosely linked to countless movies about the Sicilian mob made by Italian and foreign directors alike. Yet Torre's artistic vision deftly subverts conventional depictions of Sicily as a desolate social landscape in the thrall of terrifying Mafia bosses.

Unlike the powerful, even imposing figures constructed by conventional Mafia films, the mobsters evoked in her work are banal or ridiculous bullies, modeled on the small-time gangsters and petty criminals who populated the most notorious areas of Palermo when she first arrived in the city in the early 1990s.

In this chapter I would like to evaluate Torre's striking reconstruction of this distinctive social milieu in her three "Sicilian" films. The most compelling aspect of this body of work is the way in which documentary or ethnographic elements are recycled and transformed in the service of highly inventive cinematic storytelling. Torre began her career as a documentary filmmaker, and traces of the documentary impulse are inscribed in all her films. She has, in fact, explicitly described her approach to her subjects as that of an anthropologist (Capello 2000). Clearly the fruit of a long period of familiarization and research, her "Sicilian cycle" owes much to the willing collaboration of "native" informants. Whether articulated as a grotesque send-up of local mores (as occurs in *Tano da morire* and *Sud side stori*) or as stylized melodrama (as occurs in *Angela*), the insights delivered by these informants are nonetheless fully subsumed into the richly imaginative texture of Torre's narrative process.

Given the filmmaker's status as an upper-middle-class intellectual from the north of Italy, whose subject of cinematic inquiry is a socially marginal Sicilian population, her "anthropological" claims raise some pressing questions that must be identified at the outset: How does her deployment of parody and pastiche intersect with her anthropological objectives? What is one to make of the participation of local residents playing on-screen roles that supposedly mimic aspects of their own lives in the first two of these films? To what extent do her films reproduce or resist time-worn stereotypes of Sicily?

## North/South

A brief summary of some pertinent facts regarding the filmmaker's personal history and regional provenance may serve to contextualize these concerns. Around 1990, while still in her late twenties, Torre moved from her native Milan to Palermo, two cities at a considerable distance from each other in geographical, cultural, and economic terms, and promptly began to make short films about the fascinating and unfamiliar world she had chosen to inhabit. Her access to locations that subsequently became central to her work was facilitated at the outset by her personal and professional association with the avant-garde filmmaking duo from Palermo, Daniele Ciprì and Franco Maresco.[3] Far from adopting the dark, almost apocalyptic tone favored by these controversial directors, Torre's films suggest a warmer, more curious, less condemnatory attitude toward Palermo's human landscape. Although she obtained substantial cooperation from her Sicilian colleagues and from other local residents in her effort to document the city's criminal subculture, the obstacles she faced were considerable. While growing increasingly familiar with her adopted city, she remained an outsider on many levels: as a chronicler of everyday violence in a community bound by strict rules of secrecy and group loyalty, as a professional woman negotiating the minefields of a deeply patriarchal society, and as a northerner living and working in the south.

As a modern nation, Italy has never fully overcome the cultural, social, and economic disparities that characterized the national territory at the time of unification. The ongoing contrast between the affluence of the north and the more precarious economies of the southern regions is the most concrete symptom of that legacy. Long-standing prejudices and stereotypes also mark the division between north and south. Taking shape in the mid-nineteenth century, the discursive construction of the south, often described as the "Southern Question," rapidly consolidated the idea of a radical, essential difference between the two major sectors of the unified territory.[4] Demeaning attitudes toward the south have, in fact, endured into the twenty-first century.[5] Although the question of where the "north" ends and the "south" begins has often been a topic of dispute, the designation of Sicily as "southern" has always seemed beyond question.

The emergence of the northern populist party Lega Nord (Northern League) in the early 1990s has given new life to long-standing claims of northern superiority. In the mid-1990s, Umberto Bossi, the party leader, adopted an exclusionary, quasi-racist defense of what he described as "northern Italian culture" in his appeal for the secession of several northern regions from the rest of Italy. Bossi and his colleagues have claimed that the civic virtues of northern Italy are characteristic of "European culture," a category associated with integrity, efficiency, and hard work. In contrast to this imagined Europeanness, the south of Italy represents a "Mediterranean culture" of questionable honesty, laziness, and parasitic dependency. Although Bossi's party has by now moved beyond its secessionist ambitions, its racist rhetoric continues to be heard.

Torre began making her feature films in Sicily at precisely the point when the xenophobia of the Lega Nord, directed against southern

Italians as well as Italy's recent immigrants, was reaching unprecedented heights. As a Milanese intellectual about to embark on a cinematic exploration of everyday life in Palermo's most notorious neighborhoods, she risked being accused of the long-standing tendency of northerner commentators to pronounce judgment on the affairs of the south without sufficient knowledge of its peculiarities and complexities. According to Torre, however, condemnation is alien to her self-understanding as a filmmaker. She insists that her work is intended neither as political critique nor as a hostile caricature of the Sicilian social landscape, but rather as an ethnographic investigation of a society that has been insufficiently explored at ground level (Capello 2000).

Torre's proclaimed "ethnographic" approach is nonetheless worthy of further scrutiny. Criticisms of anthropology and ethnography as disciplines grounded in imperialism, along with feminist and postmodernist critiques, have over the past twenty years brought into focus the problematical underside of their signifying practices (Abu-Lughod 1989, Clifford 1988, Mascia-Lees et al. 1989, Ruby 1988, Trinh 2001). When applied to the study of human communities, various questions— such as "Who can represent whom?" "How?" "For what audience?" and "At whose expense?"—uncover anthropology's status as an offshoot of imperialism, and foreground the general, postmodern crisis of representation (Williams 1993). As contemporary Anglophone theorists have observed, unless anthropologists are willing to take a self-reflexive position vis-à-vis the subject of their inquiry by acknowledging the complex power relations implicit in their endeavor, they risk reiterating the imperialist mode of investigation that characterized the discipline at its inception (Abu-Lughod 1989, Behar and Gordon 1995, Mascia-Lees et al. 1989, Williams 1993).[6]

Torre's self-appointed role as investigator of the Sicilian ethnoscape suggests at least a partial internalization of a tendency already dominant in traditional anthropological practice in Italy, a tradition that Mariella Pandolfi describes as follows:

> Italian anthropologists have generally accepted the opposition of North and South, and, for political reasons, concentrated their research on the latter. Southern Italy was to them what the former colonized peoples of Africa, Asia and the Americas were to the anthropologies of the former colonial powers: England, France, and the United States. Already in the seventeenth century, Jesuit missionaries had defined the Italian South as *indias de por aca* ("our own Indies"), only marginally less savage and ripe for conversion than the *indias* of the European empire across the ocean. (Pandolfi 1998, 286)

The orientalizing nuances implicated in this type of scrutiny of the "Other" are thus enmeshed in the traditional line of approach favored by Italian anthropologists in their investigation of the south. In fact, the self/other, inside/outside dichotomies implied in traditional anthropological approaches seem to have been internalized by Torre, as her statements about her experiences in Sicily are often tinged with romantic invocations of exoticism and exceptional vitality. Admitting her fascination with the environment she encountered upon her arrival in Sicily, she claims to have drawn from her experience there a vital infusion of artistic energy: "In Palermo I found what I didn't have in Milan . . . stories, faces, bodies. An overflowing humanity that elsewhere seems to me to be a bit exhausted" (Marcus 2002, 235).

## *Tano da morire* and *Sud side stori*

The most striking aspect of the director's first two feature films is their deployment of parody and pastiche to confront troubling social issues, specifically, the ferocity of routine Mafia violence in *Tano da morire* and problems of racism and sex trafficking in *Sud side stori*. Although both films are musicals, their mordant humor and stylistic hybridity undercut the traditional, sentimental pleasures associated with the genre. In each case, the overall visual design reflects a dazzling mix of influences and citations, from comic strips to absurdist theater, from folk art to religious iconography, home movies, and live television reporting. At a moment in Italy's cinematic history when realism had largely eclipsed other stylistic registers, especially in films willing to take on burning social issues of the day, the exuberant if sometimes grotesque excess of Torre's style could be read as straightforward satire. The extraordinary aspect of this satire, however, is that it is performed on screen by Sicilian locals—including a sprinkling of real-life gangsters and petty delinquents (Capello 2000)—who were willing to engage in an exuberant send-up of their own identities, activities, and affiliations.

*Tano da morire* offers a fantastical retelling of the life and death of a low-level Mafia boss, Tano Guarrasi, who was assassinated in his butcher shop in 1988. Using a choral approach to storytelling and a lively musical score by Neapolitan singer-songwriter Nino D'Angelo, Torre infuses the narration with manic hilarity as she propels her characters toward an inevitably blood-soaked conclusion. The story of the real Tano, a resident of the run-down Vucciria neighborhood who dominated the lives of his unmarried sisters, was told to Torre by one of the man's in-laws, peppered with the kind of exaggerations that are typical of Mafia folklore. Realizing the disparity between the mythical elements applied posthumously to Guarrasi's story and the banal facts of his life, the director was inspired to make the film with the help of people who, like her initial informant, coexisted daily with the Mafia and knew the subculture firsthand.

Conventional cinematic representations of the Mafia are, according to Torre, predictable stories where good ultimately triumphs over evil. Rejecting the false comfort offered by such films, her account of Guarrasi's life is without heroes or easily distinguishable villains. At the same time, *Tano da morire* makes no attempt to present itself as an objective, documentary account. Indeed, Torre was clearly more concerned with finding a new cinematic language appropriate to her material than with "mirroring" the daily life of the Sicilian underworld in a straightforward, realistic narrative.

The film's carnivalesque tonality may seem at first to fly in the face of the filmmaker's documentary concerns. In fact, several self-reflexive embellishments explicitly point to the mediated or theatrical quality of the unfolding events, including, for example, the appearance of a proscenium and theatre curtains framing a scene that takes place outdoors. It thus becomes apparent that Torre's understanding of the documentary is not simply a matter of observing actions or facts. Rather, her elaborately self-reflexive style facilitates what Millicent Marcus has succinctly described as "an examination of the way in which chronicle becomes memory and collective memory becomes legend" (Marcus 2002, 235).

At several turns in *Tano da morire*, the vitality and playfulness of the visual and aural track are undercut by jarring references to brutality and death. The film is haunted by an iconography of death, beginning with a bizarrely choreographed funeral procession that is later revealed to be Tano's own funeral. The same procession makes an unexpected reappearance in the film's concluding sequence (set two years later), where it startles the guests assembled for the marriage of Franca, Tano's favorite sister, soon to be slaughtered by a stray bullet in the course of her wedding banquet. At regular intervals throughout the film, skulls equipped with luminous, bulging eyes float across the darkened screen, presiding over the story with their ghoulish presence. The living and the dead coexist in startling proximity. It is hardly an accident that one of the most striking song-and-dance numbers in *Tano da morire* unfolds in the protagonist's butcher shop amid hanging beef carcasses and headless chickens. These recurring images of mortality thus consolidate the impression of a community obsessed with death—courting it, flaunting it, and cultivating its rituals and symbols.

The death-oriented culture of the Sicilian Mafia is linked in Torre's film to rigid gender conventions, where manhood is aligned to a code of implacable toughness and the capacity for murderous revenge. Traditionally, all members of Cosa Nostra are bound by the code of honor known as "omertà," which literally signifies "the ability to be a man" (Jamieson 2000, 52). This ethos of "honor and silence" is formalized by participants through vows of loyalty and arcane rituals of affiliation, a process that traditionally excludes women. Thus, in *Tano da morire*, men and women inhabit separate spheres. For women, the communal meeting space is the beauty shop, where the regulars complain about their men, comment vociferously on Mafia informers, and ultimately divulge that one of them has, perhaps understandably, hired a hit man to finish off her spouse. These women are not shrinking violets, but fierce, heavyset matrons, and, as they converse, the putative killer is transformed into a threatening Medusa figure, with restless serpents coiled around her head. Although the women's raging resentment is palpable, the film implies that their dominion does not extend beyond the context of domestic life.

The men, by contrast, gather at a tavern in the piazza, at a nightclub, and at top-secret venues outside the city. They are clearly dominant in this world, disposing of their women as they please. Tano exerts strict control over his daughter and four sisters, preventing other men from approaching them at every turn. Although already murdered by the time the film begins, he makes several appearances in the mise-en-scene, not only during flashbacks, but also in the final enactment of the narrator's hypothesis that Franca's death was engineered by the already deceased Tano in order to oblige his sister to join him in the afterlife. Thus, in the world of the Mafia, dead men still hold sway over the destiny of the women who survive them.

One of the film's most compelling scenes offers a spectacular parody of the swaggering masculinity associated with mob leaders. In this, the central song-and-dance sequence, a cluster of gangsters assemble at a nightclub to cavort with each other in a lively dance number, rubbing noses, winking, kissing, and swinging their hips in suggestive fashion, while they perform a song with the refrain "Simme 'a mafia" (We are the Mafia). The mincing effeminacy of the dance routine is enhanced by the men's costumes, which include bunny ears, rhinestone buckles, and other hints of cross-gender play. Although the reference to the famous kiss of loyalty with which Mafia alliances are sealed is clear here, Torre's carnivalesque mise-en-scene converts this frequently represented ritual into a high-kitsch spectacle, laced with homoerotic undertones. The fact that the actors playing the gangsters are ordinary, often overweight and presumably heterosexual Sicilians, identified in the closing credits as bakers, parking lot attendants, restaurant workers, farmers, and clerks, adds to the incongruity of the spectacle. Torre's suggestive choreography of the all-male song-and-dance performance ultimately attributes a homoerotic counterface to the exaggerated machismo cultivated by the Mafia at the public level.

Though Torre's send-up of everyday Mafia culture in Palermo's inner city was both sarcastic and hyperbolic, *Tano da morire* was a huge hit with Sicilian audiences. Many commentators, including Leoluca Orlando, mayor of Palermo at the time, praised Torre for her willingness to ridicule rather than simply criticize Mafia culture, thus breaking an unspoken cultural taboo (Bohlen 1995). Timing, however, was crucial. Though set during one of the bloodiest periods of recent Sicilian history, *Tano da morire* was written and produced some years after the time frame of the events represented in the diegesis. In other words, the film was created at a point when a series of trials held during the mid- to late 1980s had already brought hundreds of Mafia leaders to justice, creating a significant respite from criminal activities on the island and allowing political reformers, such as Orlando, to create a semblance of civic order in Palermo.[7] The distance between the "then" of the story (the 1980s) and the "now" of its reenactment (the late 1990s) may well have contributed to the enthusiastic collaboration of the local cast and to the clamorous reception accorded to Torre's project by many Sicilian viewers, exhausted by the long reign of Mafia violence.

*Sud side stori*, the filmmaker's second feature-length musical, is set, by contrast, in the contemporary moment—the late 1990s—and the Mafia, though present, is no longer in the foreground of the story. Lawlessness and violence, however, are intricately woven into the action of the film. Recounting the star-crossed romance between an aspiring Sicilian singer, Toni Giulietto, and a Nigerian sex worker, Romea Wacombo, the narrative unfolds against a backdrop of the racial tensions engendered by the arrival of a large group of African prostitutes on the Palermo scene. Playing these women are several Nigerian sex workers recruited from the streets, while the Sicilian characters are played by local people familiar with the settings portrayed in the film. In this daring casting strategy, Torre pushes her "ethnographic" impulse to the limit, bringing together two communities still in the throes of real conflict with each other in order to construct a stylized spectacle of their mutual incomprehension and intolerance.

The film opens with a public demonstration shot on location in the city center, crosscut with a colorful tableau featuring the childlike figure of Santa Rosalia, Palermo's popular patron saint, shot against a two-dimensional backdrop that replicates devotional iconography. Rosalia, it seems, is more than agitated by the mayor's recent decision to revive interest in the city's other patron saint, Benedict the Moor, in the name of multicultural diversity. Similarly upset by the mandate to restore the "Moorish" saint to prominence, several local people are protesting in the piazza, among whom we distinguish three shrewish matrons who will soon be identified as Toni's aunts. It is only later, when these larger-than-life Sicilian women become aware of their nephew's infatuation with the alluring Nigerian immigrant, that they reveal the full force of their racism.

The arrival of several African prostitutes dragging their suitcases through the narrow streets of Palermo's inner city is presented as pure carnival. The women's sensational advance is focalized through the racially biased perspective of local onlookers, who project onto the newcomers preposterous images of exoticism and barbarity. In the midst of the phantasmagoric parade, Romea, the most visually alluring among the arriving Africans, stops in her tracks to gaze at the swooning Toni, who is watching the spectacle from a window above where she stands in the street. In this encounter, which parodies the Shakespearean balcony scene, their mutual enthrallment is forever sealed.

The manic exuberance of the arrival sequence, which was constructed on a soundstage, is intercut with gritty black-and-white images shot in the actual city streets recording a real-life exchange between a middle-aged local man and an African prostitute he propositions from his truck. Far from exoticized, the woman in this scene is blunt and businesslike. Moreover, her command of Italian is limited to the range of crude terms necessary to negotiate her services, as she names a price for each of the options she has to offer. The intercutting of this shockingly real encounter into the larger, carnivalesque fabric of the film creates a chilling dissonance. A rather similar effect is subsequently achieved in a scene where Torre's Nigerian performers restage their routine interactions with the African *maman* and the middleman at the end of each shift. Here we see the women turning in their night's wages along with a statement of net takings, only to be chastised when the money does not measure up to expectations. In these moments, the film offers a glimpse into the oppressive conditions in which the women live, circumstances that have been confirmed in studies of prostitution among recent immigrants to Italy (Achebe 2004).

The Nigerians who took part in Torre's film were already familiar with employment circumstances not completely dissimilar to slavery. After completing their journey to Italy, they were forced to relinquish their passports, which they could retrieve only by paying the huge sum of 30,000,000 *lire*. With sexual encounters worth about 30,000 *lire* in each instance, procuring the passports could entail years of indentured service on the streets. These circumstances lend special poignancy to the central song-and-dance number performed by the women in the film, the title of which is precisely "Trentamila lire" (Thirty Thousand Liras).

Despite its abundant allusions to Shakespeare's *Romeo and Juliet*, to Robert Wise's *West Side Story* (1961), and to Baz Luhrmann's *Romeo + Juliet* (1996), *Sud side stori* is above all the story of an encounter between two Souths—the Italian South and sub-Saharan Africa, a juxtaposition that comes perilously close to northern Italian stereotypes of Sicily as "Italy's Africa." Throughout the film there is frequent crosscutting from one community to the other in order to highlight the similarities between them. Preeminent in each group is an acute sense of racial hostility. Shocked to learn of Romea's growing attachment to the Sicilian Toni, the Nigerian women try to coax her away from him, offering her a list of traits that make white people unbearable. Toni, in the meantime, is treated to similar exhortations from the aunts who raised him. Also present in both communities is a reliance on magic and superstition. Romea's colleagues consult a black witch to solve the problem of the young woman's fatal attraction to a white man. Similarly, Toni's aunts invoke the assistance of a Sicilian *maga* in an effort to turn the young man's head around, eventually dispatching him to the tavern where, under the influence of alcohol, and in the presence of several elderly Mafioso types, he enters a state of distracted delirium. Finally, music has a central importance for both communities, though the film gives greater prominence to Toni's musical tastes, and particularly to his alcohol-induced hallucinations featuring the veteran Neapolitan crooner Mario Merola and the aging rock star, Little Tony, than to the African rhythms associated with the Nigerian characters. As the film progresses, Torre's humorous deployment of stereotype loses its light-hearted edge. Instead, her attempt to construct an intriguing "tale of two Souths" risks being overwhelmed by the parade of parallel exotica, delivered with broadly satirical strokes.

The uneven results achieved by *Sud side stori*, despite its remarkable visual flair, were due at least in part to the director's difficult collaboration with the African performers. While the local residents proved capable of delivering a lighthearted send-up of their own community with relative ease, the Nigerians, engaged in a comedic reconstruction of their status as undocumented immigrants and indentured prostitutes, were unable to immerse themselves fully in their scripted roles. The tensions generated by the uneven power relations inherent in this unusual "ethnographic" encounter thus become palpable in the very fabric of the film, undermining its intended humor.[8]

Though conceived as a mordant comedy, *Sud side stori* lacks the bracing energy and wit of *Tano da morire*, which looked back at a slightly earlier but significantly more violent period of the city's history from a position of relative triumph. The questions explored in the second film, by contrast—sex trafficking, illegal immigration, and racial prejudice—constituted a more daunting challenge, as they were far from resolved at the time the cameras began to roll, eventually insinuating themselves into the production process.[9] It is perhaps not a coincidence that Torre abandoned both the musical format and the use of nonprofessional actors when this project was finally completed.

## Angela: A "True" Story

While the representation of Palermo in Torre's first two feature films is filtered through grotesque comedy, the psychologically realistic register employed in *Angela* allows a more intimate appraisal of everyday life in the filmmaker's adopted city. Although the film has many of the characteristics of melodrama, its subtitle announces at the outset that the plot is based on "a true story." This claim is highlighted on the formal level by several stylistic strategies resonating with documentary practices. The use of inner-city locations, explored with a handheld camera or shot from inside a moving car, gives a number of scenes the look and feel of reportage. Images suggesting the use of surveillance cameras, as well as audio effects conveying the input of wire-tapping devices, add to the impression of documentary realism. In another of the film's self-reflexive strategies, the major narrative sequences, which unfold in straightforward chronological progression, are separated from each other by a close-up of a calendar page announcing the date of the events that we are about to witness. Although here, unlike Torre's earlier films, professional actors appear in central roles, some of the smaller parts are played by locals, creating a productive tension in the performances reminiscent of the effects of the neorealist directors' casting strategies.

*Angela* was initially conceived as a documentary based on the memories of the estranged wife of a Mafia operator.[10] In preparation for this project, the filmmaker elicited from the real "Angela," whose actual name remains unknown, an account of her marriage to a mid-level Mafia boss, her complicity in illegal operations and subsequent imprisonment, as well as her involvement in a doomed extramarital affair and the consequences that flowed from this. Ultimately, however, the plan for a documentary was abandoned and the story was adapted as a feature film with professional actors in all major roles. As occurred in Torre's previous collaborations with people living in close proximity to the Mafia, the real "Angela" served the filmmaker's project mainly as a native informant.

In transposing her interlocutor's story to the screen, Torre abandoned her earlier practice of creating "choral" narratives with several figures occupying the foreground of the diegesis, concentrating instead on just three characters, a traditional romantic triangle. It is Angela, however, who occupies center stage at all times. Through its construction of this proud Mafia wife, the film invites a critique of the position of women in Sicily's network of organized crime. While eliciting from the viewers an empathetic response, the protagonist is portrayed as both accomplice and victim of her husband's criminal activities and his commitment to an archaic code of masculine honor.

Significantly, the events recounted in *Angela* are marked as belonging to a particular moment in the past. A subtitle appearing on screen in the opening shot signals the year as 1984, conveying to a knowledgeable audience that the action unfolds at a time of intense Mafia activity in Palermo. Nineteen-eighty-four also coincided with a period in which the gains of the Italian women's movement, which had already asserted its effects in northern and central Italy, had not fully penetrated the societies of the south. In other words, the time frame locates the protagonist in a slightly different ideological landscape than she might have inhabited ten or fifteen years later, when the claims set in motion by feminism—which prompted many women to question their loyalty to patriarchal structures of power—had not yet become part of a widespread cultural awareness.

As is characteristic of the film's claustrophobic narrational technique, the opening sequence foregoes the use of a conventional establishing shot. Instead, an out-of-focus pan sweeps from right to left, coming to a halt when the protagonist suddenly comes into view, fully in focus. Framed in a tight close-up, Angela, a striking Mediterranean beauty, is engrossed in a ritual of self-grooming. Self-scrutiny and surveillance are dominant tropes in this film, as Angela perpetually polices her appearance and actions, revealing a permanent sense of anxiety regarding her visibility. Yet her concern with the maintenance of a respectable, well-groomed mask is linked to real dangers, as she is stalked, watched, photographed, and eavesdropped upon at several moments in the film.

Angela's husband Saro is the leader of a drug ring, and she assists him in the management of business, using the family shoe store as a cover. In this closed world, the punctilious observance of etiquette serves to conceal an implacable power structure, where a criminal code of honor prevails, demanding an absolute respect for hierarchies, discretion, and loyalty. Saro rules with firm authority, allowing Angela to deliver consignments of cocaine, concealed in shoe boxes, around the city, and at the same time excluding her from decision-making within the business. Enjoying the relative wealth and luxury afforded by trading in drugs, Angela colludes in her husband's activities without any show of guilt, apparently unaware of any valid code of behavior other than the rules of "honor" laid down by the mafia.

Although lacking the innovative exuberance of *Tano da morire*, *Angela* succeeds in several ways in undercutting generic representations of the Cosa Nostra. Rather than constructing the criminal world as fast-paced, glamorous, or spectacularly violent, it presents the activities of the Mafia as a closed circuit of humdrum commerce, without mystique and without heightened emotions. Within this setting, the characters observe a hardworking, punctual, carefully orchestrated routine. Angela is a consummate professional, carrying out her illegal work

**Figure 5.1**   Donatella Finocchiaro in the role of Angela.

with focus and self-discipline. The Mafia is her everyday environment; its protocols inflect her every gesture. She approaches the weighing, measuring, and packaging of the drugs she sells with the precision of a pharmacist. While undertaking deliveries in the crowded city streets, she deftly avoids discovery by the detectives who trail her, even when requested to show them the contents of her purse.

This vision of everyday commerce and domesticity is central to Torre's approach to the representation of Mafia violence and to her construction of women's roles in the hierarchy of a male-dominated subculture. Neither innocent nor entirely guilty, Angela belongs to a social world where women exist only in relation to men, a world that she has neither the courage nor the will to abandon. Despite the director's disavowal of any attitude of moral judgment vis-à-vis the world portrayed in her films, *Angela* can be read as a critical commentary on the circumstances of women who live in a deeply patriarchal community, an environment so closed in upon itself that its occupants seem unaware of any outside world to which they might escape.

An implicit critique of the gender arrangements that underpin the Mafia code of behavior is articulated in one of the most compelling episodes in the film, where a drug-dealing Mafioso is murdered by a trio of his peers, including Angela's husband Saro. Unfolding in a cramped office above the family shoe shop, the event is focalized by the protagonist, who, as a woman, is excluded from the inner sanctum of Mafia dealings and is trying to spy on the scene from a contiguous storage space. Muted lighting, impeded vision, and muffled conversation serve to downplay the precipitation of violence, despite an eventual close-up of the corpse lying on the floor, surrounded by an ever-expanding pool of blood. There are no shouts or screams, no pleas for mercy, no echo of gunshot. Ultimately, the loudest element on the sound track is the rasping noise of the packing tape used to wrap the body for disposal. Although Angela is not permitted to witness the murder directly, it is her duty to clean up the mess as soon as the men have left. We see her on her knees, wearily mopping the floor, squeezing out the blood-soaked sponge with her bare hands, and gathering up a wad of bloodied 100,000 *lire* bills abandoned at the scene. The mechanical quality of her gestures suggests she has performed this task before, and her expression indicates exhaustion rather than repulsion.

Angela's routine professionalism is gravely threatened, however, when a handsome newcomer named Masino is invited into the business by her husband. The passion that bursts into her world with his arrival undermines her disciplined way of doing things. Angela must take risks to be with her lover, and it is thanks to their imprudent use of a tapped telephone line that she eventually tumbles into a trap set by the police. The relationship between the pair is presented in a few deft strokes—even allowing a scene of pure pathos, worthy of a Hollywood melodrama. Subjected to unrelenting surveillance, the lovers are constrained to enact their romantic encounter at a physical distance from each other. Unable to speak to Masino on her compromised telephone line, Angela signals wistfully to him from a phone booth outside his apartment building, and he reciprocates her mute gestures, miming his embrace from a window high above where she stands.

Although Angela is presented sympathetically, the viewer is never allowed to overlook her collusion in the situation that oppresses her. The film clearly implies her refusal to examine her guilt in crimes routinely committed, while highlighting her emotional investment in a man who is also a criminal, and who can offer her no way out of the deadly world in which she is embroiled. Angela is not redeemed by love. Rather, love allows her to live in a permanent state of illusory expectancy. Yet, throughout the film, her irredeemable self-deception is conveyed with considerable compassion, blunting any implied critique of her ethically flawed position.

*Angela*'s concluding sequence is constructed in a particularly poignant fashion, reminiscent in its melancholy tone of the so-called woman's film. Here we find Angela waiting at the harbor café where she had agreed to meet Masino in order to escape with him to some unknown destination. As she sits anxiously by the café's rain-swept windows, a montage of cuts and dissolves suggests the slow, futile passing of the hours. Although her husband has already indicated that the younger man will be murdered for his transgression, Angela's customary self-delusion compels her to continue. In the final scene, after a night of profuse weeping, she returns to the harbor, where she continues her vigil, looking out to sea. In a move that conflates the real "Angela" with the figure on screen, a brief text is superimposed on the image, updating the audience on the woman's current circumstances, more than fifteen years after the events we have been watching. The viewers thus learn that "Angela" is now making a living as a seamstress, and that she often returns to the same spot by the harbor. We never see this presumably middle-aged woman. Instead, the words on screen are accompanied by the image of the younger Angela, looking forever out to sea, a romantic dreamer eternally in the thrall of a lover who will never return.

The nuances of "pastness" cultivated in *Angela* ultimately serve to link the protagonist's experiences to a period of Sicilian social history that has since been eclipsed by sweeping changes at both local and global levels. Anchored in 1984, the film evokes an ambiance that contrasts sharply with the realities of the transnational, big-business thrust of the Sicilian Mafia in the global era.[11] What Torre's time frame occludes from view is the transmutation undergone by the Mafia in recent years, as the organization expanded its reach both nationally and globally and began to include women in the upper echelons of its organization, particularly the widows of deceased bosses. It also occludes the unprecedented emergence of ordinary Sicilian women as an important component in the anti-Mafia movement that sprung up on the island after the murders of two judges, Paolo Borsellino and Giovanni Falcone, in the early 1990s. Women played a major part, for example, in the organization of a hunger strike in 1992 to protest these murders. Soon afterward, a group of women also launched a vibrant initiative known as the "sheets protest," where bed sheets emblazoned with anti-Mafia slogans were boldly draped from balconies throughout Palermo. Rather than cowering indoors, the women of Sicily were thus finally empowered to speak out against violence and injustice.

It was largely thanks to the lull in violence that began in 1992—dubbed "Year One of the anti-Mafia Movement" (Siebert 1998, 291)—that Torre was physically capable of making her films in the city streets without incurring considerable risk. Yet, in so doing, she focused her lens not on the vibrant women's protest of the present, but rather on fantasmatically reimagined scenes of a more violent, more colorful, and ultimately more "typical" Sicily of the recent past. The melancholy tonality of *Angela*, heightened by the use of extradiegetic music and Donatella Finocchiaro's soulful performance as the protagonist, may even conjure up an unwitting suggestion of nostalgia for that past. What is clear, however, is that Torre finds her most compelling inspiration not in the straightforward, "ethnographic" observation of contemporary realities, but rather in the way that events are transformed, through the process of remembering and retelling, into legend or romance.

# Notes

1. I wish to thank Katarzyna Marciniak for many insightful comments on an earlier draft of this essay.
2. Shortly after returning to mainland Italy, Torre made another feature film, *Mare Nero* (2003), a stylized noir set in Rome. A consideration of this film is beyond the scope of this chapter.
3. These independent and highly unconventional filmmakers have been working together since the mid-1980s, creating gags and skits for the satirical

television program *Cinico tv* before moving on to make short films, documentaries, and full-length features. Their dystopian, nausea-inducing vision of Sicily caused a minor uproar upon the release of their earliest features *Lo zio di Brooklyn* (1995) and *Totò che visse due volte* (1998). Shot in black and white, these films feature only nonprofessional actors. Women are excluded from the cast, purportedly as a commentary on the absolute dominance of a patriarchal ethos in Sicilian society. Although the images that prevail in their work may seem scandalous or repulsive, the filmmakers have developed a distinctive visual aesthetics not devoid of a poetic component. For a useful critical appraisal, see Hampson (2000).

4. Pasquale Verdicchio has convincingly argued that the annexation of the South to the new state of Italy at the moment of unification had political consequences for southerners that were tantamount to colonialism (Verdicchio 1997).

5. The accumulated perception of an essentialized north/south difference is, in fact, ideologically equivalent to what Edward Said has famously described as orientalism. In his often cited volume of that title, Said identified a cluster of cultural prejudices that characterize the construction of the "East" by Western writers since the early nineteenth century. Following Said, other scholars have found that the concept could be usefully applied not only to relations between west and east but also to attitudes adopted by the major centers of power in Europe toward other, marginal European zones. Maria Todorova's *Imagining the Balkans* is a prominent example. A collection of essays on Italy's "Southern Question," edited by Jane Schneider, also alludes to Said's work in its subtitle ("Orientalism in One Country") to describe the power relations inherent in the construction of the Italian south (Schneider 1998).

6. One of the sharpest critiques leveled against the discipline was that of Trinh T. Minh-ha who describes anthropology's quest for the Other as "an outgrowth of a dualistic system of thought peculiar to the Occident (the 'onto-theology' which characterizes Western metaphysics)," where difference becomes an instrument of self-defense and conquest. Anthropology, for Trinh, generates "nothing other than the reconstruction and redistribution of a pretended order of things, the interpretation or even transformation of [facts] given and frozen into monuments" (Trinh 2001, 14, 16).

7. The first so-called maxi-trial, which began in Palermo in February 1986 and continued for two years, resulted in the conviction of hundreds of Mafia operatives, based mainly on testimony offered by former operatives who became informants.

8. For a more detailed discussion of *Sud side stori*, see O'Healy (2007).

9. Torre reports that the women's irregular (i.e., illegal) immigration status caused long delays and entailed legal costs that she had not anticipated in advance, placing a strain on all participants in the film (Personal interview with Roberta Torre, July 2001).

10. This was not, however, Torre's first intimate exploration of women's lives in some of the city's most daunting neighborhoods. *Angelesse*, a short black-and-white film directed in 1994, offers an informal portrait of several women captured by the camera as they conjure up their memories, disappointments and frustrations as longtime residents of the mean streets of Palermo.

11. According to the filmmaker, in contrast to present-day Mafia practices, the small-time gangsters who populate her films constitute a quaint and relatively harmless anachronism (Personal communication with Roberta Torre, Palermo, July 2001).

# References


Abu-Lughod, Lila. "Writing Against Culture." In *Recapturing Anthropology: Working in the Present*, ed. Richard Fox, 137–162. Santa Fe: School of American Research, 1989.

Achebe, Nwando. "The Road to Italy: Nigerian Sex Workers at Home and Abroad." *Journal of Women's History* 15 (2004): 178–185.

Behar, Ruth and Deborah A. Gordon. *Women Writing Culture*. Berkeley: UC Press, 1995.

Bohlen, Celestine. "In a Changed Sicily, a Film Dares to Laugh at the Mob." *The New York Times*, April 20, 1998. http://query.nytimes.com/gst/fullpage.html?res=9A02EFD8103CF933A15757C0A96E958260 (Accessed on February 2, 2009).

Capello, Mary, Wallace Sillanpoa, and Jean Walton. "Roberta Torre: Filmmaker of the Incoscienza." *Quarterly Review of Film and Video* 17, 4 (2000): 317–331.

Clifford, James. *The Predicament of Culture*. Cambridge, MA: Harvard UP, 1988.

Hampson, Ernest. "Mocking the Mafia: Ciprì and Maresco's Sicilian Apocalypse." In *The Seeing Century: Film, Vision and Identity*, ed. Wendy Everett, 88–97. Amsterdam: Rodopi, 2000.

Jamieson, Alison. "Mafiosi and Terrorists: Italian Women in Violent Organizations." *SAIS Review* 20: 2 (2000): 51–64.

Marcus, Millicent. "Postmodern Pastiche, the *Sceneggiata*, and the View of the Mafia from Below in Roberta Torre's *To Die for Tano*." In *After Fellini: National Cinema in the Postmodern Age*, 234–251. Baltimore: Johns Hopkins University Press, 2002.

Mascia-Lees, Frances, Patricia Sharpe, and Colleen Ballerino Cohen. "The Postmodernist Turn in Anthropology: Cautions from a Feminist Perspective." *Signs* 15, 1 (1989): 7–33.

O'Healy, Áine. "Border Traffic: Reimagining the Voyage to Italy." In *Transnational Feminism in Film and Media*, ed. Katarzyna Marciniak, Anikó Imre, and Áine O'Healy, 59–72. New York: Palgrave, 2007.

Pandolfi, Mariella. "Two Italies: Rhetorical Figures of Failed Nationhood." In *Italy's Southern Question: Orientalism in One Country*, ed. Jane Schneider, 285–289. Oxford: Berg, 1998.

Ruby, Jay. "The Ethics of Imagemaking." In *New Challenges for Documentary*, ed. Alan Rosenthal, 308–318. Berkeley: University of California Press, 1988.

Said, Edward. *Orientalism*. New York: Vintage, 1979.

Siebert, Renate. *Secrets of Life and Death: Women and the Mafia*. Trans. Liz Heron. New York: Verso, 1998.

Todorova, Maria. *Imagining the Balkans*. New York: Oxford University Press, 1997.

Trinh Minh-ha. "Not You/Like You: Post-Colonial Women and the Interlocking Questions of Identity and Difference." In *Dangerous Liaisons: Gender, Nation, and Postcolonial Perspectives*, ed. Anne McClintock, Aamir Mufti, and Ella Shohat, 415–419. Minneapolis: University of Minnesota Press, 1997.

Verdicchio, Pasquale. "The Preclusion of Postcolonial Discourse in Southern Italy." In *Revisioning Italy: National Identity and Global Culture*, ed. Beverly Allen and Mary Russo, 191–212. Minneapolis: Minnesota University Press, 1997.

Williams, Sarah. "Abjections and Anthropological Praxis." Anthropological *Quarterly* 66, 2 (1993): 67–75.

# The Balkans: Peacekeeping and Women's (In)security

# Chapter Six

## *Vertigo in the Balkans: Karin Jurschick's* "The Peacekeepers and the Women"

### *Marguerite Waller*

Borders…are no longer conceived primarily as "lines" marking the edge of a given national territory, but more as "detention zones" and "filtering systems." As the poor are systematically regulated at points of entry, borders have become essential institutions in the constitution of social conditions on a global scale…

> —Alice Mihaela Bardan (2007) paraphrasing Etienne Balibar, "Enter Freely, and of Your Own Will" (98).

[Thirty three] female Border Patrol Unit members had been summarily dismissed by their Commander on grounds of being female and hence unsuitable for work in the border region, though it is likely to have been a pretext…to protect lucrative moonlighting opportunities such as smuggling, human trafficking (e.g. of young Timorese girls to Indonesian officers), and other illegal activities.

> —Jacqueline Siapno (2008), "Whispered Confidences: articulating the female in the PNTL (police) and the F-FDTL (military) in Timor Leste" (7).

…multiple considerations involving economics, identity, spatiality, technology, and politics converge and are placed in a complicated relationship to each other. The attempt to draw these layers together leads…to the creation of an imaginary space, a sort of theoretical platform on which different elements can be placed in dialogue with each other.

> —Ursula Biemann, "Videographies of Navigating Geobodies" (2007, 130).

A major struggle confronting transnational feminist filmmakers, wherever in the world they work, is the challenge presented by their own media and by the frameworks that potential spectators bring with them to screenings. No less than the political, economic, and military situations that motivate them, the habits of their viewers, their own perceptual and conceptual habits, and conventional understandings (academic, journalistic, masculinist, and even feminist) of contemporary forms of power and domination need to be engaged in order for the film or video to act as something other than a polemic. If it is to present an epistemological challenge that "unsettles, shatters, and disrupts domination" (Arrizón 2006, 2) and shifts the spectator's world view, the film/video maker must wrestle with what artist/theorist Ursula Biemann calls not only the "secondary, descriptive function" of images, but "a productive one as well" (2007, 133). In my own interaction with Karin Jerschick's deeply researched, wonderfully layered, and profoundly disturbing film, *The Peacekeepers and the Women*, a documentary film focused on "post-conflict" Bosnia and Kosovo/a,[1] I have discovered the effectiveness of a certain intertextuality between her documentary and classic feature films in keeping my own academic tendencies toward systematization at bay. Jerschick's *hommages* to directors such as Alfred Hitchcock and Ingmar Bergman, whether conscious or an artifact of her own expertise in using cinematic language, prevent me from cutting too quickly to frameworks that would offer a gratifying sense of "understanding" at the expense of a vertiginous engagement with what does not fit my episteme. Jurschick's film, I will argue, does not simply "explain" or "deplore" contemporary manifestations and mutations of "empire" and the intricacies of post-Cold War geopolitics, though the film is highly informative about, and deeply critical of, these developments. Rather, the multiple violences (military, economic, state, clandestine, physical, sexual, emotional, and epistemic) in which its multiple subjects, including the filmmaker herself, are caught up are placed in relation to, and (as Ursula Biemann puts it in a description of her own work) in dialogue with, each other. This work of conceptual montage, like early Soviet editing experiments, works metamorphically; it changes the signification and the impact of each of its constituent elements.[2] It follows both from Jurschick's aesthetics and from the nature of "post-conflict" situations themselves (involving huge influxes of international money and personnel) that neither Jurschick's film nor this chapter focuses on essentializing national or regional identities. The focus instead is on what border theorists call the "contact zones," on complex webs of interaction entangling subjects from the United States, Germany, France, Canada, Pakistan, Russia, Moldova, Romania, the Ukraine, and elsewhere, no less than from the Balkans.[3]

I begin, then, with Alfred Hitchcock's proto-transnational feminist thriller *Vertigo* (1958), whose aesthetic appeal lies, in part, in the loss of his world's transparency suffered by the main character, Scotty, a lawyer-turned policeman. The viewing position associated with the morally upright representative of law and order is deterritorialized and recontextualized within a fractally presented history of imperial colonialisms, involving at least two interconnected European histories. Scotty (played by Jimmy Stewart), Scottish-American both on-screen and off, is cruelly manipulated and exploited by his old school chum, Gavin, a San Francisco shipping magnate, who speaks with a conspicuously upper-class *English* accent. The history of England's relationship to Scotland implicitly haunts this interplay of accents, actors, and characters. Gavin's story of the haunting of his wife Madeleine by "Carlotta," her alleged Latina ancestress, evokes, meanwhile, the colonial histories of Spanish, Mexican, and U.S. California. A Spanish mission, which becomes the site of the transmogrification of Scotty's moral uprightness into murder, recalls the exploitation of the Native American population for the purpose of keeping the Spanish fleet provisioned.[4] The missions, established by Father Junipero Serra, provided logistical support for the Spanish military who oversaw the lucrative trade routes Spain had established with South America and Asia. They were built and maintained by the forced labor of the indigenous people, and Carlotta, if she existed, would have been the *mestiza* offspring of a Spanish soldier and a female Native American convert/slave.

British and Spanish colonial histories collide with particular irony in an episode, anticipating the fatal Mission scenes, set in Sequoia National Forest near San Francisco. During a visit to Sequoia, Scotty and Madeleine remark on the rings (photographed in close-up) seen in the trunk of a felled redwood tree, which have been correlated by the park's curators with significant dates in Anglo-American history. The signing of the Magna Carta, the foundational text of Western human rights discourse, is the particular date foregrounded by the camera. In the context of California history, though, the Magna Carta paradoxically signifies a *loss* of human rights. When the Treaty of Guadalupe Hidalgo was signed in 1848, at the conclusion of the Mexican-American War (the blatantly imperial war against which New England's Henry David Thoreau was protesting when he was jailed), the Latino population of Northern Mexico, including California, were massively *disenfranchised, dispossessed,* and *criminalized,* notwithstanding the protections that their new historical inheritance theoretically granted them.

We never find out what motive Scotty's classmate Gavin had for killing his wife, beyond a vague suggestion that he was after her money. What emerges as the greater mystery is how Scotty becomes the self-righteous precipitator of the deaths of two women, Gavin's wife Madeleine and her surrogate Judy, who, at the end of the film, falls to her death from the same bell tower that figured in Madeleine's murder. What exactly does Scotty desire, and how does this choreograph what he thinks he knows and sees? What aspects of the epistemology and sexuality of the "virtuous," all-American policeman allow Scotty to play such a central, yet unwitting, role in the violent, imperial, accumulation of wealth ubiquitously referenced by the film? I have discussed elsewhere the highly destructive "addiction to virtue" characteristic of the U.S. military and economic policy-makers of contemporary corporate globalization (Waller 2006). Here let me simply point out that by casting Jimmy Stewart, who had also starred as the hyper-virtuous mid-western Boy Scout leader-turned-senator in Frank Capra's *Mr. Smith Goes to Washington* (1939), Hitchcock adds further layers to the Scotty figure, creating an elaborate vortex (the image memorably used by Hitchcock himself to signify Scotty's nervous breakdown) that calls the legitimacy and justice of state power into question from multiple angles at once—colonial, provincial, metropolitan, racial, and sexual.

*The Peacekeepers and the Women* (2003), directed by German-based filmmaker Karin Jurschick, questions, in uncannily similar terms, the violent accumulation of wealth currently underway in several regions of the former Yugoslavia. Like Hitchcock, Jurschick focuses on the consequences for human rights and women's bodies of a chaotic intersection of multiple histories, filtered through the epistemological frames and sexual desires of those given the job of governing. Deplored by human rights advocates, NGOs, church workers, journalists, and many others, the wholesale importation of women to perform sex work in U.N.-administered Bosnia and NATO-administered Kosovo(a) has proved highly immune to efforts to slow it down or stop it. In fact, it is the presence of international peacekeeping and humanitarian personnel that appears to have enabled the shocking scale of this traffic and the success of the sex industry as the region's leading entrepreneurial activity, though exactly how these elements combine synergistically has been thoroughly mystified by both the mainstream and the tabloid press. Across the board, journalistic accounts, ranging from those in *The New York Times* and the *Washington Post* to those offered by Fox News and MSNBC, have published sensationalizing stories about the involvement of troops, U.N. police, private security company personnel, and other components of the international peacekeeping forces in trafficking and brothel ownership (Gall 2001, McElroy 2003, Lynch 2005, Watson 2007). Whatever their means and motives, the very people who are in the region to protect human rights and foster democracy are, at the same time, enabling massive violations of women's human rights through forced prostitution, rape, sexual torture, and, not least, the creation of what amounts to a slave trade in which women are bought, sold, and shipped around like so many pieces of meat. Furthermore, according to a wide range of sources, both governmental and nongovernmental, what has been happening in Bosnia and Kosovo(a) has analogues around the world, in Liberia, Sierra Leone, Cambodia, Afghanistan, Iraq, the Democratic Republic of Congo, South Korea, the Philippines, East Timor, and elsewhere (Felten-Biermann 2005, Lynch 2005, Kumar 2005, Medica Mondiale 2006, Higate 2007, Siapno 2008).

Near its beginning, Jurschick's film, in contrast to the mainstream media stories, offers the viewer an efficient, non-moralizing, non-sensationalizing way into this complex web of relations through a story told by a taxi driver to a woman activist. By carefully orchestrating her film language, Jurschick also addresses representational problems common to feminist, media, and governmental (policing) responses to trafficking. The activist, Mara Radovanovic, of the Women's Organization LARA Bosnia, tells this story directly to the camera against the background of a wintry parking lot:

> He had an old car and he wanted to sell it and buy a new one, and he was told that he could do this in the "Arizona Market." He came one day with his old car and he managed to sell it for 1000 DM. He was trying to find a better car, and he had saved another 1000 DM. He wanted to buy a car for 2000. Then he saw a very nice car, which cost 4000 DM, and he didn't have another 2000DM. The owner of the car he wanted to buy told him he could earn that money very easily. "Go to that café and buy two foreign girls—two girls from the Ukraine or Moldova—for 2000. You can drive them to Tuzla and I'll give you the address of a man to whom you can sell them for 4000. I'll wait for you." The taxi driver did this. He bought two girls, he drove them to Tuzla and sold them for 4000 and came back and bought the car for 4000 DM.

In a study of the forms taken by both anti-trafficking and anti-anti-trafficking publicity materials, feminist scholar Nancy Hesford argues that both sides construct advocacy in the same rhetorical terms that underwrite the human rights violations they oppose.[5] Singling out, in particular, the "rescue narrative"—the seductive plot in which

Hitchcock's Scotty becomes entangled—she calls attention to the ways in which the identities and identifications reproduced by its use in videos and written literature cohere with what she calls the "culture of security," the either/or, inside/outside binary logic of militarized national and regional boundaries. Binary oppositional constructions of agent and victim, prostitute and non-prostitute, she notes, reinforce notions of authenticity that perpetuate distinctions between those categories of femininity that are worthy of protection and those that are not. Conversely, she argues, an "interrogation of the cultural and political practices of rhetorical identification leads us to *question the contexts* created for and by such identification" (2005, 150. Italics mine).

The taxi driver's story, the figure of the activist retelling the story on screen, and the location within which the story unfolds all work concertedly to disrupt the rescue fantasy and its attendant identifications. Beginning with the fact of the Arizona Market itself, a free trade zone set up in 1995 by the U.S. military leadership between the Bosnian Federation and the Republicka Serbska, on the assumption that commerce would bring peace, the shot montages two incommensurable rhetorical fields, that of human rights and that of neoliberal economics. When the film catachrestically brings these two discourses together, it initiates what will become one of Jurschick's central strategies: a progressive intensification of moral and conceptual vertigo and a discrediting of the "clarity and transparency" to which both rights and economic discourses aspire. For Hesford and her coeditor Wendy Kozol, the production of this form of "knowledge" too often substitutes for other forms of action. The complexities of "trafficking," furthermore, are particularly badly served by the binary, true/false, good guy/bad guy, or, in this case, "Balkan/European" logic of epistemological "clarity" (2005, 18–21). In the sequence we are considering, for example, the spontaneous participation in trafficking by the taxi driver in need of a better car appears to be but one link in a series of informal transactions involving the seller of the car and a café owner, just to name those we hear about, who are not primarily identified as "traffickers." The evil "trafficker" who trades in innocent female flesh disappears into an infinite regress of more or less ordinary people trying to get by economically.

Operating similarly, the designation of the women as "foreign girls," although it may be a euphemism, obviates the need to categorize them as either "trafficked women" or "real sex workers." That is, the domestic/foreign binary finesses the question of whether they are victims (and by implication "good") or agents (by implication "bad") that has been the centerpiece of national and international policy toward trafficking in women. Kamala Kempadoo, Jo Doezema, and other contributors to their volume, *Global Sex Workers: Rights, Resistance, and Redefinition,* demonstrate how pervasive, even among the most progressive policy-makers and committed activists, this binarizing linkage of female victimhood with virtue and female agency with criminality remains (Doezema 1998, 46–47; Murray 1998, 62–63). Contravening this logic, an earlier inter-title in the film anticipates the taxi driver's displacement of moral categories by geopolitical ones, informing the viewer that there are towns in Moldova and Romania in which all the women under forty have disappeared. Identity categories and identifications give way to the shifting physical, economic, and sociopolitical processes that mobilize them within contexts that are also in flux. Youth, which one grows out of (if one is lucky), and location in a region undergoing rapid political and economic change trump other more stable categorizations. Meanwhile, the activist, acting here as an intermediary between the taxi driver and the viewer, blocks any impulse on the viewer's part to individualize and judge the driver, whose nationality we also have no way of knowing. Because she is positioned on screen between the viewer and the Arizona Market parking area, she also prevents the viewer from visually organizing the market space into a coherent mastershot that would offer a sense of confidence in his/her viewing position.

This sequence exemplifies the care with which Jurschick's film defines and meets the aesthetic and representational challenges presented by her subject. The film sets itself the task of subverting the rhetorical/aesthetic *conventions,* at the same time that it documents the economic and political *conditions,* that have contributed to making migration and sex work the best available option for growing numbers of people, mostly women, living in communities devastated by war and/or economic "restructuring." "Vertigo," that is, becomes both an aesthetics and an epistemology, not only addressing spectators' viewing habits but also removing the "safety" of the moral categories and essentializing identities that would impede a rigorous documentary investigation of the complicated interrelationships that are producing the sex work boom in Bosnia.[6]

A later sequence stunningly exposes the complex instability of identities and identifications by means of what appears to be a simple face-to-face interview between a young "trafficked" woman seeking repatriation and the female head of the U.N. "anti-trafficking" effort in Bosnia. The film prepares us for this revelatory sequence in densely interconnected ways. I will focus here on those that seem most crucial to my argument, with the caveat that my discussion does not begin to do justice to the film's brilliantly vertiginous montages of characters, languages, nationalities, facts, background information, interviews, testimonies, *cinéma vérité* footage, and local media productions.

Throughout the film, "peacekeepers" and "women" are presented as themselves nonbinary categories, women figuring more prominently as administrators, military officers, police, media producers, translators, and activists than as subjects of sexual exploitation and violence, though the women in the military and police forces are generally not in positions of command, and one, an American peacekeeper, is summarily fired for e-mailing her superiors about the trafficking situation. Self-identified trafficked women are presented non-voyeuristically, sometimes using a black screen with a voice over, and twice in sequences that show young women standing up to police during early morning raids on their sleeping quarters. The viewer learns that in the latter case the women who are being roused at 5:00 a.m. are trying to prove that they *are* "real" prostitutes in order to avoid deportation and repatriation to the economically devastated areas from which they come. (As we see later in the film, neither agricultural nor factory work in these regions offers even subsistence wages.) The women are aware that the United Nations forces in Bosnia have no jurisdiction over "real" "prostitutes"; they can only "rescue" "trafficked women." They also know, and the film presents these realities to viewers, that these "rescues" are themselves quite violent, involving heavily armed men in ski masks ransacking women's belongings and detaining them in prison-like quarters for deportation. "Anti-trafficking" U.N. brothel raids, therefore, both by pressuring women to categorize themselves as "prostitutes" and by depriving of agency those who do not, pick up where local mafias leave off in maintaining a cheap and docile sex workforce.[7]

The viewer also hears, through Madeleine Rees, the U.N. High Commissioner for Human Rights in Bosnia (whose subject position is that of both a "woman" and a "peacekeeper"), of the coexistence of multiple economies in the region. Rees tells of a woman earning forty dollars a month doing sex work in Bosnia, while her family in Moldova is living on ten dollars a month. "If the young woman is sending thirty of her forty dollars home, what are we doing when we say she will be repatriated to that family?" Rees asks, "It might be dreadful for her, but she is keeping that family alive." Not only violence and intimidation, that is, but a double disparity in economies contributes—perhaps to an even greater extent than rape, beatings, and brothel raids—to keeping the women on the job. If a woman's earnings for sex work cannot get her ahead in Bosnia, where a professor makes three hundred euro a month, a U.N. translator nine hundred euro a month, and a German international police force member one hundred and fifty euro a day, tax free, on top of his or her monthly salary, these forty dollars translate into food, clothing, and possibly a few years of education for family members in Moldova, Romania, or the Ukraine.

A third thread of the film that prepares viewers for the revelatory face-to-face encounter that clinches the film's destabilization of identities and identifications involves the complex development of one of the "peacekeepers," Celhia de Lavarène, as a central character in the film. Formerly a journalist—possibly French, judging from her accent, though we are never told her nation of origin—she was one of those who published sensationalizing media exposés of the involvement of United Nations personnel in sex trafficking. She was hired, she tells the camera, to develop the U.N.'s anti-trafficking efforts in Bosnia. She reports to a career member of the U.S. Foreign Service (also a Major General in the U.S. Air Force) named Jacques Paul Klein, appointed by United Nations Secretary-General Kofi Annan to serve at the rank of U.N. Under-Secretary-General as "Coordinator of all United Nations operations in Bosnia and Herzegovina." She describes being interviewed by Klein as follows: "He told me that he wanted someone who looked like a woman but had balls." "I need someone strong. I'm just fed up," she recalls his saying. "I want you to kick everyone's ass." Klein, she elaborates, wanted someone credible to the press who could convince mainstream journalists once and for all that he, Klein, had the sex trafficking situation under control. Her credentials as a staunch critic of UNPROFOR (United Nations Protection Force), he pointed out, gave her that credibility.

Klein, the head of U.N. operations in Bosnia, in other words, was not primarily concerned with understanding either the substance of the criticisms or, more fundamentally, how women's rights were being violated; it was rather his own authority and the legitimacy of his mission that he felt compelled to defend. Exactly what Colonel Klein's mission in the area really was, if it was not protecting democracy and human rights, and why it was so important to sweep sex trafficking under the rug, gradually emerge as profound enigmas to which I will have to return. Klein tells the filmmaker point blank, on camera, that there has been no involvement by U.N. personnel in trafficking and prostitution on his watch. Academic researchers and NGO personnel who were in the area at the time, however, have written that the involvement by peacekeepers in sex trafficking during Klein's tenure was widespread. Sex workers within the film speak of recognizing clients among every category of U.N. administrators, from civilian office workers to police officers and international troops. A private security company, DynCorps, subcontracted by the United Nations to supply police in the area, was, in fact, under investigation for trafficking at exactly the time that Klein was in Bosnia (Higate 2007), and Klein cannot have been unaware of this investigation.

Though the film does not explicitly mention the investigation, Jurschick approaches DynCorps's implication in trafficking and sexual exploitation (and Klein's knowledge of it) through her development of the story of the young woman police officer from Nebraska, employed by DynCorps, who was fired for sending an e-mail to her U.N. colleagues, including Klein, detailing the human rights violations suffered by the thirty-five trafficked women who had come through her office in just one month in the year 2000.[8] Klein's and de Lavarène's approach to the trafficking problem consisted, as I have mentioned, of humiliating early morning raids, questioning, incarceration, and deportation. A swashbuckling team of male police officers snappily acronymed the "S.T.O.P. Team" (Special Trafficking Operation Programme), created by de Lavarène, lent itself well to convincing journalists that the situation was being taken seriously, while bringing yet more international peacekeeping personnel onto the scene and providing dramatic video footage of police activity to the media.

With the questions of Klein's denial, de Lavarène's collusion, and the ultimate mission of the U.N. in the region in mind, let me return to the film's development of de Lavarène. Klein's "woman with balls" plays brilliantly into the vertiginous implosions of identificatory categories that Jurschick's film so fruitfully explores. She comes across as both sympathetic and repellant, shrewd and obtuse, her own femininity openly exploited by Klein, while she is also thrilled to be able to deploy heavily armed and masked police in "brothel" raids. As she says on camera during a raid being videotaped by both the S.T.O.P. team and Jurschick's crew, "This is fun!" In a subsequent daytime interview with the filmmaker in her well-appointed U.N. office, de Lavarène adds, "I just love it…My God, I'm in the middle of a movie. Honestly, you feel good." However, as in the case of the taxi driver who found himself trafficking women to Tuzla, the film does not support the viewer's impulse to categorize or to judge de Lavarène. Rather, by cutting to a black screen and the voice of a Russian-speaking woman who has been on the receiving end of such a raid, the film instead exposes de Lavarène's pleasures as neither universal nor politically neutral.

The brothel raid footage also opens out onto the question of sexuality and policing so provocatively treated by Hitchcock. While audience members are not in a position to observe firsthand the pleasures of buying sex, we can extrapolate something about the gratification of patronizing sex workers from the thrill that de Laverène derives from her power to star in a swashbuckling action adventure, from how much "fun" it is for her to play the commander in these scenes of quasi-military assault. This link between the pleasures of commercial sex and those of raiding brothels is prepared for by several contemplative pans earlier in the film of the video game machines, continuously displaying their hyperbolically violent and misogynist previews, which line the walls of a German military recreation hall, almost empty during the day but obviously crowded in the evening. Through them and later, through de Lavarène's pleasure in joining the game, the film suggests that police violence and the trade in female bodies are manifestations of some common impulse. Jurschick's inspired strategy of substituting a female figure, who is herself also a kind of "policeman," for the more conventional image of the male sexual exploiter serves to displace viewers' attention from the male/female binary in order to refocus it on the *connection* between the pleasure of enforcement and the pleasure of buying sex. Both of these, the ranks of video game machines imply, are pleasures for which a taste and a market can be created where one did not exist before.

Reinforcing the displacement of gender as fundamental to this dynamic, the young female "sex worker" whom de Lavarène interviews at S.T.O.P. team headquarters mentions that she *herself* wanted to be a police officer: "I wanted to join the police force. I saw police officers in films. In many films. I also wanted to help people." It is relevant to how one addresses these issues that the rescue narrative and the individualizing categories of victim and agent, which structure debates and legislation pertaining to the trafficking of women, appear to have configured even the "trafficked" woman's sense of who and where she is. The film proposes that, in the surreality of post-conflict Bosnia, the location of this young woman and countless others as objects of the police officer's or client's or video game player's gaze, is produced systemically—if also chaotically—by the intersections of homologous military, political, economic, and media regimes. The same could be said, of course, for those in the position of policing, gazing, and, patronizing brothels in one way or another. Not setting herself apart from this kaleidoscope of relations, the filmmaker includes a shot in which she is told by a relatively well-paid young Bosnian woman police officer working for the U.N. that she, the police officer, would have liked to do what Jurschick is doing, but there was no opportunity.

As the subject positions of de Lavarène and others in the film come to appear accidental, contradictory, and unstable, the *differences* among them begin to implode. Between de Laverène and the young woman who appeals to the S.T.O.P. team for help in getting back home, this implosion is underscored by Jurschick's brilliant choice of camera angle and framing. In a shot I read as an *hommage* to Ingmar Bergman's *Persona* (1966), two slender, artificially blond women sit talking face-to-face, the younger one with her back to the camera, the older one facing it. Recalling Bergman's blending of two women supposedly separated by class and economic status (played by Liv Ullmann and Bibi Andersson), Jurschick's two women look like mirror images of each other, except for the fact that one is young and the other middle-aged. They have the same build, the same coloring and, uncannily, exactly the same hair cut. Were they not speaking from different social positions in mutually incomprehensible languages, they might be taken for mother and daughter. (Indeed, in a context of migration, mothers and daughters quite readily find themselves on different sides of socioeconomic and linguistic divides.)

Jurschick's film language, however, also heavily ironizes de Lavarène's position, while it subtly privileges that of the young woman. In the shots just preceding that of de Lavarène's face and the back of the young woman's head, the desk chair occupied by de Lavarène is filled by a young and rather bumbling S.T.O.P. Team interrogator, whose eyes periodically drop from the young woman's face to her body as he and two other male S.T.OP. team members question her about the exact nature of her work and how much clients were charged for her services. Behind him, a poster captioned, "The Classical Elegance of Thailand," tacitly references the global scope and inter-implication of sex tourism, "Rest and Relaxation" facilities for Western military personnel, and (failed) neoliberal economic policies. (Thailand, well-known as a destination for both civilian and military clients of sex workers, was particularly hard hit by the Asian financial collapse of the late 1990s.) By means of a straight cut, de Lavarène is inserted by the filmmaker into the position of this graceless male gazer/policeman, editorialized by the Thailand poster. Should we miss the montage relationship the film sets up in this sequence between Bosnia and Thailand, or between de Lavarène and her avatars on the S.T.O.P. Team, the viewer is offered one more clue. De Laverène is wearing the same expensive shearling coat that she was wearing in the video footage of the brothel raid she commanded during which she had so much "fun."[9]

The young woman who is the object of her "maternal" concern, meanwhile, is photographed from a slightly low angle—which tends to be empowering. (The same camera position frames de Lavarène from a slightly high angle—which tends to be disempowering.) Like the Thailand poster, camera angles here visually complicate the political and epistemological hierarchy within which de Lavarène assumes she is operating. The respective screen positions of the two figures reinforce this deconstruction of power/knowledge relations. On the one hand, de Lavarène is positioned screen right, generally the stronger side of the screen, while the young woman is positioned on the generally weaker left side. On the other hand, we see de Lavarène full-face, while we see the young woman from the back or in profile. The camera obliges us to identify with the younger woman's point of view, while de Lavarène becomes the object of her and our gaze. The bewilderment the viewer experiences from being placed in an oxymoric, non-masterful identificatory position works as yet one more of the filmmaker's departures from aesthetic business-as-usual.[10]

**Figure 6.1** Celhia de Lavarène talking to a young Moldavian woman, in *The Peacekeepers and the Women.*

The conversation between the two women, mediated by a young female translator who, when she is on screen, occupies the extreme right-hand side of the screen, proceeds as follows:

> **C. de Lavarène.** May I ask you something very personal? You don't have to answer if you don't want. Why did you come back?
>
> **Translator, interpreting for the young woman**: Because of the money, but she cannot stay any longer. She cannot endure anymore to stay here, she says. Physically and psychologically, it's too much for her. So she cannot earn money to go back by herself. It's too much for her. And she says that when she is not willing to do this kind of job anymore, she can't earn the money anymore.
>
> **C. de Lavarène.** May I ask how old you are? You are very young. You can say it; I can't. (She laughs)
>
> **Translator, interpreting for the young woman**: Twenty-one.
>
> **C. de Lavarène.** You see? You have the whole life. I know that in your country it's…I mean it's not very easy to earn money. I know that. But is there a way, ah, like you could maybe learn English or computers or something like that?
>
> **Translator, interpreting for the young woman**: But again it's very expensive. Only our local mafia can support financially that kind of studies.
>
> **C. de Lavarène.** And you don't want (laughs) to have ties with them, of course.

These exchanges, in concert with the provocative framing and mirror-imaging of the two women, prompt the viewer to question who here is naïve and who is knowing. Who is coming from the center, and who from the periphery? Would the young woman be worse off having ties with the local mafia or having ties with Klein and de Lavarène? Doesn't she, in any case, have ties with both already? De Lavarène's suggestion about learning English or computers betrays her profound dissociation from the complex phenomena she has been given an enormous amount of money and resources (including arms and media) to represent and control. (It is noteworthy in this regard that top officials like Klein and de Lavarène do not speak or understand the languages of the regions they are administering.) The young woman, with her local knowledge of how access to education is controlled where she comes from, exposes the epistemological limits of the hegemonic regime at whose mercy she lies.

Though misunderstood as such by de Lavarène (and much of the legal and activist literature on trafficking), this is not a moment of choice, in the individualist sense, for the young woman. What is enacted here is the outcome of the congruence and/or collusion of the various agendas of the mafias, militaries, entrepreneurs, state powers, and U.N. agencies operating in the region. A feminist activist working with rural women in Kosovo/a in the 1990s presciently warned before the NATO bombing in 1999:

> The international community is promising large amounts of money for Kosova. But it seems that little of it will be controlled by rural women's groups or by local groups at all…Women in particular are being more excluded from decision[s] about their future than ever before…the international organizations now in Kosova have no understanding of women's issues and are actually importing sexism…along with their aid and their well-paid international consultants…anyone who has ever read a book on development knows, in advance, that these [problems] will occur. (Eli 2001, 346)

In Jurschick's film, Madeleine Rees, the U.N. Human Rights Commissioner, offers a striking analogy between the explosive growth of the sex market in Bosnia and Kosova and the proliferation of cell phones:

> It's a bit like having a mobile phone. Setting up the infrastructure and everything costs a lot of money, and the prices are prohibitive. Only if you have access to money can you buy the product. Now the infrastructure is set up. The trafficking routes are established. The buildings are there. Everything is all set up, and it's a much cheaper market.

According to Rees statistics, 100 percent of the clients in 1995 were internationals. By 2003 most of the clients were Bosnian. The activist, who told the story about the taxi driver near the beginning of the film, corroborates the information given by several others in the film, that over the past few years the clientele have become more and more local, meaning that when the internationals leave, the trafficking and prostitution won't stop. "It has become a kind of attraction," she says, "a common thing for Bosnian men to go to the nightclubs."

In a talk she gave in 2004, NGO worker Selmin Caliskan commented dryly that enforcing this kind of male/female hierarchy is not paving the way for democracy. Furthermore, though feminist activist organizations and groups, such as Women in Black and the German-based Medica Mondiale, were the main actors in developing practices and theories of inclusive, democratic civil society during the wars, they have been completely excluded from post-conflict reconstruction policymaking and funding (Corrin 2000). This originary exclusion is compounded by both the formal and informal practices of the international occupying forces. While, as we see in the film, trafficked women are criminalized, internationals involved in trafficking, if caught, which few are, face no criminal prosecution, fines, or any other consequences other than possibly being sent home. Local traffickers, who tend to be the wealthiest and most powerful members of communities, are the constituency that post-conflict reconstruction personnel choose to work *with*, not against. There is no discussion, outside of the excluded feminist activist circles, of reparations, rehabilitation, medical treatment, and follow-up services for abused women. Meanwhile, huge sums are available for jails, police, special brothel-raiding forces, prosecutors, and border guards, all of which come into play in further disempowering trafficked women.

It is time to return to the Hitchcockian question of just what the mission of Jacques Paul Klein and his ilk actually is, especially since his next posting was to Liberia where sex trafficking and sexual exploitation and abuse were/are occurring on an exponentially greater scale than they were/are in Bosnia and Kosova (United Nations Press Release 2003, Medica Mondiale 2006, Higate 2007, Watson 2007). If Klein and other participants in the peacekeeping mission are actually *not* interested in preventing or eliminating the enslavement, exploitation, and rape of young women, yet they are *deeply* invested in covering up what is happening to women in the region and around the world, then what is the logic of his project? How can a career officer in the U.S. State Department, who does not appear personally to be involved in the profiteering going on all around him, and who has no particular investment in Bosnia as either a geographical location or as a culture make decision after decision that increases the *insecurity* (economic, political, physical) of women, both "foreign" and domestic, while enhancing organized crime (also both foreign and domestic). Yet in the film he argues vociferously that Bosnia is on the road to political health. What is he, like Hitchcock's Scotty, looking at, and what is he missing?

The heavies in the film are quite literally heavy. A series of graying, overweight men, be they U.S. State Department air force colonels, local police-turned entrepreneurs, or American lawyers, are closely studied by the camera, their images in two cases framed in ways that commercial filmmaking reserves for young women (center screen, close-up, static), as if to invite the viewer to sense the presence of such figures—and the networks of power within which they operate—hidden *behind* the scenes of "trafficking." Here they are presented for our scrutiny, but also, however uncomfortably, as potential points of identification. The film dissolves "trafficking" as an anomalous activity and revisions it as part of a continuum that links neoliberal "free trade" with slave markets, militarization with "peacekeeping," and the "reconstruction" of "civil society" with organized crime. Most strikingly, the logic of the traffick in women becomes inseparable from the logic of the nation-state itself, which is still the dominant source of our political and academic epistemologies.

In light of the emphasis Klein places on borders, policing, and media representation, the questions the film raises can indeed be reframed in more provocative terms: if the "peacekeepers" are supposed to implement not an inclusively democratic peace *per se*, but rather the order of *nation-statehood*, as it is construed by and compatible with the interests of the dominant powers controlling the post-conflict process, then what does the compatibility of female abjection and organized crime with these interests suggest? What does the vertiginous collapse of binaries such as "oppression" and "opportunity," "rapist" and "peacekeeper," "slavery" and "free trade," "victim" and "agent," "trafficked woman" and "real prostitute," "organized crime" and "government," reveal about the concept and constitution of the culture of national security that Klein is trying to establish? As Hitchcock reduces to nothing the space between protection and murder, so Jurschick's film confounds the inside/outside logic, grounding and grounded by the nation-state, within which trafficking is usually addressed. The stakes of doing so are enormous. It is no longer possible to determine whether these women are agents or victims, whether their engagement in sex work is forced or voluntary, whether they are good or bad citizens, legal or illegal (im)migrants. The very *undecidability* of their situation, along with that of huge and increasing numbers of women involved in sex tourism and other forms of sex work in the globalized economy, becomes itself the agency of a reexamination and reimagining of the ways in which the world's populations are organized politically and economically. Are women's human rights, and by implication human rights generally, compatible with *any* of the current or emerging models of political organization?

# Notes

1. The spelling of the name of this region is itself a palimpsest of historical conquest, migration, and ethnically based discrimination. The Serb spelling is Kosovo, while the 90 percent ethnic Albanian majority, massively disenfranchised and persecuted for over a decade by Belgrade, signal their

   rejection of the legitimacy of Serbian rule in the Albanian spelling,
   Koso*va*.

2. In this sense, Jurschick's project resonates with that of visionary feminist
   political scientist Jacqueline Siapno, who writes in the face of the current
   situation in "post-conflict" East Timor, "It is *not inevitable* that the 21st
   century's first new nation should continue to reproduce the same mis-
   takes...—including gendered ones—that have occurred in other countries" (2008, 8. Italics mine).

3. A discussion of relations among postcolonial, border, migration, and
   transnational theory is beyond the scope of this chapter, but I draw implicitly or explicitly on all of them, along with deconstruction and an eclectic
   range of feminist and film theory. The situations addressed by the film
   embody so many different kinds of imperial and/or colonial histories
   (Greek, Roman, Papal, Ottoman, Hapsburg, Austro-Hungarian, German,
   U.S., Soviet, multinational corporate, etc.) and so many (shifting) borders
   that, as I argue throughout the body of my chapter, the point is not to read
   them through any one frame but to allow them to challenge our frames
   and the way we use them. The central role of troops of color deployed by
   the United Nations in Bosnia and Kosovo/a further complicates the picture, particularly any attempt to assimilate these post-conflict situations
   to a postcolonial theory that assumes white privilege and the disempow-
   erment of people of color. I am indebted to Gabriel Escobar, political
   officer in the U.S. Embassy in Rome, Italy, for information about the
   national and racial makeup of the U.N. troops stationed in Bosnia and
   Kosovo/a during the initial years of the twenty-first century when the film
   was shot.

4. Scotty thinks he witnesses Madeline's accidental fall from the mission's
   bell tower, but later learns that the woman he thought was Madeline was
   hired by Gavin to impersonate her in an elaborate plot that climaxes with
   Gavin's throwing his real wife's body from the bell tower in order to cover
   up his murder of her.

5. For further background about, and criticism of, the discourses of both the
   "anti-trafficking movement" and the anti-anti-trafficking movement, see
   also *Global Sex Workers: Rights, Resistance, and Redefinition*, ed.
   Kamala Kempadoo and Jo Doezema, especially the chapters by Jo
   Doezema entitled, "Forced to Choose: Beyond the Voluntary v. Forced
   Prostitution Dichotomy," and by Alison Murray, "Debt-Bondage and
   Trafficking: Don't Believe the Hype." Briefly, Doezema, Murray, and
   Hesford argue that the dichotomy enshrined in both international legislation and the mission statements and literature of many NGOs between
   "voluntary" prostitution and "forced" prostitution has become a way of
   denying sex workers their human rights. Only "trafficked women" have
   rights that are violated; "voluntary" prostitutes do not have rights. A
   Human Rights Watch report on India, for example, explains, "Sex workers who are imprisoned and detained, subject to cruel and degrading

mistreatment, who suffer violence at the hands of the state or by private individuals with the state's support, are disqualified from human rights considerations if their status is 'voluntary' " (Doezema 1998, 46). Amalia Cabezas cites similar police harassment of, and violence against, women arrested as sex workers (whether they are or not) in the Dominican Republic, and more generally in Latin America, the United States, and Europe (2005, 202–203). Meanwhile, opportunistic alliances between anti-trafficking projects and antiprostitution projects in the United States have led to interpretations of all forms of women's migration toward economic betterment and sex work as trafficking, enabling paternalistic narratives of rescue and rehabilitation to operate as alibis for tightening immigration policies and restricting women's mobility and autonomy (Hesford 2005, 152–153). Anti-anti-trafficking advocates argue that "migration policies and the closing of borders may in fact contribute to the increase in prostitution and trafficking world-wide…because states…forbid women to migrate for work in other professions" (Hesford 2005, 158). In this sense, they implicitly reinscribe the distinction between "legitimate" female labor that should be protected and "illegitimate" sex work.

6. Katarzyna Marciniak, in her forthcoming essay entitled "Pedagogy of Anxiety" brilliantly works through the ways this "unsafety" has played itself out in her classrooms when she has taught the film *Calling the Ghosts* (1996, dir. Mandy Jacobson and Karmen Jelinic), which addresses the wartime sexual violence that preceded that of "post-conflict" Bosnia. Selmin Caliskan has argued that, in fact, the post-conflict sexual violence should be classified as a war crime and be made prosecutable by the War Crimes Tribunal in the Hague (Caliskan 2006).

7. One NGO in the region reports, further, that while teams were built up to combat trafficking through brothel raids, women were relocated to private houses to which the raids had no access. Clients and traffickers thus protected themselves from the policies they were also responsible for creating and implementing, while they made the women more invisible and thus in greater danger (Caliskan 2004).

8. This story also allows the film to address the gendered nature of military/police authority, which I and others have described elsewhere as a contributing factor to the intensification of the subordination and oppression of women in militarized societies (Kirk and Okazawa-Rey 2001, Waller 2006).

9. For me, the "wolf in sheep's clothing" image resonates humorously with Klein's "woman with balls" metaphor. Jerschick's admittedly black but very funny comic use of the resources of her medium is relevant to my argument about the film's aesthetics, but beyond the scope of this paper.

10. The image below is from *The Peacekeepers and the Women*. Germany 2003, Director: Karin Jerschick. Courtesy of the director.

# References

I wish to thank my colleague Amalia Cabezas for her groundbreaking activist and theoretical work on sexual rights, which has greatly influenced my reading of Karin Jurschick's film and of the phenomenon of sex trafficking in the Balkans. I am also deeply grateful to Selmin Caliskan of the German-based NGO Medica Mondiale, who first called my attention to forced prostitution in Bosnia and Kosova and to Jurschick's film, and who has generously provided me with further references and information. To Karin Jurschick herself, thanks for taking so many risks in making this beautiful film.

Arrizón, Alicia. *Queering Mestizaje: Transculturation and Performance.* Ann Arbor: The University of Michigan, 2006.

Bardan, Alice Mihaela. " 'Enter Freely, and of Your Own Free Will': Cinematic Representations of Post-Socialist Transnational Journeys." In *Transnational Feminism in Film and Media,* ed. Katarzyna Marciniak, Anikó Imre, and Áine O'Healy, 93–107. New York and London: Palgrave/Macmillan, 2007.

Biemann, Ursula. "Videographies of Navigating Bodies." In *Transnational Feminism in Film and Media,* ed. Katarzyna Marciniak, Anikó Imre, and Áine O'Healy, 129–145. New York and London: Palgrave/Macmillan, 2007.

Binder, David. "Country Report, Bosnia. In A Postwar Zone, the Sex Trade Flourishes." (2001) http://www.musnbc.nsm.com/id/3071976. (Accessed on January 1, 2007).

Cabezas, Amalia Lucía. "Accidental Crossings: Tourism, Sex Work, and Women's Rights in the Dominican Republic." In *Dialogue and Difference: Feminisms Challenge Globalization,* ed. Marguerite Waller and Sylvia Marcos, 201–229. New York and London: Palgrave/MacMillan, 2005.

Caliskan, Selmin. "Roundtable Gespräch mit den National Human Rights Institutes." Unpublished paper, 2004.

———. Oral presentation at "The Global Women's Court of Accountability" held at the Joan Kroc Institute for Peace and Justice in San Diego, California, November 17–18, 2005.

Corrin, Chris. "Gender Audit of Reconstruction Programmes in South Eastern Europe." *The Urgent Action Fund and the Women's Commission for Refugee Women and Children,* 2000. http://www.bndig.de/~wplarre/ GENDER-AUDIT-OF-RECONSTRUCTION-PROGRAMMES— ccGAudit.htm (Accessed on March 7, 2008).

Doezema, Jo. "Forced to Choose: Beyond the Voluntary v. Forced Prostitution Dichotomy." In *Global Sex Workers: Rights, Resistance, and Redefinition,* ed. Jo Doezema and Kamala Kempadoo, 34–50. New York and London: Routledge, 1998.

Doezema, Jo and Kamala Kempadoo, eds. *Global Sex Workers: Rights, Resistance, and Redefinition.* New York and London: Routledge, 1998.

Eli. "Women's Activism in Rural Kosova." In *Frontline Feminisms: Women, War, and Resistance*, ed. Marguerite Waller and Jennifer Rycenga, 343–347. New York and London: Routledge, 2001.

Felten-Biermann, Claudia. "The 'disaster after the disaster' is a reality: Why a gender perspective is needed in the tsunami context." Report written for Medica Mondiale on the work of women's center Flower Aceh the organization supports in Indonesia (2005).

Gall, Carlotta. "Macedonia Village Is Center of Europe Web in Sex Trade." *The New York Times*, July 28, 2001, A1.

Hesford, Wendy S. and Wendy Kozol, eds. *Just Advocacy? Women's Human Rights, Transnational Feminisms, and the Politics of Representation*. New Brunswick, New Jersey, and London: Rutgers University Press, 2005.

———. "*Kairos* and the Geopolitical Rhetorics of Global Sex Work and Video Advocacy." In *Just Advocacy? Women's Human Rights, Transnational Feminisms, and the Politics of Representation*, ed. Wendy S. Hesford and Wendy Kozol, 146–172. New Brunswick, New Jersey, and London: Rutgers University Press, 2005.

Higate, Peter. "Peacekeepers, Masculinities and Sexual Exploitation." *Men and Masculinities* 10 (2007): 99–119.

Jurschick, Karin. *The Peacekeepers and the Women*. DVD. 80 mins. New York: Women Make Movies, 2003.

Kirk, Gwyn and Margot Okazawa-Rey. "Demilitarizing Security: Women Oppose U.S. Militarism in East Asia." In *Frontline Feminisms: Women, War, and Resistance*, ed. Marguerite Waller and Jennifer Rycenga, 159–171. New York: Routledge, 2001.

Kumar, Corinne. "The South Wind: Towards a New Political Imaginary." In *Dialogue and Difference: Feminisms Challenge Globalization*, ed. Marguerite Waller and Sylvia Marcos, 165–199. New York and London: Palgrave/Macmillan, 2005.

Lynch, Colum. "UN Faces More Accusations of Sexual Misconduct." *The Washington Post*, March 13, 2005, A22.

Marciniak, Katarzina. "Pedagogy of Anxiety." *Signs: A Journal of Women in Culture and Society* (forthcoming, 2010).

McElroy, Wendy. "Is the UN Running Brothels in Bosnia?" (June 11, 2003) http://www.foxnews.com/story/0,2933,43603,00.html (Accessed in November, 2005).

Medica Mondiale. 2006. Press Release, Bonn/Cologne, March 7: "War crimes against women." Received by the author in an e-mail from Selmin Caliskan. (November, 2005).

Murray, Alison. "Debt-Bondage and Trafficking: Don't Believe the Hype." In *Global Sex Workers: Rights, Resistance, and Redefinition*, ed. Jo Doezema and Kamala Kempadoo, 51–68. New York and London: Routledge, 1998.

Siapno, Jacqueline. "Whispered Confidences: Articulating the Female in the PNTL (police) and the F-FDTL (military) in Timor Leste." *IIAS Newsletter* 48 (2008): 7–8.

United Nations Press Release. "Secretary-General Appoints Jacques Klein as
  his Special Representative for Liberia." (July 11, 2003). http://www.
  un.org/news/Press/docs/2003/sga848rev.1.doc.htm (Accessed on October
  16, 2007).
Waller, Marguerite. "Addicted to Virtue: The Globalization Policy-Maker."
  *Social Identities: Journal for the Study of Race, Nation and Culture* 12,
  5 (2006): 575–594.
Watson, Steve. "UN Child Sex Slave Scandals Continue: Wave after wave of
  child abuse reports pour forward from all over the globe." Infowars.net.
  http://inforwars.net/articles/January        2007/030107UN_Sex.htm
  (Accessed on January 3, 2007).
Wölfe, Sonja. "Armed Conflict and Trafficking in Women: Desk Study."
  Eschborn, Germany: Deutsche Gesellshcaft für Technische
  Zusammenarbeit (GTZ) GmbH, 2004. http://www.gtz.de/traffickingin-
  women. E-mail: antitrafficking@gtz.de (Accessed on January 1, 2007).

*Greece: Women's New Roles and Identities*

# Chapter Seven

## Maria, Irene and Olga "à la recherche du temps perdu... "[1]

*Maria Paradeisi*[2]

## Introduction

Since the beginning of the restoration of democracy in 1974, Greek cinema has shifted its attention from the sociopolitical subjects of the 1970s and 1980s to portrayals of identity issues, gender roles, private stories, relationships, and feelings. Filmmaker Elissavet Chronopoulou explains this change of direction by stating, "we are trying to allow emotion to pass into our films. The manner in which you use it is a matter of personal taste. But there is no reason why we should not allow our heroes to live" (Katsounaki 2003, 1). *Starting in the 1980s, directors began to* produce films about the representation of the new sociocultural roles of the contemporary Greek woman (e.g., *I dromoi tis agapis inai nichterinoi/Love Wonders in the Night* (1981) by Frieda Liappa, *Revanche* (1983) by Nikos Vergitsis, *I timi tis agapis/The Price of Love* (1984) by Tonia Marketaki, and *I ores/The Hours* (1990) by Antouanetta Angelidi). Continuing this trend, more women directors contributed to Greek cinema with several interesting portraits of female characters. Films such as *I diakritiki goitia ton arsenikon/The Mating Game* by Olga Malea (2000), *Kleftis I pragmatikotita /Thief or Reality* (2001) by Antouanetta Angelidi, *Pame gia ena ouzo/Let's Go for an Ouzo* (2002) by Kleoni Flessa, and *I nostalgos/The Woman Who Missed Home* by Eleni Alexandrakis (2004) all present stories of modern women struggling with professional self-realization and personal fulfillment.

The annual production Chof Greek films is limited to about twenty, of which about one-fifth are directed by women. Katerina Evangelakou and Elissavet Chronopoulou are among the most prominent filmmakers who have produced films about women's private, public, and political roles in contemporary Greece. Katerina Evangelakou (Pireus, 1962) studied Film Direction at the Evgenia Hatzikou School of Film and Television Studies. She has produced and directed more than forty documentaries for television as well as many episodes of the *Backstage* program over the past fifteen years. She has also worked with visual artists[3] in video environments[4] and has directed three feature films: *Iagouaros/Jaguar* (1994),[5] *Tha to metanioseis/ You Will Regret It* (2002),[6] and *Ores koinis isychias/False Alarm* (2006).[7] Elissavet Chronopoulou (Athens, 1981) graduated from the Stavrakos Film School and started her career in film in 1987 as an editor. In 1995 she began directing the shorts *Na pou Ginete/Lean on Me*[8] and *Chtes to apoyevma/Yesterday Afternoon (1998),*[9] the documentary *Politikos Englismos stin Ellada toy 20ou eona/Political Confinement in 20th Century Greece (2000),* and the TV films *Treis efhes/Three Wishes (2002) and Moni ex amelias/Alone out of Negligence (2005). Ena tragoudi de ftnanei/A Song Is Not Enough* (2003)[10] is her feature debut, and her second film, *Annivas pro ton pylon/Hannibal Before the Gates* (2007) has not yet been distributed.

Evangelakou's *You Will Regret It* and Chronopoulou's *A Song Is Not Enough* portray charismatic female characters, respectively Maraki and Irene, struggling with their individual choices and societal expectations. More specifically, the two stories follow the evolution of lower-middle-class women from the late 1960s to the early 2000s, a period of economic development and major cultural change in Greece. Both films subvert culturally based gender roles and offer stories of fulfilled women in contemporary Greece. Maraki and Irene lead professionally successful lives: Maraki is an entrepreneur, and Irene is a theater actress and a political activist. They disregard the strong gender patterns prevalent in Greek society and remain uncompromising in asserting their individual goals and in defending their right to be respected like men. The male characters, however, hold merely supporting roles and are represented predominantly in relation to the female protagonists.

Evangelakou and Chronopoulou establish portraits of women using similar innovative narrative styles and present characters through allusions and "distantiation" devices. Such techniques are referred to as "Brechtian alienation effects…which recondition the spectator and 'make strange' the lived social world" (Stam 2005, 147) and "reflexivity, a technique whereby art reveals the principles of its own construction" (Stam 2005, 148).

The two directors also present cinematic "space" subjectively, superseding the distinction between the private and the public spheres.

Private space is often enriched by a lyrical and poetic dimension as it inspires characters' moments of reflection and relaxation. Motherhood and complex cross-generational relationships between women occupy a significant emotional space in both films. Narrative fragmentation and chronological discontinuity between the present and the past, as well as the alternating use of black/white (for the past) and color (for the present) constitute the aesthetic features of both films. Furthermore, both Evangelakou and Chronopoulou express the complexity of their heroines' lives with gentle humor. Although the directors use similar narrative devices, the differences between the two main female characters, Maraki and Irene, can be expressed as follows:

| businesswoman | small city | single woman | present | outside |
| female artist | capital | divorced woman | past | inside |

The narrative style of both films reflects the artistic conventions of European art house cinema and of the "new Hollywood" of the mid-1960s. Bordwell explains that in art cinema, "Specific sorts of realism motivate a loosening of cause and effect, an episodic construction of the '*syuzhet*' (plot), and an enhancement of the film's symbolic dimension through an emphasis on the fluctuations of character psychology...The film will deal with 'real' subject matter, current psychological problems such as contemporary 'alienation' and 'lack of communication.' The mise-en-scène may emphasize verisimilitude of behavior as well as verisimilitude of space (e.g. location shooting, non-Hollywood lighting schemas) or time (e.g. the *temps mort* in a conversation)" (Bordwell 1995, 206). Mast and Kawin explain that "...the new American cinema did not ask to be taken as reality, but constantly announced that it was artificial...Slow motion, freeze frames, jump cutting, self-conscious camerawork, mixtures of black and white and color were all standard tricks of the new trade" (Mast and Kawin 1996, 463–464). The narratives in *You Will Regret It* and *A Song Is Not Enough* are structured around consistent fragmentation between the present and the past and are characterized by the use of slow-motion actions and freeze-frames. In *A Song Is Not Enough* the use of a combination black and white (for the past) and color (for the present) film is prevalent.

Stam explains that textual analysis "explores the mesh of cinematic codes (camera movement, offscreen sound) and extra-cinematic codes (ideological binarisms of nature-culture, male-female) either across a number of texts or within a single text" (Stam 2005, 188). Stam also summarizes film analysis as "an open-ended and historically shaped practice oriented by diverse goals…a genre of film writing open to diverse influences…to diverse grids…to diverse '*schemata*'…and to diverse principles of pertinence, both cinematic (camera movement, editing), and extra-cinematic (representation of women, blacks, gays and lesbians)" (Stam 2005, 192).

Textual analysis, as the blend of cinematic and extra-cinematic elements of analysis, will be used to discuss *You Will Regret It* and *A Song Is Not Enough*. This article will also explore the two films' non-linear narrative styles and will examine the complex nature of gender roles as represented in the female characters' public and private lives.

## You Will Regret It

Using a light comic tone, Evangelakou presents the different nature of female and male desires, by focusing on women's fear of facing the unknown and overturning familiar situations. The director also shows the vacuity of accepted social and moral norms and the high cost of compliance with traditional roles. She depicts the intricate nature of relationships between mother and daughter, siblings, and men and women through a complex plot and constant leaps from the present to the past, and vice versa, over a period of time that covers more than twenty years.

Evangelakou's film is about Maraki (a diminutive of Maria), a middle-aged woman who lives in a provincial area of Greece. Brilliant in math, as a teenager she has the deep desire to leave her hometown and continue her studies. However, in the end, she never leaves her hometown and does not pursue her academic aspirations. She decides instead to help her elder sister study and marry her beloved, their high school professor. (Maraki herself had been in love with "the handsome basketball player" when attending school, but in the end he preferred her younger sister). Maraki lives with her neurotic mother and runs her own pastry shop. Her business is so successful that she can support her mother and sisters. Her fortieth birthday finds her pregnant by Kyriakos, a much younger friend of hers.

The film starts on the seashore, with a mother sitting on the sand reading and at the same time telling her young son an improvised fairytale about a princess who did not want to grow up. The little boy cannot wait to reach the happy ending and, interrupting his mom at a critical moment in the story, he says, "And then the prince arrived in a spaceship and married her!"[11] "No my child," the mother answers, "the prince will come at the end…running late, but he will come," thus anticipating the plot's development. These first images are interrupted by the opening credits on the screen. After the credits, the film flashes back and the plot takes a surrealist turn: as Maraki rehearses, in a voiceover monologue, different possible ways to announce her pregnancy to her lover, she faints and collapses in the street. However, this "accident" has a dreamlike quality: wearing elegant clothes and high heels, she lies on the ground, changes positions trying to get comfortable on the concrete sidewalk, and smiles while listening to her best friend's comments, but no one comes to help her. She is pondering over at least three different ways of announcing her pregnancy to her much younger lover, while she also wonders whether she should reveal the news or hide it from him. After several attempts to find the best way to announce her pregnancy, Maraki realizes the uselessness of every possible variation. The humor, spontaneity, tenderness, and sincerity of this monologue make this intimate moment the most important in the film.

This monologue is often interrupted by the interference of third parties, who disagree with Maraki's decisions (she is elected councilor at the municipal council) about her support, in a local newspaper article, of the lazy cleaning lady, whom everyone else wants to fire. Important examples of these interruptions, as interesting elements of distantiation, are the sudden appearances of Anthi and Lena, Maraki's two sisters, and her best friend Poppy, a hairdresser. In their first appearance, when the two sisters wish Maraki happy birthday, one wears a surgeon's gown as she accompanies a stretcher; the other, with her hair in rollers, has just picked up her daughter's doll from the bed. In their second appearance, they are hosting a child's birthday party and complain about not being able to look after their melancholic mother. Through these visual representations, the director defines the first sister as a dynamic woman and the second as a passive person (characteristics that will be confirmed later on in the story).

The storyline is regularly interrupted and becomes more and more fragmented as streams of flashbacks continue the narrative. A series of disconnected events adds tension to the story: a montage of Maraki's preoccupations is intermittently juxtaposed with quick flashes of a young biker. In this sequence, Maraki and the biker move in opposite directions: when the young man moves from right to left, Maraki walks from left to right, and vice versa. Their opposite directions lead toward an imaginary point of convergence. With such concise narration Evangelakou informs the viewers how their different directions will lead them to meet at a crucial point in their lives.

Just after the first introductory section, the young man on the bike changes direction with a U-turn and arrives at a cottage where he is welcomed by middle-aged Menis. His movement is followed by an effective visual metonymy. Maraki has just left the hairdresser, where she has announced the results of the pregnancy test, when Poppy realizes that Maraki has left her cardigan behind. She shakes it out and at that moment the scene turns into slow motion: the cardigan hovers, immobile in the frame, while voices are heard, and the hairdresser's salon empties in the blink of an eye. The next scene presents Maraki lying on the pavement while she, in a voiceover, expresses her wish to live her life again from the start. Viewers then watch a review of her life presented in segments: every time Maraki narrates certain past events, the camera shows them through flashbacks regularly intercut with snatches of other characters' actions taking place in the present.

Maraki remains on the pavement in an unnatural position almost until the end of the film. Often she opens her eyes and answers questions in a voiceover, all the while making small movements in order to get comfortable. The first flashbacks, which concern her, take the viewer back at least twenty years and to a different place, when it seemed that everything would turn out very differently. Maraki as a student is dreaming of going to university, later she is shown in a classroom, excelling in all her studies. The most important flashback shows Maraki at the decisive moment of her teens and with her inseparable companion, Kyriakos. The son of her mother's friend Adonia, he is thirteen years her junior and like a younger brother to her. The headmaster announces that Maraki has won the first prize in essay writing and that she has been awarded a scholarship. This happy close-up is followed by a shot of her and Kyriakos' legs as they run along the corridor (the little one holding on to the edge of her school uniform). Then, in a subjective shot from Maraki's point of view, her favorite basketball player is seen in the playground. As she passes from discouragement to hope, in a voiceover monologue, the miracle she had waited for takes place: the basketball player invites her, along with her sisters, to the game the following day. Jumping of joy, in an imaginary dialogue with him, she states her case, "If you want a casual relationship, I am available as long as it lasts, after all I'm leaving next year..."

The next scene shows Maraki sitting with her friend Poppy on a bench, sharing their news, while Kyriakos is playing next to them and looking at his older "sister." In a close-up, Maraki announces the news about the scholarship and "The Date," but Poppy informs her that her beloved is seeing her sister. The following shots reveal the strong friendship between the two teenagers as they share their joys and sorrows and support one another—Poppy has been expelled from school and Maraki's romantic hopes have been crushed. The camera has already repeatedly revealed to the viewer the intense flirtation between Lena, Maraki's sister, and the basketball player, something that takes Maraki completely by surprise. The overwhelming shock is expressed through the freezing of her movement in the frame.

A sudden cut interrupts the narrative, leaving the action suspended and increasing tension for the viewer. The story is again set in the present with Maraki's sisters traveling to town. When the camera is back on the two girlfriends, it shows in close-ups their sad expressions due to what has just been said. Maraki tries to choke back her tears and says that "she was just joking" while the almost equally surprised Poppy says the same offscreen. Surprisingly, little Kyriakos reassures her by saying, "Don't worry, I'll marry you!"

The story continues in the present. Maraki's former headmaster learns of her "fall" and, as he approaches her lying down on the sidewalk, he asks out loud, "Why, my child, didn't you accept the scholarship? Why were you left behind?" and Maraki replies in voiceover, "Honestly, I don't know..." (possibly suggesting that Maraki was afraid of pursuing a life more suited to her extraordinary academic abilities). The next flashback shows Maraki's sisters, each in turn, departing from their little town with their partners. The last to leave is Kyriakos, who will return to his childhood idol, twenty years later, handsome and with a high-performance motorbike. A romance then develops between him and Maraki, despite their differences in age and lifestyle.

Most of the action in the present concerning Maraki refers to her powerful presence in the public domain, her genuine interest in the common good, and her unique fighting spirit when defending her beliefs—something that makes her unpleasant to the people who disagree with her. (Her aggressive style is attributed to the fact that she is unmarried). Maraki doesn't hesitate to openly confront situations and publicly condemn members of the local council when she realizes that they are abusing their power for their own interests.

Maraki is not, however, the only member of the family who was afraid of "pursuing her life." A series of flashbacks shows a long-term "silent" romance between her shy mother, Ioulia, a widow since she was twenty-eight, and the even more timid Menis, a well-off neighbor. When Menis, encouraged by Maraki, finally asks Ioulia to marry him, her friend Adonia intervenes. A singer in a nightclub and Kyriakos' single mother, Adonia pursues and wins Menis. So Menis, who never got over Ioulia, lets himself be carried away by events. When Ioulia recalls this old romance, she refuses to admit her fear of starting a new life. Evidently, as time passed, these events plunged her into melancholy and agoraphobia.

Maraki's two sisters, Anthi and Lena, were also carried along by the flow of events. Their conservative suits and matching shirts, sunglasses, and tight lips made them conform to the traditional image of the married petit bourgeois woman. As they travel toward their home town (Poppy has informed them about Maraki's "collapse"), viewers learn about their stories through more narrative flashbacks. Anthi, a bad pupil at school, dreams of becoming an actress and in a moment of adolescent impulse flirts with her literature teacher. The teacher reciprocates, and while she seems to regret this recklessness, she ends up leaving town with him. Following his encouragement, and with financial support from Maraki, Anthi studies to become a paramedic. Lena is the first to get married (to the basketball player), when she is already expecting a baby.

Both Anthi and Lena, unlike Maraki, have conformed to social conventions and "have realized their lives" as wives. However, in their conversation, cinematically rendered in shot/reverse shot, they complain about the high price they have paid for getting married. Lena cries hysterically as she describes her husband's constant infidelity (the charming basketball player, who ended up becoming a taxi driver). Anthi tells her to stop being a victim and to divorce him, adding "Men are kids…there are no men…real ones. We reckon they exist…but it's our fault, we give them the license to fool around." Anthi, on the other hand, after saying that her husband's highest virtue is being faithful to her, complains about the monotonous routine of life with a hypochondriac.

It is obvious that the two sisters are jealous of Maraki's freedom from the responsibilities of marriage. In contrast to hostile and unfair Anthi, Lena is riddled with guilt toward the "perfect" sister who gave up the dream of becoming a mathematician in order to support them, and who is carrying the burden of their melancholic mother. Lena has also learned from Poppy (probably when they were in school) of Maraki's feelings for the basketball player, a fact that now magnifies her guilt. Furthermore, while Anthi holds Maraki responsible for getting mixed up with the much younger Kyriakos, Lena strongly states that she should not interfere with Maraki's life. Soon after, Anthi turns Lena against "Saint Maraki," whose "fall" has made things difficult for both of them. Both sisters break in hysterical laughter as they imagine Maraki and Kyriakos together, insinuating that a relationship between an older woman and a much younger man is inappropriate.

The women's fears, guilt, and insecurities are reflected in similar reactions by their men. The basketball player, full of worry and guilt (since Lena caught him flirting with another woman), looks for his wife at her sister's house, afraid that she may have left him. At the same time, Menis, in a discussion with Kyriakos, hints at the fact that when he feels deeply in love he faces sexual problems, which explains why he finally preferred Kyriakos' mother over Ioulia. During a discussion between the two men, Kyriakos seems lost in his own thoughts, having just confessed his fear about Maraki's pregnancy. Menis loses his temper and starts hitting him wildly, screaming at him that he should be ashamed of himself, since Maraki could be his mother. His violent reaction is indicative of a conservative mentality. Kyriakos, on the other hand, does not seem to understand the cause of such rage, thus showing that this social prejudice is foreign to him. Soon, though, Menis regains his composure and rules out the possibility of such a pregnancy because, as he says, Maraki is a calculating woman (reinforcing another cultural negative stereotype). Finally, after Menis' insistent encouragement, the two men decide to attend Maraki's birthday party.

One of the key final scenes shows Maraki's guests meeting up in a car park. This encounter and moment of revelation involves a wide range of emotional shifts that leave their marks in a series of rapidly alternating close-ups. The announcement of Maraki's "fall" is followed by the confusion of the guests' reactions, with everyone talking over one another. The celebratory mood turns suddenly into anxiety, and Lena concludes that her sister has lost her mind since, for the past forty years, she has kept everything bottled up. Kiriakos' apprehension gradually increases, while Anthi declares that she knows absolutely nothing about the causes and consequences of the fall, and entertains various hypotheses. In the midst of this chaos, the basketball player calls to make up with his wife, and while they exchange sweet nothings, the camera turns toward the sky as the cheerful music from the opening monologue is played again.

With a fast-paced crosscutting, the film shows Maraki (lying there all on her own, still in the same position: another unnatural event) wishing for something important to happen. At that very moment, and in keeping with the comic tone of the film, pigeon droppings land on her forehead. This brings her to her senses while the cleaning lady (the only person there next to her) wipes her forehead and helps her to her feet. Maraki's smile draws to a close her review of the relationship with Kyriakos. In a voiceover, she concludes that it was beautiful while it lasted.

As the women walk off into the distance, the voice of a child asks for the end of the fairy tale, and the film returns to the opening scene where Maraki gives her son a math problem to solve. A close-up of a puzzled child holding an exercise book with a problem written in it is followed by a close-up of his mother reading a math book. Then, in the background, the figure of a tall man is seen from behind (with a silhouette similar to that of Kyriakos), as he fishes along the edge of the rocky shoreline, while the camera tracks back to include the mother and son in the frame, suggesting that these people belong to the same family.

## A Song Is Not Enough

**Chronopoulou**'s film revolves around four characters, one child and three adults. Set in the early 1970s, during the politically and socially difficult military dictatorship in Greece, this film explores relationships of friendship and love, motherhood and fatherhood, highlights the pressure of historical demands, and portrays the inevitable collision between family responsibilities and political militancy. The director powerfully addresses Irene's moral conflict between the commitment to fight against a tyrannical state and her need to preserve family harmony, explores the protagonist's intense mother-daughter relationship and the trauma that results from its sudden ending, examines Irene's struggle in juggling the multiple roles of a modern woman, reveals the damaging consequences of a triangular relationship (Irene, Manolis, and Vasia) on the lives of those involved, and portrays vividly tempestuous relationships among family members.

Olga, a woman in her thirties, is faced with her mother's political activism and the recent history of her country. In the winter of 1972, twenty-eight-year-old Irene is arrested by the Junta[12] for subversive activities and sent to Korydallos prison. Her imprisonment has a devastating effect on her own life and the lives of those close to her. Her nine-year-old daughter Olga does not understand what is happening and considers her mother's disappearance as abandonment and betrayal. For Manolis, Irene's irresponsible and bohemian ex-husband, this is the first time he is fully responsible for his daughter. However, Olga does not get along with her father. Meanwhile, in prison, Irene discovers another side of life and of herself. When she is released in August 1973, she finds that nothing is the way she left it. Olga finds a way out of the vicious cycle of anger and resentment toward Irene only when she discovers the story of the old man who experienced a fate similar to that of her mother and her fellow prisoners. Set in two narrative time planes, the film deals with the difficulty of coming to terms with the past.

Twenty-eight-year-old Irene tries to juggle her roles as actress (the lead in a youth theatre), mother of her young child Olga, divorcee, and political activist. The fragmented and nonlinear narrative shows Irene and Olga twenty years later, still suffering from the wounds of the separation. Although most of the film deals with the past, its ramifications in the present are the central part of the plot. The film starts with photographs of political exiles, while in a voiceover interview with a member of the resistance the audience is informed of prison and exile experiences.[13] This interview, divided into four different fragments and inserted at different moments in the film, does not last long, but it is significant because it shows the efforts made by the young daughter, Olga, to comprehend her mother's "betrayal."

In addition to the intermittent use of parts of the interview, the narrative moves on different levels blending into one another with a fragmented chronology and leaps in time from the present to the past and vice versa. The first level deals with the past, around the axis of the mother-daughter relationship presented in Irene's rehearsals at the theatre, her relationship with her best friend Vasia, her militant involvement in the resistance, and Irene's and Olga's relationships with Manolis. The second level concerns Irene's life in prison and the relationships that develop in the context of the female community there. Parallel to Irene's time in prison, the film presents the characters whose lives are most affected by her prolonged absence: little Olga with her father and his family, and Manolis and Vasia. The third level is about Olga's life as it is in the present with her own family, her companion Dimitris, her son Dodo, and her alcoholic father (whom she often retrieves from bars), juxtaposed with her mother's successful artistic career in the theatre.

Chronopoulou's cinematic narration declares little and implies a lot. Many nuances and tensions can be inferred from the positions that the characters hold in each frame, their gazes, their small gestures, and the charged silences exchanged between them. From the start, the director depicts the characters lucidly, and their roles and temperaments are then confirmed by the development of events in the story. The relationship between Irene and Olga, in the first level of the film, seems to be a relation between equals (despite the differences in age and roles) due to the dynamic personality of the young girl and the single-parent structure of the family. The first depiction of this central pair takes place in the theatre. The inventive theatrical direction brings to the fore the rehearsals between Irene and her colleagues, thereby pointing at the obliquely critical nature of the plays that the left-wing theatre company decides to produce. While the mother in the foreground is working creatively, in the background of the scene Olga is trying to concentrate on her study of Roman history (she is forced to follow her mother to the theatre). It becomes clear that Olga is very sensitive to her mother's scolding and yet she is very testing with Irene. (Olga often pushes her mother to the limits and punishes her and, later on, her father by ignoring them.) Olga's tantrums are usually followed by expressions of tenderness and support toward her parents, especially when they are in an emotionally vulnerable state of mind.

The following scenes present the main features of the characters playing key roles in the plot. Irene's relationships with Vasia and Manolis are complex and tumultuous, and Chronopoulou highlights Irene's relationships of attraction and repulsion with people around her. Vasia is competitive with her childhood friend (Irene is undoubtedly the leading lady of their theatrical company) and she also accuses her of elitism and arrogance (an opinion that Argiro, Irene's cell-mate, seems to share at times). Irene has left and rejected her reckless husband Manolis; however, there remains a physical attraction between them, shown by her hospitality during his occasional late-night visits. With an effective montage of seemingly parallel situations, the camera portrays these visits along with corresponding circumstances in which twenty-eight-year-old Olga goes around retrieving her alcoholic father from bars.

This relative balance in relationships and situations is overthrown when Irene is arrested and put in prison. The theatre company is left without a lead actress, Manolis has to face responsibilities he is incapable of handling, and Olga suffers deeply due to her mother's absence. What follows in the narrative distinctly implies the predictable difficulties: Olga often reproaches or does not talk to her father, marking the near reversal of the parent-child roles. These conflicts, however, alternate with moments of love and tenderness, like when the two smile at each other while playing piano and singing together.

In the second level of the narration, Chronopoulou presents the contradictory feelings and circumstances created by isolation and confinement. The humor, solidarity, support, and small acts of resistance in prison, which bring the political prisoners together, alternate with the tensions, breakdowns, tears and despair, and longing for their loved ones. Emphasis is also put on the relationship between political and criminal prisoners. Finally, the director presents the nervousness and insecurity that prisoners experience when faced with the unexpected amnesty and their imminent release. Key to this second section are the two meetings between Irene and Manolis in the prison visiting room, where they are both filmed with classic simplicity and in expressive shots/reverse shots. Both meetings are characterized by the exceptionally rich nuances in the exchange of gazes and in the charged silences; the couple communicates silently in the midst of the raucous crowd surrounding them.

Equally important are Irene's two letters written in prison, one to Olga and the other to Manolis, about her inability to express her feelings and her attempt to reevaluate her actions. In the first letter, read in voiceover, Irene describes with nostalgia the morning ritual of getting Olga ready for school. In juxtaposition to these images, Olga is seen preparing breakfast like her mother used to, while her father is asleep in another room. The letter ends with Irene imploring her daughter to come and visit her at least once in prison. The second letter, in a voiceover again, reads, "everything was wrong...nothing is the same anymore..."[14] Irene, longing for Olga, Manolis, Vasia, and "a walk on a Sunday afternoon...," concludes admitting, "...Olga is right...everything I have done is wrong..."

When the letter-reading begins, the female prisoners are playing football in the yard; they are wearing their little woolly hats and look like little girls. The heavy snow gives a dreamlike atmosphere to this rare moment of joy and play. This scene, as the place of "artistic motivation" (Bordwell, 1995),[15] has an appealing element justified by the plot, but it is also present purely for its artistic beauty.

A critical change occurs during Irene's confinement: she is gradually replaced by Vasia in the relationship with Manolis, and in her position in the theatre. Chronopoulou brings to the fore the two women's conflicting emotions and moods by using two very distinctive close-ups: Vasia's guilt and her powerful desire to replace her best friend and eternal rival in the leading role in the theatre; Irene's hesitant feelings of understanding for what has happened and her bitter response to her best friend's competitiveness. The resolution to this rivalry occurs when Irene overcomes her feelings and actively supports Vasia at the premiere.

When the second level of the story ends, a new scene anticipates the development in the present. Irene is released from prison and enjoys the sunny journey back home in Manolis' car. Just as the relationship of the ex-spouses seems to be restored, when they arrive at home little Olga, hiding on the balcony, reacts coldly to her mother's warm hug. The drama erupts when Vasia arrives. After a violent emotional reaction, she collapses, thus confessing indirectly her new relationship with Manolis. Still in love with his ex-wife, Manolis thinks that having had a relationship with Vasia while Irene was in prison, and restarting the relationship with Irene now that she has returned home, is simply normal. As Irene shows him the door, little Olga, with her characteristic determination, announces that she will stay with Manolis. (The child rarely calls him "father.")

The third level of narration presents the story twenty years later, shifting the attention from the mother to the daughter and focusing on their total inability to communicate. During these years, only one relationship has been restored: the one between Irene and Vasia. Now a famous theatre actress, Irene has little or no contact with Manolis, and sees him only at premieres. Olga, who has her own family with a loving, supportive companion and a beautiful son, is still angry with her mother. Her hysterical outbursts every time her father or partner tries to convince her to go to the theatre reveal the depth of the problem caused by her mother's "absence" for twenty years. On the other hand, Olga's constant study of material concerning political prisoners reveals her efforts to understand her mother and hopefully to resolve their conflicts.

The greatly anticipated moment of reconciliation takes place in the theatre where Chronopoulou shows Olga backstage (instead of among the audience), watching her mother from the wings as she plays the role of Alexandra De Lago in *The Sweet Bird of Youth*.[16] When the heroine talks about her despair—the moment of withdrawal from theatre performances—her lines symbolically refer to the painful separation from her own daughter. As Irene turns around (with her back toward the audience), she recognizes her daughter and her eyes fill with tears as she continues her lines. Now her words are clearly addressing her daughter, "...sooner or later, at some point in your life, what you considered to be the purpose of life, you lose it or you let it go...and then you die..." Olga turns around, goes to her mother's dressing room and, with a smile of relief, lies down on the couch looking at the big picture in the room, of herself and her mother as they were twenty years earlier.

## Conclusion

*You Will Regret It* and *A Song Is Not Enough* are characterized by the presence of strong female characters both in leading and supporting roles. The protagonists' charismatic personalities transcend culturally defined gender roles and come in conflict with their social communities' values and family members' expectations. The female main characters acquire an important role in the public sphere, often paying a high price on a personal level or in their family life for their unpopular choices and courageous decisions for independence and autonomy. However, the social obligation of getting married and complying with traditional roles often comes with a much greater cost. All the male characters play supporting roles and are presented only in relation to the films' heroines. The reversal of the dominant social model of male-female relationships in cinema, man superiority vitality spirit woman inferiority passivity body (Clement and Cixous 1975, 115), and the fluidity of contemporary gender identities are effectively portrayed. Evangelakou's and Chronopoulou's films point out that reactions to traditional gender-defined roles in recent decades still coexist with the rooted social norms and moral prejudices, usually more common in smaller towns and among older generations.

These themes are presented through cinematic narrative styles that include the artistic conventions of the European art film and of the "new Hollywood" of the mid-1960s. Examples of these features are: projections of the ambiguous and intricate character of human nature, and the frequent use of distantiation devices. In these films, the use of the camera is the very opposite of the unseen observer that typically characterizes classical narration. Relevant and unique features of both films are the consistently fragmented nature of the narration, the systematic disruption of the space-time continuum, the sudden cuts to set transitions from different time planes, and the disarray of the subjective and objective realities.

Space often acquires a subjective and lyrical-poetic dimension when expressing the characters' feelings. *A Song Is Not Enough* is also characterized by the mixture of black/white and color film, whereas what is distinctive of *You Will Regret It* is the use of slow motion and the unpredictable happy ending. Finally, both films leave any sexual encounters offscreen. *A Song Is Not Enough* presents a very few discreet shots of female nudity, thus evading "the representation of woman as spectacle-body to be looked at, as a place of sexuality, and object of desire…" (de Lauretis 1982, 4) eluding spectators' voyeuristic desire of the woman's body as object of visual pleasure.

# Notes

1. The title of this essay is adapted from the title of Marcel Proust's novel *À la recherché du temps perdu* (1913–1927).

2. I would like to thank Flavia Laviosa and my colleagues Alexandra Halkias from Panteion University and Zacharias Palios from University of Crete for their important help. I also wish to thank Theo Hutchinson and Roza Maragopoulou for their translation of this essay into English.

3. Opi Zouni, Annita Argyroheliopoilou, and Michel Feris.

4. Evangelakou is also the author of the children's fairytale entitled *The Unsmiling Queen and the Unruly Bow* illustrated by Denis Lhomme and published by Polis (2002).

5. This film is about the Greek Civil War and based on the Greek novel by Alexander Kotzias with the same title, published in 1987.

6. The film has been released also with the international English title *Think It Over*.

7. This film is a contemporary fictional story.

8. The film was awarded the 1995 Hellenic Ministry of Culture State Awards, First Prize GFC Distinction/Incentive Award; and at the Short Film Festival of Drama in 1995 it was awarded the Best New Director Award, Best Woman Director Award, Actress in a Leading Role Distinction, and Artistic Achievement Distinction.

9. The film was awarded the 1998 Hellenic Ministry of Culture State Quality Awards, and the Quality Distinction GFC Distinction/Incentive Award.

10. WorldFest-Houston International Film Festival, 2004: Independent theatrical feature films, Platinum award.

11. Translations of the dialogues of the film *You Will Regret It* are mine.

12. On April 21, 1967 the military Junta was imposed. A group of right-wing Greek Army colonels, lead by Georgios Papadopoulos, Brigadier Stylianos Pattakos, and Colonel Nikolaos Makarezos, successfully seized power in a coup d'état on the pretext of imminent "communist threat," establishing what became known as the Regime of the Colonels. During this time (1967–1974), all political parties, including the United Democratic Left (EDA), were dissolved, and civil liberties were suppressed for all Greek citizens. Socialist Labor Party of Greece (KKE) members were persecuted along with other opponents of the Junta. The military dictatorship abolished political freedom, while imprisonments, torture, and exile were widely and severely enforced. Greek women were actively involved in the Resistance against the repressive military regime. After the restoration of parliamentary democracy in 1974, Constantine Karamanlis legalized the KKE.

13. After the defeat of the democratic army in the civil war in Greece (1946–1948), the left-wing partisans were sent to prison or exiled on various arid islands in the Aegean Sea, whereas those who had collaborated took over the means of suppression from which right-wing terrorism ensued.

14. Translations of film dialogues are taken from the subtitles of the DVD *A Song Is Not Enough*.

15. David Bordwell defines four kinds of motivation. Viewers may justify the material in terms of its relevance to the requirements of the story

(*compositional* motivation); or they may apply a notion of plausibility derived from some conception of the way things work in the world (*realistic* motivation); or they may justify an expectation or inference on *transtextual* grounds (*transtextual* motivation); or something could be present for its own sake—as an appealing, or shocking, or neutral element (*artistic* motivation).

16. Tennessee Williams' 1959 play. Although there is no specific connection between *The Bird of Youth* and *A Song Is Not Enough*, or Alexandra De Lago and Irene as Olga's mother, the lines "...sooner or later, at some point in your life, what you considered to be the purpose of life, you lose it or you let it go...and then you die..." are used to express Irene's emotional state (as a woman has lost her daughter, and therefore the purpose of her life) and to reconnect her to Olga.

# References


Bordwell, David. *Narration in the Fiction Film*. London: Routledge, 1995.

Clement, Catherine and Cixous, Hélène. *La jeune née*. Paris: 10/18, 1975.

De Lauretis, Teresa. *Alice doesn't. Feminism, Semiotics, Cinema.* Bloomington: Indiana University Press, 1985.

Katsounaki, Maria. "Greek Cinema: Time to Look Within." November 12, 2003. www.greekembassy.org/embassy/Content/en/Article.aspx?office=3&folder=419&article=12354 (Accessed on April 25, 2009).

Mast, Gerald and Kawin, Bruce. *A Short History of the Movies*. Boston: Allyn and Bacon, 1996.

Stam, Robert. *Film Theory, an Introduction*. London: Blackwell Publishing, 2005.

# *Turkey: Harsh Living Conditions*

# Chapter Eight

# Hard to Bear: Women's Burdens in the Cinema of Yeşim Ustaoğlu

S. Ruken Öztürk

The history of female Turkish feature film directors began in the 1950s, but, amongst more than twenty women directors, only a few have made a significant contribution to Turkish film history. Furthermore, since 1990, the most important characteristic of these directors has been that they have ignored women's issues in their films. Instead, they have focused on relevant political matters and events, including the Kurdish problem, Armenian emigration, relationships between Turks and Greeks, and the 1980 coup when the Turkish military overthrew the civilian government (Öztürk 2004). The release of some of these films caused much debate in Turkey, but they were shown at international film festivals and released abroad with less controversy. Relationships with "Others," namely Kurds, Armenians, and Greeks, have always been sensitive topics in Turkey, especially after the military coup, and have been virtually taboo in mass media such as film. Liberal Turks consider the diversity of other nationalities and ethnic groups to be enriching, but right-wing conservatives have often found "otherness" to be threatening, particularly when linked to past hostilities. Women directors are among the brave artists who have risked their careers to raise these issues. Clearly, their films were not made for mainstream commercial markets.

Yeşim Ustaoğlu is the twentieth female director in the history of Turkish cinema, and the most famous of the few contemporary women directing feature films: she has won numerous awards at international film festivals.[1] After studying architecture at university, for the first seven years of her career she made short films. Following this period, she directed four feature films that focused on the themes of identity or memory: *İz/The Track* (1994), *Güneşe Yolculuk/Journey to the Sun* (1999), *Bulutları Beklerken/Waiting for the Clouds* (2004), and *Pandora'nın Kutusu/Pandora's Box* (2008). Her only documentary,

*Sırtlarındaki Hayat/Life on Their Shoulders* (2004), is set in the same location as *Waiting for the Clouds*. What makes Yeşim Ustaoğlu worthy of academic attention is both her depiction of different cultural identities and her use of sophisticated cinematography with a strong visual impact. Although she does not consider herself a "woman director" (Dönmez-Colin 2006, 131), her more recent films have acquired a distinct woman's perspective, and women characters have increasingly taken center stage in her work.

This chapter examines the representation of women in the documentary film *Life on Their Shoulders* and the feature film *Waiting for the Clouds*.[2] These two films have been selected because Yeşim Ustaoğlu's focus on women exemplifies a kind of counter-cinema or art cinema, and because both films are politically courageous. The two films are also closely related, feeding off one another since they share the same setting, a plateau high in the mountains, bordering the Black Sea in northeastern Turkey. Furthermore, in both films the director uses local people as actors and focuses on problems common amongst women, such as early marriage and illiteracy. In the documentary *Life on Their Shoulders*, the Laz villagers migrate to the plateau for the summer months. Likewise, the feature film *Waiting for the Clouds* depicts the journey of these people, and of one woman in particular, as they ascend to the plateau. But the film also evokes the tragic exile that Ayşe, the central character, faced in the past. Thus, the theme of migration shifts from one film to the other and from migration to exile by way of Ayşe's memories. The analysis of these films also demonstrates how the director embraces women's and minorities' issues, and how she enables the viewer to feel her subjects' burdens. The hopelessness and apathy that the women in the documentary experience as they endure physical and emotional burdens motivated the director to present an alternative response to their desperation. She expressed this alternative response in *Waiting for the Clouds*, through the reaction of an empowered woman who experienced exile. This empowered character challenges the feelings of guilt and desperation that arise in the women featured in the documentary. Finally, this chapter discusses how the strong female character of the feature film solves her problems, mainly through cooperation with other women, examples of which are shown in both films.

The origin of the story of *Waiting for the Clouds* lies in the exile experienced in the early twentieth century. During the difficult period of transition from the Ottoman Empire to the Republic of Turkey (1923), the need to forge a new national identity was paramount. Thus, the situation of the ethnic minorities posed a serious problem. During the Balkan Wars (1912–1913), as Greek troops poured into Salonika, Greek nationalists endeavored to create ethnic homogeneity, as did the Turks. Consequently, the rising nationalism of both Greeks and Turks determined the minorities' fate in the regions that remained in the Ottoman sphere and in those areas newly invaded by the Greeks. During the First World War many Greeks (*Rum*)[3] were driven out of the Black Sea coastal regions for reasons of security. Some were exiled to Russia, others to Greece or to the interior of Anatolia (Yıldırım 2006). This is the broad historical background of *Waiting for the Clouds*. The female protagonist, Ayşe or Eleni (as she was once called), is one of the Greek citizens exiled in 1916, when she was only a child. Ayşe's trauma is symbolic of a national and ethnic trauma in Turkey's history that resonates even today. These historical events become more significant in the film as Ayşe remembers her past: memories portrayed without the use of narrative flashbacks.

## Heavy Burdens

Within their mountainous home, the Laz people[4] move to cooler dwellings on the high plateaus for the summer months, where they adapt themselves to the natural environment without any form of luxury, including electricity. *Life on Their Shoulders* revolves around the story of this seasonal migration, the climb and the descent, highlighting the role of women within this environment. The first scenes show people preparing for their journey and closing up their houses in the Laz village of Topluca. The end of the film, which mirrors the beginning, shows the same people on the plateau preparing to return, closing up their summer houses and setting out. *Life on Their Shoulders* is both visually and aesthetically effective due to the remarkable beauty of the region, captured by the director's extraordinary cinematography. The viewer's attention is constantly drawn to the women who walk across steep slopes and along the cliff edges with heavy loads on their backs. Leaning on their walking sticks, they move with difficulty through the mud, and some become exhausted and fall sick under the weight of their burdens.

Day-to-day life for the men of the village consists of smoking, drinking tea, and singing Laz songs. In one domestic scene, a man plays a musical instrument while a woman works and cooks. In numerous scenes the women tie their loads to their backs with long, thick ropes, as the men help them to load up. Some women are so heavily laden that they are bent double and their faces are hidden. Tellingly, the animals are loaded with the same things and in the same way as the women. Women also do all kinds of work, from carrying loads of baskets, beds, furniture, and wood when they migrate to the plateau, to working on the farms, milking cows, and baking bread when they settle into their houses. In *Life on Their Shoulders*, the director visually and cumulatively draws attention to the experiences and problems of women in the Black Sea region, such as damage to their health, illiteracy, early marriage, and bearing too many children. The enormous weight of the loads that they carry and the huge amount of daily work for their own families and the larger community take a significant toll on their health. Inevitably, women in this region age quickly, and their faces are wrinkled and dry.

At the beginning of the documentary, the camera focuses on the wrinkled and worn hands of an old woman as she describes how she carries heavy loads and works constantly. Another woman explains that she can no longer go up to the plateau with everyone else because of osteoporosis and rheumatism, so she is left behind, alone in the village for the entire summer. At the end of the film, a young woman describes how she suffers from a slipped disc and serious kidney problems. Although their health rapidly deteriorates due to the hard physical work, these women do not complain much, they have grown accustomed to their harsh living conditions. Their experiences are vividly captured in what the camera shows: the woman's wrinkled hand reveals her lifetime of hardship, and her endurance.

Another serious problem in Turkey in general, and in this area in particular, is early marriage. In *Life on Their Shoulders*, when the women talk amongst themselves, the topic of marriage inevitably comes up, often making the young girls smile and giggle. Marriage is a constant topic of conversation and the ultimate goal in these girls' lives. With marriage come children, and these women usually have many; one of them claims to have had ten. Early marriages and large families are quite common amongst the rural poor, and it is the girls, not the boys, who usually marry at a very young age. In *Waiting for the Clouds*, a woman states that when she got married she "wasn't even fourteen."[5]

Education seems to offer some hope of overcoming these problems. Women tell the director that educated girls no longer cover their heads as they did in the past. To be educated means to break with tradition. A young woman holding children in her arms says that in the past it was not desirable for a girl to go to school, but that today there are few girls who do not attend lessons. Gradually traditions change, and the overall, literacy amongst girls has increased. However, in Turkey the illiteracy rate is still above 12 percent, and women, in comparison to other groups, are at a greater disadvantage: 20 percent of women do not know how to read and write (Nohl and Sayılan 2004). Illiteracy is also one of the themes subtly mentioned in *Waiting for the Clouds*, in a dialogue in which a female neighbor who, after delivering a letter to the protagonist Ayşe, humbly admits that she cannot read or write.

The heavy loads borne by women in poor rural areas like the Black Sea region of northeastern Turkey are numerous: the physical burdens of overwork, illness, and premature aging, along with the cultural problems of illiteracy, early marriage, and large families. Desperation and hopelessness are often the results of such harsh living and working conditions.[6] In an interview, Yeşim Ustaoğlu shared a tragicomic anecdote that occurred during the shooting of the film: "Once I asked a young man to help us carry the heavy equipment, he said, 'wait a minute' and went to call his mother!" (Dönmez-Colin 2006, 140).

Figure 8.1  Laz women climbing the plateau in the Kackar Mountains in summer, in *Life on Their Shoulders*.

# The Burden of Guilt

In *Waiting for the Clouds*, the director creates a strong female character who overcomes desperation and hopelessness. The film is based on Yorgos Andreadis' story *Tamama: The Missing Girl of Pontos* (1993). Ayşe, whose real name is Eleni, is the daughter of a Greek family. She and her family were exiled, and they made the long and painful journey on foot from the Black Sea region to southern Turkey. Many of the people forced to migrate on foot faced harsh conditions and died. Eleni lost most of her family during this march, and by the time she reached the city of Mersin on the south coast she had only her younger brother Niko left. While Niko preferred to stay with the Greek exiles, Eleni chose to live with a Turkish family who took her in and adopted her. Ultimately, Niko was sent to Greece with all the other orphaned Greek children. Eleni, however, now named Ayşe, stayed with her new family and years later, when her adoptive parents died, moved from the South back to the Black Sea region. There, she and her adoptive sister, Selma, bought the house in which Eleni/Ayşe had lived with her real family as a child. Hiding the fact that Ayşe was an adopted exile, the sisters lived there together for years.

*Waiting for the Clouds* covers the period from the haunting experiences of the early twentieth century until the 1970s. The opening sequence of the film is composed of black-and-white images illustrating the misery of exile and enforced migration that occurred at the beginning of the past century. This introduction ends with a girl holding her little brother in her arms, a scene that will recur in the final part of the film. This image of the two children is followed by shots of the misty scenery of the Black Sea region. The date of the story is identified as 1975; the political discourse of the film reflects issues of Turkish identity in the 1970s, such as communism and nationalism. The film's introductory images add another historical past to this political period, that of the forced exile in 1916, to which the story is closely connected.

Folklore also contributes to the identification of different ethnic identities as "Others." The only child character in the film, Mehmet (so attached to Ayşe that she will later identify him with her brother Niko), tells her that he is scared of elves and that they come whenever he wets his bed. Ayşe in turn tells him a story about elves, villagers who cannot get away from them, and a young girl who loses her family because of them. Selma, her ailing sister, responds to Ayşe's story with an unhappy look that may at first seem meaningless to the viewer. However, in retrospect, this scene is meant to suggest that Ayşe, like the girl in the story, lost her family, and that the elves represent the political and social forces that shaped and implemented the policies of exile. As a child, Ayşe was not only separated from her immediate family, she was also forced to renounce her identity, her language (Pontic Greek), and even her name (Eleni) when she moved in with her Turkish family. Now she is Ayşe and she speaks Turkish.

The death of Selma, ill since the beginning of the film, triggers Ayşe's confrontation with her past. Having spent all her life with her sister and having cared for her through her illness, Ayşe is now completely alone for the first time. Subsequently, she remembers Niko and she feels remorseful for having abandoned him. Nevertheless, the transition in which she recalls her former identity does not occur immediately or spontaneously. Soon after Selma's death, on the first night when she is at home alone, Ayşe cannot sleep. The following morning she enters a dusty room and goes through old belongings in a chest. She comes across some old photographs, but this is not just a coincidence, it is actually the result of the gradual inner journey that started during her lonely and sleepless night. Because she has just lost her sister, as she once lost her brother, she walks almost unconsciously toward the old chest: this action leads her to find the pictures and remember Niko. Looking through the old photos, she pauses suddenly. At this point, Yeşim Ustaoğlu does not let the audience see which picture has astonished Ayşe. Instead, with the first fade-out, the director indicates that the protagonist will start a new period of exploring memories, which will lead her to a suppressed past.

After her sister's death, Ayşe does not speak. She has concealed her ethnic identity for fifty years, and by never speaking her own language she has also buried her past. But now she wants to do the opposite, and in order to cope with her feelings of remorse, she rejects the Turkish language, and remains silent. As the women migrate up to the plateau, carrying wood on their backs, the tops of the mountains are covered by fog; it is as if the clouds have descended to earth. This collapsing of the sky onto the earth suggests that time has frozen, thus foreshadowing Ayşe's collision with her memories. As she ascends the plateau, Ayşe stops for a moment, stunned by this foggy scene. This is the crux of the film, when it seems that she has lost her way. The fog impairs her vision, forcing her to rely on memory alone. Although the viewer is not yet aware of it, this walk up the mountain and Ayşe's memories of a more dramatic walk in her past as an exile intersect in her mind.

## Her Own Voice Discovered

Neighbors on the plateau understand that Ayşe is suffering. She stands still for several hours, still carrying the wood on her back, and then she develops a high fever from sitting outside her front door all night. In her febrile state, she hallucinates, hugging Mehmet (her neighbor Feride's son) and saying "Niko, don't go." On the film's poster, Mehmet, symbolizing the young Niko, is in the foreground, while a faint image of Ayşe appears in the background. Mehmet's association with Niko is underscored by his position in the poster. Ayşe's words—Niko, don't go—mean nothing to Feride, who continues to care for Ayşe. However, after this episode she resumes her silence and stays motionless like the foggy mountains. Eventually, when Ayşe seems to recover from her silence, or what might be called her illness, the first words that she speaks are in her own language, Pontic Greek: "God, please forgive me. Please help me." Her native language has sprung from her subconscious, while her true identity and original idiom have resurfaced. This is the turning point in the story: as Ayşe reclaims Eleni and reacquires her own language, Turkish viewers are deprived of *their* language in their own land because the language of the film has changed.[7]

When it is time to move down from the plateau, the women in the community try to persuade Ayşe to leave with them, but she refuses. With a second fade-out the director establishes a new point of transition in the narrative. A stranger comes to the village whose arrival changes everything. Viewers first see the visitor getting off a minibus and entering a hotel. Then they see him in his room, absentmindedly looking out of the window into the distance, with a look that is reminiscent of Ayşe's in her hypnotic state. Viewers later learn that the visitor's name is Tanassis and that a Turkish fisherman helped him escape to Russia in 1916. Tanassis tells the story of how he traveled from Russia to Greece two years later, and how he joined the partisans in 1947 to save the country from the imperialists. He was later exiled by the Greeks back to Russia. Eventually, he was allowed to return to Greece, and has now come back to visit old friends and see the house, now in ruins, in which he had lived. When Mehmet tells Tanassis that he speaks just like Aunt Ayşe, Tanassis goes to see her. During this visit her tongue is untied. First in Pontic Greek and then in Turkish, she tells all that had happened to her. "Why did they do this to us, Niko? They told us only two days. You'll have to walk only two days. But what happened?" she asks. Now that a fellow exile has emerged from the past, viewers finally discover the secret that Ayşe has hidden for so long.

The time between Ayşe's sudden silence and her first words in her native language can be interpreted as a struggle to regain her original identity. Silence is not only deprivation of speech in a physical sense, it is also a conscious choice by the main character. As Cameron has noted, "Silence can also mean censoring yourself for fear of being ridiculed, attacked or ignored" (Cameron 1990, 4). Ayşe, as Eleni, has been neglected, even unwanted, by the state's official ideology. Now it is Eleni who resists the state's language and brings her own to the surface from the depths of her subconscious. Although she temporarily stops speaking Turkish, and despite her lapse into silence, she does not reject Turkey, the Turks, or their language. In the scene where she tells her story to Tanassis, she uses both Pontic Greek and Turkish. Furthermore, when Tanassis suggests that they move to Greece together, Ayşe/Eleni says that she wants to die in her homeland, which is now Turkey.

After she has reacquired her language and recovered her past memories, Ayşe states that her real name is Eleni and that it was changed when she was adopted, a change that holds more than one underlying meaning. The adoptive family accepted the little girl by changing her name and raising her as their natural daughter. On the other hand, they knew that keeping her Greek name would be dangerous for her, so they changed it to a new Turkish name in order to protect her. Her past, however, is inevitably, and consequently, erased along with her name, native tongue, and culture. When Ayşe tells her story to Tanassis, she says, "Niko is my brother. I'm Eleni Terzidis, the daughter of Prodromos and Marika Terzidis." She names herself and makes this statement aloud, symbolically regaining her identity, and using assertive language to emphasize her realization. She also explains that she has always lived with a feeling of guilt: her sin of betrayal—the abandonment of her brother in the past—has never left her. In Ustaoğlu's own words, "Ayşe wants to be cleansed of her feelings of guilt, and she prepares for the journey to find her brother no matter what may happen" (Dönmez-Colin 2006, 136). Therefore, to free herself of this sense of guilt, she has to rebuild her own original identity and look for her brother. She then sets out on a new journey.

## Confrontation

Tanassis has returned to Greece, and when a letter arrives for Ayşe/Eleni from Salonika, viewers understand that she had asked him to find her brother. She comes down from the plateau with her neighbor

Feride, who brought her the news. Tanassis has found Niko. While Feride makes some soup for Ayşe/Eleni, she prepares for the journey to Greece. The beauty of the Black Sea region is reflected on the window of the bus and on her face as she looks through the window. Ayşe/Eleni is bravely pursuing her past, seeking closure in a foreign country without knowing what awaits her. With the third fade-out the director signals that the film is approaching its finale.

When she arrives in Salonika, Ayşe/Eleni finds Niko's house and goes to visit him. When she finally sees him, she says directly and confidently, "I'm Eleni, your sister." But Niko, intimidated by her decisiveness, closes the door in her face. His wife opens it again and lets her in, saying in a welcoming and reassuring tone, "You must be cold. Come inside and warm up…Don't think now." Later, when Niko and his wife are alone, she becomes angry with him for hiding this secret from her for so many years. Nevertheless, Niko continues to reject his sister, replying, "There is no secret. I lost my entire family during the long march." During this scene, Niko tells his wife about the exile and their arduous walk. Interestingly, he recalls those events in the same way as Ayşe had, using almost exactly the same words. The past that they have preserved in their minds is indeed the same, even though one has been living in Turkey and the other in Greece. After listening to Eleni's and Nikos' stories, she asks her husband to talk to his sister.

In the final part of the film, while Niko is looking at some old black-and-white photographs, Eleni takes his hand, but he suddenly pulls it away. He cannot muster the courage to approach her and he continues to reject her expressions of affection. Eleni, on the other hand, is determined to get closer. The photos that Niko is looking at are from the days after he arrived in Salonika. "These photos represent my life. You aren't in any of them," he tells Eleni, as if the pictures were proof that he never had a sister. Eleni is surprised by this stubborn attitude and she pulls out a different photo from her pocket. This is the picture the director had concealed from viewers earlier in the film. The photo is an old, worn, and faint image of two adults with two children: Niko, Eleni, and their parents. Although the faces are faded, Niko is surprised; here is the visual and tangible proof he needed. His shoulders sink in this final scene: he can no longer reject Eleni and he accepts the existence of his forgotten sister. These emotions are conveyed entirely through facial expressions, rather than words, as neither of them speaks. Confident, proud, holding her head up high, Eleni looks at Niko.

After the scene in which Niko looks at the photo, the film shifts to the sister and brother shown in the black-and-white documentary snapshots from the opening sequence. Combining these two images by means of montage, the director shows that Niko finally believes that they are siblings. The purpose of Eleni's journey was right: she has achieved her goal to find her lost brother. The film had started with black-and-white images and it ends in the same way. With these conclusive images, sister and brother are brought together.

## The Power of Sisterhood

One of the major factors contributing to Eleni's brave and effective realization of her past—the exile, her feelings of guilt, and her brother—is the solidarity of women, a cultural element that pervades the whole film. Cooperation among women is evident in *Waiting for the Clouds* as the source of sisterhood and mutual understanding. In contrast, men are shown to be indifferent and sometimes hostile. In one scene, for example, drunken men harass a young boy whose father is living in Russia. They also throw stones at Ayşe's house because they have learned about her Greek origins. Significantly, it is a woman who challenges the men and protects the insulted boy.

Throughout the film, women in the village discuss how to help Ayşe and put an end to her silence. They resort to a traditional remedy based on superstition. Although she objects to it, they melt lead in order to save and relieve her soul. In addition to this scene, female solidarity often provides Ayşe with emotional and practical support. The film's first scenes demonstrate the bonds that hold women together, such as Ayşe's life shared with her older sister, Selma. Ayşe carries the old and ailing Selma on her back and tends to her every need. Ayşe is not troubled by this burden; she looks at Selma affectionately, and Selma kisses her hand lovingly. Both of them know that they are not really sisters, but they care for each other just as if they were.

The sense of solidarity is equally present in *Waiting for the Clouds*. In one scene, for example, shot at first from a high angle, the women are working and chatting together on a sunny day. They are talking about a young girl's wedding, and one woman says that she got married at a very early age. In another scene, the women working on the farm promise a young girl that they will help her with her wedding dress. The aim of such forms of cooperation is to relieve other people of some of their preoccupations, as, for example, in the scene when the women discuss where to bury Selma, because the rest of her family is buried in Mersin. Feride in particular often attempts to relieve some of Ayşe's burden, she persuades Ayşe to come down from the plateau, and sees her off to Salonika. When Ayşe arrives there, her brother Niko closes the door on her because he is scared of her determination, but his wife lets her in and offers her warm hospitality in their home. In both films, *Waiting for the Clouds* and *Life on Their Shoulders*, the power of sisterhood lies between the lines, as the director consistently emphasizes women's relationships with one another.

## Conclusion

Yeşim Ustaoğlu is the first female director in Turkish cinema to depict the women of the Black Sea region realistically. She shows that these women work harder than the men and that they suffer more. In the feature film, the inner journey from Ayşe to Eleni and the external journeys—the protracted exile of the Greeks in the past, the migration of the Black Sea people to the plateau, and Ayşe/Eleni's journey to Salonika—take place one within the other, and all intersect. In her films the director is sensitive to the diverse national and cultural identities living in Turkey, especially the minorities, representing all the "Others." In her films Ustaoğlu looks at all the citizens of the Republic of Turkey, not only Turks but also Kurdish (*Journey to the Sun*), Greek (*Waiting for the Clouds*), and Laz people (*Life on their Shoulders*) as sub-identities, not through nationalistic eyes but in a very positive light. In the director's opinion, these groups are all facets of Turkey's diversity and richness. Luce Irigaray recounts an interview with Hélène Rouch, a scientist, which sheds some interesting light on this film. In the interview Rouch explains that a fetus is half stranger to the mother's body, since half of it comes from the father. The mother's body prepares to reject the strange half, but then her tolerance mechanisms are activated and the fetus and mother live together peacefully. The mother's body always knows "the other," and makes the placenta know it as well. She naturally accepts "the other" (Irigaray 1990, 24–54). Similarly, Ayşe/Eleni accepts all "the others" in her life without any objection, both her adoptive family of Turks and the adult Niko, whom she does not know after all. She does not see them as the threatening "Others." Conversely, Niko does not possess the ability to tolerate "the other," namely, Ayşe, and therefore does not give her a warm welcome. Ayşe/Eleni is more willing to understand and to make an effort, as she is more interested in living peacefully. She is like Niko's wife and also like the director, who is sensitive to "other" identities.

In *Waiting for the Clouds*, Niko is a character who has changed his disadvantages into advantages. He arrived in Greece as a child, alone, orphaned, and penniless. However, as time passes, he gets a job in Salonika and starts a new family for himself. Moreover, he does not feel remorseful and does not think about his past or the people he has left behind. He also erases his sister from his memory. Ayşe, by contrast, takes up a burden that is not of her own making, and bravely deals with the consequences. It is significant that it is a woman who confronts feelings of guilt and goes looking for her brother, regardless of how many years have passed.

Although Ustaoğlu says that the film *Waiting for the Clouds* "tries to find answers to the thorny questions of identity and nationalism" (Dönmez-Colin 2006, 137), the director also shows in her films the differences between women and men. Although Suner points out that *Waiting for the Clouds* seems to downplay the question of gender (2007, 63), it should not be ignored that Ustaoğlu gives priority to a brave woman in her feature film. According to Suner, this film belongs in the category of "transnational feminist cinema," which "conceives the construction of gender not only in terms of the relations between men and women, but also the relations among women of various classes, races, and ethnicities" (2007, 66, 68). Moreover, Suner correctly writes that Ayşe/Eleni finds a voice to express herself and that she cannot be characterized "as a victim of patriarchy in a clichéd way" (2007, 63). Ayşe/Eleni brings all of her secret past out of the closet, sets free all that she has suppressed, and moves to the other side, which for her is Greece. There, she embraces her brother who has lived in a different culture. The film describes the struggle for identity of a woman who has experienced exile, confronted her feelings of guilt, and healed herself by journeying to find her brother. The mountains' pervasive fog is symbolic of a hidden past, and when Ayşe/Eleni transforms her inner journey to an external one and finds her brother, she is relieved of her burden. It is as if the burden, like the clouds, has lifted from the earth.

In her feature film, Ustaoğlu relieves her character of a serious burden and shifts that burden to the shoulders of her viewers. She aims to make the audience look critically at events by portraying different lives. Neither Ustaoğlu's documentary nor her feature film provides any comfort for her viewers. On the contrary, the director shakes their beliefs and wants them to look at history from a different perspective (*Waiting for the Clouds*), or to witness women's harsh lifestyle and miseries (*Life on Their Shoulders*). Furthermore, *Waiting for the Clouds* is a film that might cause the viewer to be uneasy, not only because of the historical perspective of the theme but also because of its style: it has long scenes and unfolds at a slow pace. *Waiting for the Clouds* does not have the vocabulary of image and language found in mainstream films, rather it belongs to the European tradition of art cinema. As Hayward points out, "There is no safe narrative, no beginning, middle and end, no closure or resolution" in counter-cinema/oppositional cinema (2004, 76). Another feature of Ustaoğlu's films to which viewers may not be accustomed is the central role of women. Men are only faintly present, while women are at the core of both the documentary and the feature film.

Women are subject to heavy burdens. The load that they carry is sometimes tangible, like firewood, and sometimes psychological and emotional, like the feeling of guilt; in either case these burdens are painful. In the documentary, women carry their physical burdens as if it were their destiny to work so hard. They suffer physically, but they cannot free themselves of their burdens because of the circumstances of their lives. In the feature film, the main character suffers from a personal burden, but she brings the suppressed past into consciousness so that she can cope with this emotional burden; then she rediscovers herself in order to unload it.

Women in Turkey are restricted by unbearable problems, both physical and psychological; however, solutions will be found in the actions of strong women. This is also the view of the director, as she lifts the inevitable problems portrayed in the documentary by creating a strong female character from the Black Sea in the feature film. Ustaoğlu cannot intervene in the lives of women in the documentary, but she does try to understand them. The women in the documentary bear their burdens and do not complain much; indeed, they talk about themselves only when asked. They are brave, but cannot easily escape their fate. In the feature film, however, the director creates a strong female character and allows her to cope with her troubles and overcome them. Thus, Ustaoğlu challenges women's desperation and hopelessness, and in so doing she demonstrates the importance of sisterhood.

# Notes

1. *Waiting for the Clouds* (2004, France/Germany/Greece/Turkey) was awarded the following prizes: Haifa Film Festival 2005, Best Film Award; Yerevan International Film Festival 2005, Fipresci Prizes of the Armenian Association of Film Critics and Cinema Journalists for the Best Feature Film; International Istanbul Film Festival 2004, Special Jury Prize, Best

    Actress (Rüçhan Çalışkur); Orhon Arıburnu Awards (National) 2004, Best Actress (Rüçhan Çalışkur); Sundance Film Festival 2003, NHK International Filmmakers Award; and DAAD Script Development Scholarship, 2001.

2. The documentary, shot in 2002, is the earlier film. The feature film was shot in 2003. Postproduction and release of both films took place in 2004 (Yeşim Ustaoğlu, e-mail message to the author, June 28, 2008).

3. The Turkish word *Rum* is commonly translated into English as *Greek*. However, this term refers to non-Muslim citizens living in Turkey who speak Pontic Greek, which is different from Modern Greek.

4. The ethnic group that lives in this geographical region is called the Laz, and they mostly speak Laze, or Lazce; this becomes obvious in the documentary. They have their own cultural traditions, cooking, music, and lexical items. Both the documentary and the feature film depict wedding scenes, dances, and various other aspects of their lifestyle.

5. Translations of film dialogues are taken from the subtitles of the DVD *Waiting for the Clouds*.

6. The image below is from *Life on their Shoulders*. Turkey 2004, Director: Yeşim Ustaoğlu. Courtesy of the director.

7. The company that released the DVD of the film did not include Turkish subtitles among the options in the main menu. They can be selected using the television remote control only when the film is running. This omission has an ironic, if inadvertent, message to convey. The civic system has deprived Eleni of her language. How can the audience sympathize with Eleni unless they are made as language-less as she is? Lacking comprehensible subtitles, the uneasiness of viewers who do not understand Pontic Greek might accomplish that end. Yeşim Ustaoğlu explains that this was not a deliberate choice and adds: "Unfortunately, I found out that obtaining the subtitles was problematic after the DVDs were published. However, in the film *Life on Their Shoulders*, I did not translate anything, particularly when they were speaking the Laz language. I did this on purpose in the documentary because I wanted us to listen to the Laz language attentively and figure out what we do not understand. We should comprehend the language by listening to its music" (Yeşim Ustaoğlu, e-mail message to the author, June 28, 2008).

# References


Cameron, Deborah. *The Feminist Critique of Language: A Reader.* London: Routledge, 1990.

Dönmez-Colin, Gönül. *Cinemas of the Other.* Bristol: Intellect, 2006.

Hayward, Susan. *Cinema Studies: Key Concepts.* London: Routledge, 2004.

Irigaray, Luce. *Je, Tu, Nous: Pour Une Culture de la Différence.* Paris: Grasset, 1990.

Nohl, Arnd-Michael and Fevziye Sayılan. "Teaching Adults Literacy in Turkey. Technical Report to the Support to Basic Education Program." 2004.http://www.meb.gov.tr/duyurular/duyurular/Proj/TEDPBilgilendirme.pdf (Accessed on June 11, 2008).

Öztürk, S. Ruken. *Sinemanın Dişil Yüzü: Türkiye'de Kadın Yönetmenler* (Female Side of the Cinema: Women Filmmakers in Turkey). İstanbul: Om, 2004.

Suner, Asuman. "Cinema without Frontiers: Transnational Women's Filmmaking in Iran and Turkey." In *Transnational Feminism in Film and Media*, ed. Katarzyna Marciniak, Aniko Imre, and Áine O'Healy, 53–71. New York: Palgrave MacMillan, 2007.

Yıldırım, Onur. *Diplomasi ve Göç* (Diplomacy and Emigration). İstanbul: İstanbul Bilgi Üniversitesi, 2006.

*Syria: Female Identities and
Political Resistance*

# Chapter Nine

## This Woman's Work: Filming Defeat in the Arabic Idiom: Poetry, Cinema, and the Saving Grace of Hala Alabdallah

*Rasha Salti*

The Arab world claims an increasing number of women filmmakers. Nevertheless, it is indeed surprising that Syria should claim barely a handful of women filmmakers considering that, in its discursive representation, the ideology of the Ba'ath[1] made a point to address inequities in the status of women in society. A cursory look at gender ratios, however, reveals unexpected results; in countries where state ideology and policy purport a commitment to redressing the gap between men and women, like Syria, Tunisia, and Algeria, the number of women filmmakers is notably low in comparison to their male counterparts. Conversely, in countries where women's rights have not been a chief concern of the state or regime, but where society remains (relatively) open, tolerant, dynamic, and politically plural, like Palestine and Lebanon, the ratios come closer to being equal.

Yet, it might very well be that the most remarkably bold and compelling of experimental filmmakers in the contemporary Arab world is a woman. Hala Alabdallah Yakoub, born in Syria, living in France, working (save for a few exceptions) between Syria and France, is a curious filmmaker. Her story, career, and filmmaking are composed of the most conventional elements (motifs) that brew to produce a peculiarly unusual narrative. She will not go into the history books as the experimental filmmaker who broke ground with the nonlinear form, nor with abstraction. Rather, with her two nonfiction nonnarrative feature-length films, *I Am the One Who Carries Flowers to her Grave* (2006) and *Hey! Don't Forget the Cumin* (2008), she is already recognized for having crafted a singularly poetic cinematic vocabulary that couples, miraculously, a disciplined cerebral conceptual approach with an overwhelming emotional charge, a cinema that engages subjectivity with a dizzying nakedness and yet steers clear of inane navel-gazing. Hers is the cinema of an Arab world that has witnessed revolutions transform into sinister tyrannies and liberating ideologies into murderous demagoguery, where men and women believed they could reverse a prevailing order of injustice and autocracy and were defeated. Hers is the cinema of a generation that was disillusioned, broken, jailed, tortured, humiliated, exiled, silenced; a cinema of the present moment in this sorry *fin de règne*, not captive to the past; a cinema of unfinished sentences, whose chronology or linearity comes undone; a cinema that does not operate as "a mirror of the world," her world or ours (the viewers), rather hers is a cinema that journeys and transposes a poetic chronicle of journeying in sound and image. She believes that art saves one from succumbing to despair or dementia. Her cinema, she claims, saved her from drifting into the abyss. Hers is the cinema that restores music to sorrow and poetry to despair, cinema as art, an art that saves.

This chapter will explore Hala Alabdallah's singular career, her cinematic language and its poetics, in the two films that make for her experience as a director, *I Am the One Who Carries Flowers to her Grave* (2006) and *Hey! Don't Forget the Cumin* (2008). Of Hala Alabdallah's generation, there are few, Antoinette Azriyé being slightly older, who have been working for nearly two decades now as a film editor at the National Film Organization (NFO), the state-run body that oversees film production in the country, and only ventured into directing a few years ago, making short fiction films. Waha al-Raheb, an artist, screenwriter, and director, slightly younger than Alabdallah, is also affiliated with the NFO, her cinema has been decidedly mainstream and predictable. Hala Mohammed studied film at the University of Paris VIII with Hala Alabdallah. A published poet as well as film director, she completed two documentary films for the al-Jazeera news channel in 2005/6 for their *Prison Literature* series, and works independently. Finally, in the past few years, two other women (in their early thirties) joined the community of filmmakers: Joude Gorani, who graduated from the FEMIS in Paris in 2005, where she trained as a cinematographer and affiliated to the NFO as such, has directed two short films of her own; and finally, Diana el-Jeiroudi, who was not trained as a filmmaker but worked in production management, and has directed two documentaries independently. Hala Alabdallah stands out as an oddly lone figure in this rare community of women filmmakers because she is a central figure in the making of some of the most remarkable masterpieces of Syrian cinema (directed by men), some produced by the NFO, yet without ever having been herself affiliated, and maintaining her position as a singularly individualistic and fiercely independent filmmaker.

Since its establishment in the late 1960s, film production in Syria has been entirely under the control of the NFO, a relatively autonomous appendage of the Ministry of Culture. The organization's mandate oversees the production, licensing, commercialization, and distribution of films, in addition to import and export of films and management of the countrywide network of state-owned theaters. Only those filmmakers affiliated with the organization are eligible for production funds, and their affiliation provides them with a regular salary, health and social benefits. For all intents and purposes, private film production companies were rendered defunct by the late 1960s, and privately owned movie theaters became a rarity. Mohammad Malas's *The Night* (1992) was the first film produced by the NFO to feature a French coproduction. Oussama Mohammad's *Sacrifices* (2002) was the second film to be coproduced, also with French funds. The momentum remains too slow to be identified as a trend, but independent filmmakers working either in Syria or between Syria and Europe can only make films with European funding. This is the case for Hala Alabdallah, veteran documentary filmmaker Omar Amiralay, and the emerging generation of filmmakers like Diana el-Jeiroudi, Orwa Nirabia, Meyyar el-Roumi, Ammar Albeik, and Hisham el-Zouki, to cite a few. Sadly, this constellation of names does not cohere to form an independent cinema circle, movement, or community, for a variety of reasons too complex to recount; suffice it to note that in this disjointed grouping of names, Alabdallah and, to a lesser extent, Amiralay are the only two with meaningful connections to the list of filmmakers cited. In several different ways, formal and informal, she has been involved in the films they have directed. This is another manner in which Hala Alabdallah is an important insider/outsider figure able to transgress the paradox of her position with admirable grace. She explains these independent filiations, intimate associations and significant collaborations, her ability to give intensely and consistently yet remain self-effaced and maintain a distinctly individualistic voice, as the outcome of her passion for cinema: "I draw extreme pleasure from contact and exchange with others," she confessed, "to be able to visualize what another filmmaker has inscribed in words is an inspiring challenge. I don't see it like a sacrifice at all, rather an intense training for the brain."[2]

Hala Alabdallah was born in Hama, in 1956. She graduated in 1978 from the University of Damascus with a degree in agricultural engineering. She earned a second degree in genetics from the University of Paris VII in 1982, a third degree in anthropology from the Ecole des Hautes Etudes en Sciences Sociales in Paris in 1984, and a fourth degree in film and audiovisual studies from the University of Paris

VIII in 1989. In spite of these scholarly peregrinations, cinema was always her passion. At the Damascus ciné-club, barely eighteen years of age, she is remembered as one the most assiduous and fiery attendees. Even before she finished her university degree, she became involved in film production. In fact, from late into the 1980s onward, she became a deeply felt presence behind some of Syrian cinema's most compelling cinematic œuvres, and she has worked as a close and vital collaborator with Syria's eminent filmmakers, Oussama Mohammad, Mohammad Malas, and Omar Amiralay.

She was assistant director to Oussama Mohammad for *Nujum al-Nahar* (*Stars in Broad Daylight*, 1988), and Mohammad Malas for *al-Leyl* (*The Night*, 1992). Moreover, she coauthored and codirected *Tahta al-Raml, Fawqa al-Shams* (*On the Sand, Under the Sun*, 1993) with Malas, a documentary on political prisoners in Syria. She was also coauthor and producer of Amiralay's documentary on slain former Lebanese prime minister Rafiq Hariri, titled *Rajol al-Hitha' al-Thahabi* (*The Man with the Golden Soles*, 2000) and producer and artistic director of *Sunduq al-Duniya* (*Sacrifices*, 2002) directed by Oussama Mohammad. She is the general director of Ramad Films, a production company based in France, cofounded with Omar Amiralay. She has been the executive producer of a good number of films he directed, including *Fateh Moudaress* (1994) and *Nouron wa Thilal* (*Shadows and Light*, 1994), *Par un jour de violence ordinaire, mon ami Michel Seurat* (*On A Day of Ordinary Violence, My Friend Michel Seurat*, 1995), *Un Plat de sardines* (*Plate of Sardines—Or The First Time I Heard about Israel*, 1997) and *Il y a tant de choses à dire…* (*There Are Many Things Still To Say…*, 1997). Alabdallah has also worked on several other films, shot in Lebanon and Syria, directed by French filmmakers. She coauthored *Les Défis de Marcel Khalifé* (*The Challenges of Marcel Khalifé*, 1998) directed by Pierre Dupouey, a documentary on Lebanese militant leftist singer and composer Marcel Khalifé; she was executive producer and artistic collaborator on *Le Sourire d'Hassan* (*Hassan's Smile*, 2003), *Le taxi collectif de Damas* (*The Shared Taxis of Damascus*, 1996), *Yahya Khaldi affichiste à Alep* (*Yahya Khaldi, Postermaker in Aleppo*, 1996), and *Le Chant des norias* (*The Song of Norias*, 1998) directed by Frédéric Goupil; and executive producer on *Du particulier au particulier* (*From the Particular to the Particular*, 2004) directed by Brice Cauvin. Finally, her collaborations with Lebanese filmmakers include, *Nisa' Hezbollah* (*Women of Hezbollah*, 1999), *Duwwar Shatila* (*Shatila Roundabout*, 2005) directed by Maher Abi Samra, and *L'Orient au petit feu* (*The Simmering East*, 1999) directed by Jacques Debs.

Her life and her career in film have been imprinted with back and forth travel between France and Syria, with frequent stopovers in Lebanon. Alabdallah left Damascus in 1980. She, as well as her husband, Youssef Abdelké (a renowned artist and printmaker), were overtly affiliated with a radical leftist political organization; when Hafez al-Assad cracked down on all the political parties in opposition to the Ba'ath, they were both sentenced to jail. Upon their release, knowing full well they would summarily be incarcerated again, they decided to flee to Beirut, and from there to Paris. Abdelké's charges would not be "pardoned" by the Syrian government for twenty-five years. Alabdallah, on the other hand, managed to negotiate reentry. It was never an easy process: this implied regular meetings with internal security or military intelligence, interrogation, and paperwork at nearly every entry and exit, wherein she had to prove her intentions were "innocuous" or harmless.

In 2006, Hala Alabdallah turned fifty years old and directed her first film. It could not be so simple as a consciousness of a coming of (middle) age, but in her own words, "[she] decided to give [herself] a gift, a birthday gift, as well as to [her] three closest women friends from Syria."[3] She called upon Ammar Albeik, a promising young Syrian filmmaker in his mid-thirties, to codirect the film with her. The impetus for the film shall remain foremost this coming of middle-age, or the realization that "[she] did not have much time left to do what [she] yearned to."[4] However, beneath the veneer of that initial impetus, there are pages and pages of scripts, film treatments, notes, and footage of locations that she scouted for films that have never (or not yet) seen the light of day. When it was still in production, the film's provisional title was *Repérages de l'amour et de la mort*, or *Scouting Locations for Love and Death*. Ultimately, she titled it *Ana al-Lati Tahmilu az-Zuhur ila Qabriha* (*I Am the One Who Carries Flowers to her Own Grave*), borrowed from a verse by Da'ad Haddad, one of Alabdallah's favorite Syrian poets.[5] The film premièred at the 63rd edition of the Venice International Film Festival (official selection Orizzonti), where it was awarded the prize for documentary film. Afterward, the film traveled the world and earned more awards, including the Grand Prize for Documentary at the International Festival for Mediterranean Cinema in Tétouan, Morocco.

She had barely begun to accompany screenings of the film when she started working on the next one. This time she planned to direct it on her own. The critical acclaim and worldwide travel of *I Am the One Who Carried Flowers to her Grave* suggested she might be able to line up production support for her next project prior to beginning filming. Although there were tangible signs to that effect, none effectively materialized, and Alabdallah found herself working with sparse means, marshalling modest earnings from awards, as she did with her previous project. The second film, also nonfictional and feature length, is titled *Hey! Don't Forget the Cumin*. It is less autobiographical and introspective but no less subjective. On why she waited for so long before directing, Hala Alabdallah reflects:

> I never felt that the other projects I worked on were not my own. When I am working, I become fully invested and that feeling is thrilling. I was always guided by my intuition; only recently have I become introspective. When I turned fifty years old, I realized there was not much time left. Friends used to assure me that directing one's own film would leave a different taste, and I dismissed the notion. They were right however, it does feel different. There is more freedom in directing one's own film. You set a different ceiling; that's all.[6]

Essentially, *I Am the One Who Carries Flowers to her Grave* is a film about a return to the home-country: home to the geography of youth, home to the setting for first times and first things, first friendships, first loves, coming of age, dreams for changing the world, beginnings. It was not her first return home from her Parisian exile; Alabdallah had traveled home to Syria several times prior to that trip in 2005. Effectively, however, it was her husband's first return home after twenty-five years of estrangement. This is an important element in the story, and several sequences in the film document his arrival at the airport, the opening of his exhibit—which "occasioned" his return—and the dancing party afterward, but that return is not principal. The film is Hala Alabdallah's own return to the homeland where her story as an adult woman started, the geography upon which her emotional map was first drawn: the scenery, sites, and scapes where she cast countless films and imagined countless scripts. Decidedly nonlinear, she combines several narrative elements to paint this return.

At the heart of the film are intimate conversations with three of her closest friends (Fadia Lazkani, Roula Roukbi, and Raghida Assaf), the three women, *camarades de combat*, with whom she came of age, dreamed of a better world and was sentenced to jail. She visits each in her home, the intimate interiors films in close-up, her camera scrutinizing but remarkably tender. They revisit episodes of their shared past and reflect on the trajectory from then until the here and now. Theirs are pain-stricken stories of lives fashioned to overcome disillusionment, endure past disappointments, and devise ways to heal deep wounds to the heart and soul—fiery souls, dampened, whose life ambitions were derailed. In these conversations, where they are obviously speaking with Hala (sometimes we hear her voice, rarely do we catch a glimpse of her presence), we seldom hear the question she is asking. These sequences are the exact opposite of the talking head interviews of conventional documentary films. The silences, the unsaid as well as whatever was edited out, are as audible as what is heard.

Besides Hala Alabdallah, there are two other women in the film. Da'ad Haddad, the poet to whose verse the film owes its title, and Fekrya Miro, Youssef Abdelké's mother and Hala Alabdallah's mother-in-law. In the chronology of the film, we are first introduced to Da'ad Haddad. A cherished friend to Alabdallah, Haddad was a passionate but tortured soul, whose profound melancholy had turned to deep depression and tragically led to her end. Alabdallah visits the home of Nazih Abouafach, a friend she and the poet shared. They recount stories and anecdotes from Haddad's life, resurrecting a ghostly presence, vibrant and fiery. In other sequences, as Alabdallah travels to the small island of Arwad, and the camera lingers on the open horizon of the Mediterranean, Alabdallah confesses this is where she believes Da'ad Haddad to have really settled in her final resting place, where her tomb belongs. In Haddad's life story, we are presented with the narrative of a woman with immense talent and sensibility who was driven to the verge of dementia from coping with everyday life in Syria. Her depression and suicide are neither explicated nor analyzed, but there are hints and suggestions of a soul whose yearning for freedom was stifled and whose soar was shot down in its flight. In the conversations with Fadia, Roula, and Raghida, we hear stories of women who have learned to pick up the broken pieces and move on; in contrast, Da'ad Haddad could not live with those breaks.

Fekrya Miro's story is different. A woman in her eighties, she is a wise Penelope-mother figure who has learned to live side by side with a longing for her son whom she has not seen for twenty-five years. If her son's absence has coalesced into a negative space over the years, it is nonetheless a clement ghostly presence. She, like Fadia, Roula, and Raghida has endured a life with wounds and ruptures. She is filmed in her house, in the days preceding her son's return. While the anticipation ought to be overwhelming, her seasoned resilience gives her awe-inspiring composure. She does not want to believe her son will soon be near until it actually happens; she describes longing and anticipation in frank, measured words. When the camera captures the reunion with her son at the airport, the emotion is finally released.

The film is interspersed with landscape shots. Long, brooding shots of open horizons in the Syrian countryside, autumnal and wintery, a captivating palette of grays drenched in melancholia. Hala Alabdallah and Ammar Albeik appear on screen intermittently, each instructing the other to shoot a particular angle or take. From the abbreviated and sparse exchanges, the viewer understands they are scouting locations. They visit Arwad, a small piece of land off the Mediterranean coastline and popular vacation destination for families: the geography of childhood summers. The time being late fall or early winter, the island is practically deserted, and the landscape evokes a sense of desolation. The locations are scouted for film projects the viewer is never intimated to, but the hope-filled motivation rescues these sequences from succumbing to the sorrow that shrouds the palette of grays and sense of suspended time. In these sequences, Albeik's presence is deeply felt. Their exchanges, in spite of gender and age difference, underscore the complicity of their collaboration: their film is also a long conversation piece between them. They are not together all the time; he is definitely absent in Hala's conversations with her *camarades de combat*, and she is notably absent when he films Youssef Abdelké, her husband. Alabdallah claims Albeik came in to "put together sequences and pieces of films [she] had long yearned to complete,"[7] however, her presence, stories, poetics, and sensibility ultimately overwhelm the film.

In spite of Ammar Albeik's presence, the visit to Nazih Abouafach and to Elias Zayyat (an artist who repairs religious icons), there is really "only" one man in the film, namely, Youssef Abdelké. He is filmed by Ammar Albeik in his studio in Paris. Surrounded by black chalk drawings of fish, severed hands, worn out men's shoes and stilettos, Abdelké's disposition is decidedly (and unapologetically) masculine. His longish unruly white hair frames the handsome face of a man with the aura of a lion; even though what he says is sad and harsh, his large brown eyes remain alight with playfulness. Abdelké talks about his artistic practice, the space of his studio, exile, return, broken dreams, and never surrendering to despair. In a separate sequence, Ammar Albeik films him at a protest rally to demand the release of political prisoners in Syria. Albeik also filmed Abdelké's return to Damascus, his arrival at the airport, the opening of his exhibition, and his reunion with family, friends, and *camarades de combat*. All the sequences documenting the return are in stark contrast with the remainder of the film: they are crowded with people; they are loud, lively, dynamic, and descriptive, documentary, not introspective.

Abdelké was greeted at the airport like a national hero; a crowd of some two hundred people or more waited at the arrival terminal and broke into chant when his figure emerged. This was an eminently political moment in defiance of the regime, a peaceful celebration of a dissenting artist. At the exhibition opening, where the dark charcoal drawings hung ominously, the crowd swelled (some two thousand people attended that evening). The uncanny gathering of the band of comrades and its celebration were an act of defiance as well. Abdelké is filmed shaking hands, hugging and holding the fists of men marked by long jail sentences, hunched from the darkening weight of years of disillusionment and defeat. We are not intimated to the world of the male militants. The journeying into Youssef Abdelké's story stops there. We are, however, intimated to Hala and Youssef's Parisian home, the privacy of the interior arrangement of spaces, everyday gestures, and commonplace conversations. And yet the intimacy of their joining, their story as husband and wife, man and woman, remains off-limits. The most private scene in the entire film shows Alabdallah in her bathroom, looking at her face in the mirror, noting casually signs of aging. It is the only "physical"—sensual—moment in the film, where she acknowledges her body with a disarming spontaneity. It is interesting how codes are truncated in Hala Alabdallah's film; whereas the convention of the binary between body and spirit deems matters of the heart and mind more profound or complicated to expose, in this case the filmmaker lays bare so seamlessly "interior" realms of herself and characters that the body, physicality, and sensuality become the realm with a less straightforward access. Yet coming-of-middle-age is a remarkably physiological experience.

*I Am the One Who Carries Flowers to Her Grave* is as much a *mise-en-abîme* on a coming-of-middle-age as it is a *mise-à-nu*: the story of a return home told with meanders and journeys. The coherence of the film is woven like a poem, where metaphors and allegories unravel—as if in serial—one onto the other; we are led from one sequence to the next following motifs and metaphors. From the wide scapes of the island of Arwad charged with a meditative melancholy, we are led into conversations with captivating women whose faces are etched with melancholy. As they tell stories of enduring hardship, making sense of a world undone, we visit the ghost of Da'ad Haddad, a woman whose emotional and psychological universe was undone to the extent of collapse. From scenes of an abandoned home on the island of Arwad we are led to the home of Fekrya, whose son's forced departure has accompanied her for twenty-five years. In spite of the nonlinear narrative, there is an emotional dramatic buildup that culminates with Youssef Abdelké's return and reunion with his mother and friends. The end of the journeying comes when the camera meanders into Alabdallah's Parisian home and films its intimacy. Masterfully avoiding the all too predictable full circle motif, or contriving a concluding note of wisdom, the camera begins to gaze weightlessly from the windows of the apartment toward the street. The film ends like poems do, open-ended and with a long-drawn breath.

*Hey! Don't Forget the Cumin*, Hala Alabdallah's second directorial venture, explores alienation when it verges on dementia, veers toward suicide, or rescues itself through artistic expression and creation. In describing the leitmotiv, Alabdallah uses the word *"al-ghorbah,"* Arabic for estrangement. In Arabic, as in English, the word contains the root for *ghareeb*, Arabic for strange and stranger. Although estrangement and alienation are synonymous (aliens often being the legalese for foreign nonnationals), in estrangement, as in *ghorbah*, there is no suggestion of pathology, of a straying to clinically identified dementia, whereas alienation has permeated the language of psychology and is associated with a whole host of emotional, psychological, and existential states. The film articulates around three characters, three stories: Jamil's, Sarah's, and Darina's. Jamil Hatmal was a beloved friend of the filmmaker; he took his life at age thirty-eight, in Paris, in November of 1994. Sarah Kane was a British playwright whose work and persona captivated the filmmaker; she took her life at age twenty-eight in 1999. Darina al-Joundi, a friend of the filmmaker, is an actress, the steadfast survivor among the three characters, she was thirty-eight years old when she was filmed. *Al-ghorbah* straddles between the cultural and emotional out-of-placeness Alabdallah, her husband, and their friends (also political refugees in Paris) experienced in making a life for themselves in France, and the *mal-être* of profound alienation that the characters in her film are beset with.

Very early on, Jamil Hatmal had a troubled life. His mother died when he was six years old and he developed chronic heart problems at age eighteen. He became affiliated with a leftist political party at a young age, published short stories at a young age, and was sentenced to jail at a young age. In 1982, Hatmal left Syria, seeking political asylum in France. It seems he was unable to settle there and make a life for himself. The burden of loss and rupture were crosses too heavy to bear: he attempted suicide several times. He also underwent two heart surgeries. He ended his life six months after publishing a novella titled *Narcicism*, excerpts from which the filmmaker uses in the film. A year earlier, in one of his columns, Hatmal had addressed a letter to God, in which he described how much he missed his son, and yearned to return to Syria and be with his son, "even as a cadaver" . . . and thus he would return. The last time Alabdallah saw him, he was in the hospital. She recalls he was cheerful, they had a good laugh together.[8] His appetite was back and he craved a bowl of hummus. As Alabdallah was stepping out of his room, she offered to bring him some; he stopped her and said: "Hey! Don't forget the cumin."[9] In one of the film's sequences Alabdallah stages him in a hospital bed; a stream of women and his failed loves hover around him. He becomes invigorated, playful, and seductive. His mother appears amongst the women; he recognizes her and asks her to fetch him a bowl of hummus. As she steps out the door, he calls to her and says: "Hey! Don't forget the cumin." During the interview, Alabdallah confessed she was still unable to believe he was gone for good.

Sarah Kane, a British playwright, was celebrated very early in her career but committed suicide in 1999. Her published plays include *Blasted, Cleansed, Crave,* and *4.48 Psychosis.*[10] Alabdallah was smitten by Kane's work and felt haunted by the young woman's alienation within. In her last play, *4.48 Psychosis,* Kane had announced her suicide. Unlike Jamil Hatmal, in as much as Kane's *ghorbah* was internal, it was nonetheless at par with the world or social universe around her.

Darina al-Joundi is the survivor amongst the three, the fighter: she is a Syrian-Lebanese actress who grew up in Lebanon during the difficult years of the civil war. Compounded by a troubled childhood, al-Joundi was radically defiant of prevailing social values in Lebanon, which resulted in her family forcing her to "seek treatment" at psychiatric institutions. One day she took her fate into her own hands, left everything behind, and settled in Paris. She made a life for herself and exorcised her alienation, *ghorbah,* and dementia by writing her ordeal[11] and then performing it on stage. Alabdallah filmed rehearsals and the performance itself at the famed Avignon festival.

It is certain that Hala Alabdallah experienced *ghorbah* in her Parisian exile, but she also experienced *ghorbah* in Syria, back home. Her estrangement was never homesickness or a longing for a space, a world, or a culture; she has affixed her rootedness in her work: in film. She describes Syria as the geography of her childhood, and France as the place where she continues to live. Her longing for Syria, the realm of her childhood, was never marked by bitterness: "In any case, I don't have a lot of memories of my childhood," she says, "even less so visual memories."[12] She explains further:

I am very settled in France, I don't feel particularly alien; I actually feel secure there, not anxious. However, I don't feel the impetus to invest my soul in projects in France; nothing there stirs my sensibilities. By the way, even though I have lived there for twenty-five years, I still don't have a passport. Syria, on the other hand is the geography that holds the landscapes where I imagine my films. Every time I go back, I rediscover it with a curiosity that has yet to be quenched. I am always positively surprised. I know the country well, not every corner of it, but I have traveled quite extensively throughout its expanse, and yet every time I am someplace, I feel the thrill of first time discovery. It is actually at once familiar and surprising. In many ways, I belong in that landscape, that place. I wonder if deep down inside, it is not merely the geography of my escape. I know that I don't go to Syria unless I have a project.[13]

If Alabdallah's estrangement is neither tinged with bitterness nor with madness; her motivation in making this second film, then, is exploring how art can rescue from alienation—regardless of how profound or clinical. This is where her relationship with the film's characters dwells. The initial idea was inspired by Darina al-Joundi's, as well as another friend's, story. Darina was on a healing path from having told her story; the second woman (an Argentinean) had checked herself into the hospital. On madness, Alabdallah says:

For some reason, people (friends) have a habit of confiding in me. They tell me how they feel, what happens to them. I suspect they could sense their struggle with alienation was something I could relate to. With experience acquired over time, I have come to realize that the manner in which we are raised in our part of the world forces us to develop two voices within. Our relationship with the outside world, with our families and expression is coerced, repressed. Madness is all there, in these two voices. It fascinates me.[14]

Visually, the film is structured around a rhythmic interplay of light and darkness, inspired from the architecture of psychiatric and mental hospitals in the Levant from the twelfth and thirteenth century, where a specific ordering of light and darkness in space was believed to wield therapeutic and healing power. In the film's dossier, Hala Alabdallah writes, "light that heals a wound; light that purifies the soul."[15] Sequences filmed in the infamous *bimaristan* (a psychiatric and mental hospital from the thirteenth century) of Aleppo are interspersed in the film. Some feature Darina al-Joundi appearing and disappearing, sometimes her image reflecting on the surface of water fountains and small pools. The performance rehearsals are also filmed with a strong interplay between light and darkness. Light is sculptural: it carves bodies and emotions.

Hala Alabdallah has few filmmaking kin in the Arab world. There is a shared sensibility in deconstructing linear narratives, infusing subjectivity, casting autobiography in elements, and drawing on allegory and metaphor with Mohammed Soueid and to some extent Akram Zaatari, both Lebanese filmmakers described as experimental. Subjectivity, the use of the first person singular, and nonlinear narrative have acquired considerable currency with the new generations of filmmakers from Lebanon as well as Palestine. However, their animus and motivation are wholly different from Alabdallah's or Soueid's. Theirs is a rebellious rejection of the canons of the previous generation of filmmakers, the abstracted collective "we," the linear construction of argument and the representation of reality or lived experience as a coherent whole. Their struggle is to proclaim the personal and the private to be more truthful and legitimate than the collective and public (or national), in part because they inherited a world where collectivities had been dismantled or disbanded and state power dulled. For Hala Alabdallah the first person singular is not meant to undermine systematically the collective "we." Her usage is instrumental, it alternates with a "we" and serves, with dexterity and grace, to weave stories of a fractured and wounded collectivity. Her subjectivity sets the story; her introspection drives the narrative, and as such they allow the unraveling of so many other stories and the casting of a myriad of other characters. In other words, the point is not to transpose her personal experience only, but rather to wander into worlds that she inhabits or inhabit her. They intersect with history writ large with a capital H, and lived experience stifled in the official record. Hala Alabdallah has never stopped being a dissident; her cinema is boldly defiant, anti-conformist, experimental, and eminently poetic. *I Am the One Who Carries Flowers to her Grave* is one of the rare documentary films, as well as works of art, that tells the story of a generation disillusioned, deceived, and defeated. Along with Omar Amiralay's *Flood in Ba'ath Country* (2003) it is one of the most sharp and effective critiques of Hafez el-Assad's regime.

Her feat, also her gift, is the ability to make poems with films, or films from poems. Poetry reigns supreme in her imagination, the sky, sea, light, and music of her interior world:

> I cannot imagine life without poetry; it makes me drunk, giddy, high, and it can draw tears. Nothing levels that much power, this ability to communicate beyond language. Poetry is the expressive form with the most profound ability to be free and challenge the limits of imagination. There is a similar or shared spiritual drive with cinema.[16]

In her passionate attachment to poetry, Hala Alabdallah is a thoroughly Arab artist. Only until very recently, poetry had set the prevailing paradigms for articulating a poetics, and for canonizing the allegorical and metaphoric vocabulary in modern and contemporary artistic and creative practice in the Arab world. In that regard, she adheres to a long-established tradition in the modern Arab world. She is also, however, a diasporic artist and filmmaker (from the kind of diaspora of political dissidents), in which time and place do not cohere into a cogent whole, or even a continuum, and escapes all attempts at fastening to categories and conventions. Her cinema records the memory of a lived experience that the state claims never took place, or that society banishes to the oblivion of dementia. Surely a defiant and subversive cinema, but foremost the work of a filmmaker forged from within a here and now, whose political and moral ideals have collapsed, from the belly of a world that has come undone—a filmmaker who believes cinema is art, and that art can rescue from the ruthlessness of being in the world.

# Notes

1. The Arab Socialist Ba'ath Party (also spelled Ba'th or Baath) was founded in Damascus in the 1940s. It is amongst the nationalist anticolonial liberation ideologies, socialist, secular, but also pan-Arabist. In Arabic, *ba'ath* means renaissance or resurrection. The party had branches and affiliates in various Arab countries. It was strongest in Syria and Iraq, coming to power in both countries in 1963. In 1966 the Syrian and Iraqi parties split into rival organizations mainly for ideological reasons—the Regionalist Syria-based party being aligned with the Soviet Union while the Nationalist Iraq-based party adopted a generally more centrist stance. Both trends retained the same name and maintain parallel structures in the Arab world. The Ba'ath Party came to power in Syria on March 8, 1963 and has held a monopoly on political power since then.
2. Hala Alabdallah in an interview with the author, July 2008, Beirut (Lebanon).
3. Ibid.
4. Ibid.
5. Da'ad Haddad is a Syrian poetess whose life ended under mysterious circumstances in 1991; most speculate it was suicide. Haddad was a distinctively singular voice amongst the three generations of contemporary modern poets in Syria. Her poetry was profoundly anchored in her subjectivity, a sensibility deemed vanguard and countercurrent to prevailing trends. She was a prolific writer but published sparsely; she dated her poems to the day and hour, yet only two collections of poems were published in her lifetime, and a third posthumously. Her poetry has often

earned her affinities and comparison with Emily Dickinson. The published collections are: *Tasheeh Khata' al-Mawt* (Correction of the Error of Death) and *Kasrat Khobz Takfini* (A Piece of Bread Suffices Me) in the 1980s, *Al-Shajarah al-Lati Tameel Nahwa al-Ard* (The Tree that Leans Toward Earth) in 1991, shortly after her death. She is not translated into English.

6. Hala Alabdallah in an interview with the author, July 2008, Beirut (Lebanon).

7. Ibid.

8. Ibid.

9. Ibid.

10. Sarah Kane (1971–1999) was an English playwright. Kane's published work consists of five plays, one short film, *Skin*, and two newspaper articles for *The Guardian*. *Blasted*, her first play, premiered at the Royal Court Theater Upstairs in 1995 (directed by James Macdonald); *Phaedra's Love* was commissioned by the Gate Theater in 1996, loosely based on the classic text by Seneca; *Cleansed* premiered at the Royal Court Theater Downstairs in 1998, also directed by James Macdonald; *Crave* was directed by Vicky Featherstone and presented at the Traverse Theater in Edinburgh in 1998; *4.48 Psychosis*, completed shortly before she died, was directed by James Macdonald and performed in 2000 at the Royal Court. Critics, including Aleks Sierz, have regarded her work as part of a movement that broke away from the naturalistic tendencies prevailing in twentieth-century English theatre. Publications include: "Blasted" (with an Afterword by Sarah Kane) in Edwardes, Pamela (ed), *Frontline Intelligence 2: New Plays for the Nineties*, London: Methuen, 1994, 1–50; *Blasted & Phaedra's Love*, London: Methuen, 1996; *Cleansed*, London: Methuen, 1998; *Crave*, London: Methuen, 1998; *4.48 Psychosis*, London: Methuen, 2000; *Complete Plays: Blasted, Phaedra's Love, Cleansed, Crave, 4.48 Psychosis, Skin*, with an introduction by David Grieg. London: Methuen, 2001.

11. Darina al-Joundi is a Lebanese-Syrian actress; she has appeared in several Arab films and television serials, including Yousry Nasrallah's *Bab el-Shams* (*The Gate of the Sun*, 2004), and Danielle Arbid's *L'Homme Seul* (*The Lone Man*, 2007). She cowrote her story in French with Mohamed Kacimi, titled *Le jour où Nina Simone a cessé de chanter* (*The Day Nina Simone Stopped Singing*), which she performed on stage at the Avignon Festival in 2007, and published by Actes Sud in 2008.

12. Hala Alabdallah in an interview with the author, July 2008, Beirut (Lebanon).

13. Ibid.

14. Ibid.

15. Ibid.

16. Ibid.

# References

Bazin, André. *What Is Cinema? Volume 1. Essays Selected and Translated by Hugh Gray.* Berkeley: University of California Press, 1967–2005.
Blaetz, Robin, ed. *Women's Experimental Cinema. Critical Frameworks.* Durham and London: Duke University Press, 2007.
Deleuze, Gilles. *The Movement-Image.* Translated by Tomlinson, Hugh, and Barbara Habberjam. Minneapolis: University of Minnesota Press, 2006.

*Turkey, Jordan, Palestine: Honor Killings*

# Chapter Ten

# "Death is the fairest cover for her shame"[1] Framing Honor Killings

*Flavia Laviosa*

## Introduction

The United Nations Development Fund for Women (UNIFEM) defines honor killings as crimes committed against women who are rape victims, suspected or accused of having premarital sex, or women thought to have committed adultery. The women are typically killed by male relatives in order to restore the family's violated honor. Radhika Coomaraswamy[2] (2005), in her nine-year tenure as U.N. Special Rapporteur on Violence against Women (1994–2003), addressed "honor crimes" as an indisputable infringement of human rights and a form of unjust violence perpetrated against women. She explains that in many societies the cultural concept of maleness is defined by the principle of "honor," which is deeply connected to the control of female sexual behavior in the family and community.

This chapter is a contribution to and an expression of support for women's daily struggle for their lives in honor-centered societies in Mediterranean regions. Divided into two main sections, it aims, first, to develop a composite description of honor-based crimes, to identify the multifaceted culturally defined reasons for this prevalent phenomenon, and to illustrate the varied manifestations and insidious forms of manipulation of such practices intended to punish women who are accused of tarnishing their family's reputation. Through a review of the works of prominent human rights activists and journalists, this chapter also intends to report on the pervasiveness of honor killings and to examine the intrinsic weakness in the legal enforcement of punishments for these crimes, which often hinders the prosecution of the murderers. Second, this chapter analyzes the seminal work of four women filmmakers whose films denounce the practice of crimes of honor in countries around the Mediterranean, and play a major role in raising international public awareness of the victims and perpetrators of honor killings. The films discussed in this chapter are *Crimes of Honour* (1999) by Shelley Saywell, *In the Morning* (2004) by Danielle Lurie, *Vendetta Song* (2005) by Eylem Kaftan, and *Magharat Maria/Maria's Grotto* (2007) by Buthina Canaan Khoury.

# "Death is the fairest cover for her shame…"

## Women's Outcry

Families attach their moral reputation to their female members and in particular to the women's bodies, so "honor" and its outcome "shame" are instruments used by the men to monitor women's sexuality and freedom of movement. Women who have premarital (not necessarily sexual) relationships, fall in love with a person outside their family's social class, ethnic, or religious group, adopt the customs (or religion) of a different community, (allegedly) commit adultery, seek a divorce (usually from an abusive husband), refuse arranged or forced marriage and want to choose their own spouse, or are raped (often by a member of their own immediate or extended family),[3] are perceived to contravene socially and culturally approved (sexual) behavior, and to violate their community's moral codes. There is some evidence that homosexuality (for women and men) can also be grounds for honor killing by relatives (Jimenez 2004). The merest suspicion of any of these types of behavior can turn into a death sentence for the person accused. Rana Husseini reports that often "all that is needed to incite murder is a deliberate and malicious campaign of gossip" (2009, xiii). Husseini also denounces the fact that "in many cases, the crimes have serious hidden intentions far removed from honor—such as the murder of female siblings in order to claim sole inheritance of the family estate" (2009, xiii). Perpetrators rely on the leniency of their countries' legal systems toward honor killings, abusing this practice to their advantage. Regulation of women's behavior involves horrific forms of violence called honor crimes, including honor killings, dowry deaths/bride burnings,[4] acid attacks,[5] death threats, or the withdrawal of family benefits and security. These crimes cross socioeconomic classes and education boundaries, and are part of cultural practices rather than of specific religious beliefs.

In societies where honor killing occurs, the male relatives of the woman in question convene a family council to decide her punishment and designate the male family member who will kill her. As Diane King clearly states, the explanation for such decisions lies in the belief that "without the murder, the lineage that the victim and perpetrator share would suffer irreparable harm to its reputation. With the murder, this wrong is righted and the lineage restored to a place of respect in the community" (2008, 318). This practice is regarded as a private family matter, so nonfamily members do not usually become involved. Courts do not prosecute the perpetrators because they treat the defense of family honor as a mitigating circumstance in a crime, thus legitimizing the killing.

While there is a general association of honor killings with Muslim-majority societies in the Arab world,[6] or within Muslim immigrant communities in North America[7] and Europe,[8] there is in fact widespread incidence of such crimes among Christian-majority groups in Latin America[9] and southeastern Europe,[10] as well as in Uganda, and among Hindu and Sikh communities in India. It is estimated by the United Nations that as many as 5,000 women and girls are murdered by relatives each year in so-called honor killings around the world; but Diana Nammi,[11] founder of the London-based International Campaign against Honor Killing, declares that no reliable statistics are available. These crimes are committed in fifty-four countries and often in rural areas where no birth or death certificates are issued. Nammi estimates that more than 10,000 cases occur every year (El Ouali 2008).

Crimes of honor still elude international control mainly because they are described as "traditional or cultural practices," thus implying acceptance and leniency. Ideological discourses on cultural relativism (which recognizes and requires respect for diverse culturally defined practices) have aimed to explain violations of women's rights through atrocious forms of violence perpetrated by families and communities. Contrary to international human rights law,[12] which rejects justification of violence against women on the basis of custom or tradition, crimes of honor breach a woman's right to life, freedom and equality, human dignity, and physical integrity.

When families immigrate to other countries, they bring with them their traditional codes and forms of punishment against women who stain their family's reputation. These practices inevitably cause intercultural and intergenerational clashes when young people, born and raised in the host country and society, show an interest in education, freedom to socialize with other groups, choice of partners, and aspirations to professions. A recurrent phenomenon is the disappearance of teenage girls who fail to return from trips to their countries of origin. It is suspected that they are lured to these communities and then forced to marry men chosen by their families. If they refuse, they are subjected initially to death threats and ultimately to murder (Smith 2008). In February 2008, Commander Steve Allen, a senior British police officer, gave evidence to the Home Affairs Committee of the House of Commons showing that around five hundred cases of arranged marriage and honor killings are reported to the police and Foreign Office's forced marriage unit every year.[13] He stated, "Is it under-reported? Massively. What we will never know, or cannot know at the moment, is the extent to which it is under-reported" (Smith 2008, 11). Honor crimes differ from domestic violence in that they pose new problems for the criminal justice system in many Western nations, because these crimes are often disguised as unreported disappearances, suicides, or accidents, and are often performed in the families' home countries or carried out by hired killers. Generally they are planned in advance and involve close male relatives acting together to enforce the rigid norms of their community. Furthermore, these men believe that they are acting in the best interest for their family since their reputation is at stake, and that they have a moral duty toward their own communities.

A relatively recent phenomenon associated with honor crimes is the widespread practice of "honor suicides." Traditionally, a close relative of a dishonored girl, usually a brother younger than eighteen, would carry out the murder and receive a short prison sentence because of his young age. But since 2006, Turkey[14] has reformed its penal code and tightened punishment with life sentences for honor killings, regardless of the killer's age. However, these legal changes have given rise to new methods: some families, trying to spare their sons from the recently enforced harsher punishments associated with murdering their sisters, now order their daughters to kill themselves, and disguise their deaths as suicides (Bilefsky 2006).[15] Since the newly increased number of suicides has coincided with stricter laws and sentencing related to honor killings, Yakin Ertürk,[16] the U.N. Special Rapporteur on Violence against Women (2003–2009), was sent to Turkey to investigate suspicious cases of suicide among Kurdish girls. In fact, Ertürk reported that some suicides that occurred in Kurdish-inhabited regions of Turkey were forced suicides, in other words, they were "honor killings disguised as a suicide or an accident" in order to avoid arrest (Bilefsky 2006). This phenomenon has also been denounced by Turkish Nobel Prize-winning writer Orhan Pamuk in his novel *Kar* (2002) /*Snow* (2004), which chronicles a journalist's investigation in the small town of Kars (in reality Batman), near

Turkey's eastern border with Armenia and Georgia, where a suicide epidemic among teenage girls brings attention to the town.

Turkish journalist Ayşe Önal strongly believes that countries in the Middle East and neighboring regions cannot end the practice of women's killings through legislative reforms alone, because these crimes are imbedded in the sociocultural-religious tapestry of the communities. She explains that, "in a society where values were not in line with the law, stricter sentencing did not serve as a deterrent" (2008, 253). In fact, the occurrence of these new suicides shows that law-centered policies alone are inefficient and insufficient, and that other culturally sensitive strategies of intervention are needed. As Coomaraswamy suggests, "states should seek to adopt appropriate education measures to modify social and cultural behaviors that sanction violence against women," while women working within their communities to protect women's rights need stronger support, otherwise "any other strategy risks creating a backlash" (2005, xiii).

Although crimes of honor against women have always taken place in numerous societies around the world, and the legal language defining these crimes has been present in the penal codes of many countries, academic publications only began to discuss the culture of honor and shame in the Mediterranean area and Latin America in the 1970s, while media did not start to pay attention to these issues until the 1980s (Khan 2006). Activists and journalists working on issues of honor-related violence have often been threatened and prosecuted. Asma Khader, a prominent Jordanian human rights lawyer and leading advocate of the campaign to strengthen legislation outlawing honor killing,[17] has been harshly attacked and criticized for her work. Rana Husseini, a journalist and human rights defender, also from Jordan, who has investigated cases of honor killing and provided wide media coverage of forms of violence against women since 1994, has received multiple threats to her life.[18] Ayşe Önal, an award-winning journalist from Turkey,[19] who has revealed the difficult lives of both the female victims and the male perpetrators of crimes in an honor-based society and interviewed men imprisoned for honor killings in Turkey, thus giving tragic accounts of ruined lives, has also been repeatedly threatened and severely persecuted.

The recent surge in media coverage of crimes of honor has generated controversial sociopolitical and academic debate worldwide. Reimers' in-depth study (2007), for example, examines the Swedish media's representation of the famous case of Fadime Sahindal. A twenty-five-year-old Kurdish woman, Fadime was killed by her father on January 21, 2002. He was sentenced to life imprisonment on April 3, 2002. Reimers discusses how media coverage drew on the concept of honor in order to understand the motive for her murder, and contributed to the change in public notions of cultures of honor in comparison to the characteristics of Swedish culture. Remarkable is the work done by Maria Hagberg, President of the Network Against Honor Crimes in Sweden, through the blog *Stop Honor Killings.*[20]

Vociferous attention from the news media and brisk journalistic coverage, human rights activism and policy making, the work of NGO's and civil society groups worldwide, academic research, international political focus, and recent legislative reforms have all inspired a transnational discourse that delves into religion and moral norms. Information, data, statistics, and results produced by the work of these agencies have infused a heated debate on "cultural relativism" versus the universal respect for women's lives. These widely discussed topics have increased research on case studies and the publication of academic volumes and books for a general readership. The number of mainstream and independent films released and educational TV and radio programs broadcast has also increased, as has the amount of information distributed through the proliferation of new Internet-based platforms (e.g., Web sites, blogs, Facebook, YouTube, community forums, various networking sites, cell-phone video-recording) that, as educational agents, synergetically contribute to addressing the causes, highlighting incidents, and raising international public awareness of crimes of honor.

## Framing Honor Killings

The dramatic confluence of events—social and cultural—that have made honor killings a worldwide crisis crossing cultures and religions is portrayed in poignant and compelling films that focus on this prevalent, rarely denounced, and leniently punished practice. A recent feature film, *Land Gold Women* (2009), by Indian director Avankita Hari, entirely shot in Birmingham, is the fictional story of a seventeen-year-old British-Asian girl, Saira Khan. She has an English boyfriend but is forced into an arranged marriage by her family. Her father is enraged by her rebellion against traditional norms and her refusal to marry an approved suitor, so he takes matters in his hands. Another dramatic film, *Niloofar* (2008), award-winning editor Sabine El Gemayel's debut,[21] is the story of a twelve-year-old Iraqi girl, who is promised in marriage to an older man when she becomes a woman.

When she reaches womanhood, however, she runs away with her uncle, thus dishonoring the family, so her stepbrother is sent to find her. Other films on the practice of honor killings include *Malaf Khas/Private File* (2008), a documentary by Egyptian director Saad Hendawy; *Mutluluk/ Bliss* (2007) by Turkish director Abdullah Oguz, an adaptation of Zülfü Livaneli's international best-selling novel *Bliss* (2006); *Honor Killing* (2007), a documentary by Dutch director Frans Bromet and codirectors Seren Dalkiran and Yeter Akin of Turkish/Kurdish origin. The documentary *Karanlikta Diyalograr/Dialogue in the Dark* (2006), by Turkish director Melek Ulagay Taylan, is a journey through the southeastern region of Turkey to investigate stories of women living under the threat of being killed by their male relatives over honor-related cases. Interviews with people and a representative of the Tribal Court lead the director to question the concepts of honor and shame, which victimize both men and women. The director meets local women who run the *Ka-Mer* (Women's Center). Another interesting documentary drama is Australian director Anna Broinowski's *Forbidden Lies* (2007), which investigated accusations against Norma Khouri, the Jordanian author of the novel *Forbidden Love* (2002), after she wrote a fictional biography of a Muslim friend, Dalia, who was killed for dating a Christian man.

Films reporting and condemning unambiguous truths about the practice of honor killings specifically in Mediterranean cultures, and directed by women filmmakers, include *Crimes of Honour* (1999) by Shelley Saywell, *In the Morning* (2004) by Danielle Lurie, *Vendetta Song* (2005) by Eylem Kaftan, and *Maria's Grotto* (2007) by Buthina Canaan Khoury. Of these four directors, Saywell and Lurie are from North America, Kaftan from Turkey, but living in Canada, and Khoury from Palestine. They bring different cultural perspectives to their films and use diverse narrative styles, but they all pioneer unchartered territories and are at the forefront of efforts to denounce and combat crimes of honor. Their films document stories of female victims and survivors as well as of male victims and perpetrators of honor killings, and they are discussed here in chronological order.

## Crimes of Honour

Prolific independent Canadian documentary director Shelley Saywell[22] provides evidence for the terrible reality of honor killings in her documentary *Crimes of Honour*.[23] Filmed in Jordan and in the West

Bank, the narrator takes viewers through the tragic lives of three Jordanian women, all brutally murdered by their own family members. Relatives and neighbors notice changes in women after they begin to attend university. Education gives them self-confidence, independence, and a feeling of equality, which contrasts with the strict lifestyle and rigid codes of behavior imposed by their communities. The film tells the stories of young women running away from their families because they are being forced into arranged marriages but love someone else, or because they have had sexual relationships and fear their family's punishment. These young women live in constant fear for their lives and some of them are given protection in shelters. Saywell visits the Jeiwedeh Prison in Amman, one of the shelters where threatened young women live secluded lives without access to education, work, friends, or any relative, in order to avoid being killed.

One of the three stories is about twenty-three-year-old Rania Arafat. Throughout the film her story is interwoven with the passages read from yearning letters describing how she misses her family, but at the same time expressing her need to live freely. Rania was promised in marriage to her cousin as a very young child, but she later told her family that she wanted to marry the man she loved. She ran away twice, the second time only two weeks before the arranged marriage. Whilst in hiding, she wrote to her mother and pleaded for forgiveness and understanding. Her letter was read on a popular national TV program in Jordan. Her parents called the TV station and promised that she would not be harmed. She believed them and when, on the night of August 19, 1997, she returned home accompanied by her family, her youngest brother, Rami, shot her five times in the head and chest, killing her immediately. The autopsy showed that Rania had remained a virgin. Rami was underage, and for this reason he served only a six-month jail sentence for his crime. In Jordan, the plea of honor is recognized as a legitimate defense and usually results in a lenient sentence.

Amal is the second Arab victim of honor killing documented in the film. She also ran away from home twice because she wanted to be independent. Her family was ashamed and worried about her reputation because their neighbors had started to gossip. One night, when she returned home and went to sleep, her brother Ahmed and her father strangled her. Saywell examines the reasons behind these crimes by interviewing Ahmed, who was convicted to serve a seven-year sentence in Swaga Prison for strangling his sister Amal (he was given such a severe sentence thanks to Khader's legal battle). Ahmed tells his sister's story and explained why he killed her. He states in the interview, "I strangled her. She didn't fight back. I recited the Holy

Koran as she was dying...it took a few minutes and she was dead."[24] He concludes that he had no choice. If necessary he would do it again for his other sister, his daughter, or his wife.

Ahmed's brother, when interviewed at home surrounded by his mother, sister-in-law (Ahmed's wife), and niece (Ahmed's daughter), explains that losing Amal was very painful for everyone in the family. About four years after her death, they still miss her and pray for her soul. They did not want to kill her, because they loved her and always will. Shots of a quietly crying mother still mourning her lost daughter give a full sense of the multilayered tragedy within a family with one son in prison and one daughter in the grave. The practice of honor killings generates strong and irreconcilable ambiguities in family's reactions as members express sympathy for the victim, but nonetheless simultaneously state that the woman's murder was inevitably just and unquestionably necessary. This conflicting duality suggests a very complex sociological phenomenon with the culturally bound notion of honor at its core.

The third story is a case of rape. Women are punished even when they are the victims of rape, not only by strangers but also by their own fathers and brothers. In the case documented in this film, the family believed that Kefaya, a victim of incest as she was repeatedly raped by her brother, deserved to die, because neighbors had started to gossip. Victims of incestuous rape are murdered by their own attackers who plea the honor defense for a more lenient sentence, as rape ordinarily carries a fifteen-year sentence.

The film also profiles three remarkable human rights activists, who provide protection and legal assistance to women threatened by their families: Rana Husseini, an award-winning investigative reporter for the *Jordan Times*, who documents the stories of female victims of honor killings. Jordanian human rights lawyer Asma Khader, who fights for women's protection through a change to a section of Jordan's two-hundred-year-old penal code, and campaigns for more severe sentences for men accused of murder. She was instrumental in creating a legal literacy/legal assistance program for Jordanian women. Nadera Shalhoub-Kevorkian,[25] who set up the first hotline in the West Bank and Gaza at the Women's Center for Legal Aid and Counseling in 1993–1994, and who offers legal assistance to Palestinian women in situations of domestic violence and at risk of honor killings.

From the jails where perpetrators are imprisoned to the hiding places of frightened young women, Saywell captures the culturally pervasive tragedy of honor killings and explores the complex societal reaction to this phenomenon through revealing interviews with family members and the dramatic individual experiences of survivors and perpetrators. Through a combination of voiceover narration, letter reading, interviews, and dramatic photos of the dead women's brutally disfigured bodies and faces, the documentary brings to the fore a composite picture of honor crimes. Filmed against the backdrop of the desert and in the bustling streets of the cities, through the gates and the bars of the jail cells, and in the privacy of people's homes, the documentary portrays female and male characters with respect and dignity. The young women living in the shelters, shot in extreme close ups, with their identities concealed by the veil, talk to the camera with terrified, piercing eyes, thus connecting directly with the engaged viewer.

## In the Morning

The short feature *In the Morning*,[26] by American director Danielle Lurie,[27] is a courageous drama confronting the multilayered cultural and ideological dimensions of honor killing. The director was struck by Dexter Filkins' article published in the *New York Times* (2003) about a young woman murdered by her brother for becoming pregnant out of wedlock. Moved by what she had read, Lurie was determined to draw public attention to the urgent issue and alarming practice of honor killings. Before writing the screenplay and directing the film, the director conducted extensive research in Turkey and worked closely with journalist Dexter Filkins and Nebahat Akkoç, the leader of *Ka-Mer* (the Women's Center of Diyarbakir), an organization that finds shelter for women and helps them to apply to the courts for restraining orders against relatives who have threatened them. The film is loosely inspired by a true story—the murder of Kadriye Demirel in Diyarbakir, in November 2003. Demirel's case received considerable attention both in Turkey and internationally. She was six months pregnant when she was stabbed and then beaten to death by her older brother. Apparently she had been raped by a cousin. When the family tried to force the cousin to marry her, he refused. Her older brother, Ahmet, then decided to kill Demirel (Eissenstat 2006).

Set in contemporary Turkey, but filmed in Lurie's own apartment in Los Angeles, the film is spoken in phonetic Turkish by American actors.[28] As Lurie explains in an interview, no professional Turkish actors would agree to be part of a film that touched on this sensitive topic.[29] When fifteen-year-old Derya is brutally attacked, raped, and beaten by a stranger while walking home one evening, the male members of her extended family gather to discuss and plan her murder in order to restore their lost honor. Because he would serve the short-est jail sentence, it is decided that Derya's youngest brother, thirteen-year-old Baran, will kill her. Soon after the men's deliberations, Derya's father gives his young son a pistol and instructs him to kill his sister the following day, "in the morning."

The film's narrative is constructed around regular juxtapositions of scenes of the young woman's repeated rape and shots of the men making decisions regarding her murder. Shifting from Derya's subjugation to physical violence in a dark and deserted street at night to the men's irrev-ocable judgment about her ineluctable destiny, passed in a dimly lit backroom of the family business, the editing intervals suggest a contin-uum in the male sexual and moral cruelty, and a crescendo of brutality culminating in premeditated murder. Interspersing the scenes of the rape produces the dual dramatic effect of extending the duration of the physical violence (throughout the ten-minute feature, thus conveying a realistic duration of the crime), and expanding the emotional impact of Derya's fear, screams, and struggle throughout the traumatic experi-ence. The rhythm of the intercut between the rape and the meeting pow-erfully reminds the viewer of Derya's helplessness to protect herself from the sexual attack and of the impossibility of her defending herself against the family's accusations. Lurie's narrative style builds up dramatic ten-sion, while establishing an escalation of frightening emotions and fear-ful expectations, which inevitably ends with Derya's sudden and conclusive execution at the hands of her younger brother. The terrified expression on Derya's face, as her body lies abandoned and bleeding at the roadside after the rape, turns into an expression of horrified surprise as she is left quietly dying on the floor of her family home. In a spiraling progression of events, the feature comes full circle: linking Derya's vio-lated body on the street with her punished motionless body in her home, while her wide open eyes, looking straight into the camera, seem to interrogate the witnesses and accuse her perpetrators. While Lurie focuses more on the men's blunt hatred for the girl, her film in part also addresses the inextricable aspect of family fear and pain surrounding the crime in two instances: when the younger brother resists and rebels against his father's order to kill Derya; and later, when he is left standing in tears of sorrow, fear, and regret, looking at his dead sister.

## Vendetta Song

The bio-documentary *Vendetta Song*,[30] by independent Turkish-Canadian director Eylem Kaftan,[31] describes the filmmaker's own journey from Montreal to Turkey to solve the thirty-year-old mystery of her aunt Güzide's murder. As Kaftan explains, there was no record of her aunt's existence or her death—no letters, and only one grainy, faded, sepia-colored photograph of Güzide's mother-in-law with two men (Güzide's brothers-in-law, Kadri and Baki) and a little boy (Güzide's son). Kaftan's father (and Güzide's brother), who lives in Istanbul, tells his daughter about his mother's and sister's misfortunes. He also recalls an old story about one of the two men in the photo, the man who killed Güzide.

Kaftan's grandmother was only seventeen when she got married, but her husband left her for another woman when she was pregnant with Güzide. Her family decided that her fatherless baby would bring shame on them, so they sent Güzide as a baby to a distant Kurdish village to be raised by her father's family. They also forbade Kaftan's grandmother from ever seeing her daughter again or keeping in touch with her. In fact, they did keep in touch and managed to meet once in secret when Güdize was about fourteen years old. Güdize married at age fifteen and had five children, four of whom died at birth, and her only surviving son drowned at the age of five. Her husband was killed in a blood feud with another village. Now a childless widow, her husband's family expected her to marry Baki, one of her two brothers-in-law. Güzide married Kadri instead, the brother-in-law she loved, but she paid for her decision with death. Out of vengeance, Baki killed her.

Kaftan, determined to unravel the family secrets surrounding her aunt's life, made this film to avenge Güzide's unjust death. The docu-travelogue, written and narrated by Kaftan, is the poignant story of the director's search for truth, reconnection with her aunt's ancient culture, reconciliation, and closure as she tenaciously pieces together the few hazy family memories that will lead to her aunt's husband. The journey begins on the busy streets of modern Istanbul where Kaftan's parents live and where the director gathers some information and photos from her father. Then she travels to Diyarbakir (the spiritual capital of the Kurdish people, near the Iraqi border) and visits her grandmother's house, where Güzide was born (and where Kaftan's father lived before he moved to Istanbul). The difficult search takes Kaftan to the rural and unmapped village of Millan in the Kurdish mountains were Güzide grew up, then to Karacaören where her two brothers-in-law lived, and finally to Tepecik where Güzide was murdered. When the director traces her roots to eastern Turkey, she meets people who remember her aunt as a good-hearted and much loved person, and a tall, beautiful, strong, brave woman (who very much resembled her niece, Kaftan herself). They have developed legends and folklore around her life and unresolved death. Traveling back in time, from village to village across Turkey, and through political instability, Kaftan follows a series of word-of-mouth clues and manages to meet Kadri, who tells her about Güzide's last days.

*Vendetta Song* is not only the director's journey into her family's past, more importantly it is the exploration of a world of marked gender inequalities, the traditional practice of arranged marriages, a semifeudal tribal social structure, and blood feuds and civil conflict between Kurdish separatists and the Turkish army. As the director sheds light on the mysterious causes of her aunt's death, she also addresses issues relating to the traditional practice of honor killing by interviewing Pinar Ilkkaracan, founding president of Women for Women's Human Rights, a leading women's advocacy organization in Turkey.[32] Ilkkaracan explains the cultural origin of such crimes in Mediterranean countries and the critical work done by women's NGOs to educate people and attempt to eradicate this common practice. The film's effectiveness lies in the rich portrayal of a kaleidoscope of people and ethnic communities whose customs, values, and traditions are presented through interviews and intense moments of human intimacy, warm hospitality, and mutual respect, as well as instances of tension when going through a military check point, cultural divergence with men when interviewed on issues of honor, and verbal confrontation with some men when questioned about what really happened to Güzide.

Special effects are used in a visually captivating narrative that reconnects past and present through black-and-white and color photos, family memories, traditional ceremonies, dancing, singing, and storytelling. The director's photographic choices, as the expression of the narrating viewer and traveler, document concrete human encounters and critical events, thus orchestrating social and cultural situations in the framed moment in time and space. The photographic style of using snapshots, as a form of character-narrative, offers a privileged view of how Kaftan tells the story. Through the re-elaboration of the visual memories preserved in the family photo album, and the rediscovery of the family tree with the recognition of the universe of women's portraits, Kaftan's personal and familial stories become intertwined. As she approaches Güzide's figure and reconstructs fragmented episodes of her life, the director, through her aunt, redefines her own identity and ethnic roots. In the absence of photographic portraits of Güzide, drama is added to the story through the instrumental and recurrent use of blurred and slow-motion recreated flashbacks of Güzide's life. The documentary is also vital and engaging in its use of imagery of the vast and bare landscape, always with an entrancing oriental sound track commentary that together visually and musically frame the stories being told.

Kaftan herself is the protagonist in this bio-documentary, as her own life gradually merges with her aunt's destiny. After her visit to Millan, the director chooses to wear a traditional Kurdish black silk scarf with gold embroidery (a gift from Leila, a young girl she befriends with during her stay in Millan), which modestly holds and covers her hair (she had worn her very long dark hair loose throughout most of the film), and frames her face, neck, and shoulders, making her resemblance to her aunt even more apparent. This moment marks the beginning of a process of gradual self-identification and emotional reconnection with Güzide. While Kaftan regrets not having found any photos of her aunt, Leila tells her to look at herself in the mirror to see Güzide's image. Through her journey and search, Kaftan restores broken family ties and reestablishes the interrupted continuity with Güzide's lost ethnic heritage. Finally, however, Kaftan, as the director, writer, narrator, and leading character, prevails in the narrative with a narcissistic performative presence, while the film is at times contrived and fabricated in the unrealistic attempt at, and display of, reconciliation between male members of rival tribes.[33]

## Maria's Grotto

The documentary *Maria's Grotto*,[34] by independent Palestinian director and producer Buthina Canaan Khoury,[35] is a character-driven dramatic portrayal of victims, survivors, and perpetrators of honor killings in Palestine. Khoury is the first female director from Palestine to tackle this problem from within her own culture, and to interview her own people about their customs and values. The director reports the practice of this crime through the true stories of four women, and she tackles the topic from a sociohistorical, legal, political, and psychological perspective. She also addresses issues pertaining to controversial tribal law deliberations that take place in the absence of an official legal system and penal code that recognizes and punishes honor killings in Palestine as murders. The director clarifies that within Palestine, in the West Bank people follow Jordanian law, and in Gaza they implement Egyptian law. These laws were promulgated in 1966 and later modified in their respective countries. But they were not changed in Palestine, because Palestine is not recognized as a country and therefore the Palestinian people cannot reform their legislation.[36] Khoury also explains that family, civil, and social disputes, including cases of honor killing, have been subject to tribal court decisions, even under the Palestinian National Authority. Tribal law recognizes the principle of "honor," so killings intended to restore family honor are not defined as crimes, and the killers are not considered guilty of murder.[37] While touching upon the complexities of this phenomenon, Khoury also takes on a thorny prismatic point of view that largely problematizes the notion of honor and denounces the criminal behavior.

Dedicated to her mother, Azizeh, and to all women, the film begins in Khoury's hometown, Taybeh.[38] The director's voiceover introduces a story that she had known since she was a child. In 1936, a young Christian Palestinian woman, Maria, was murdered by her own family. She was the sole heir of the family property, but her stepmother had her killed, so that the rest of the family would inherit the property. Prior to her death, Maria had been victim of false accusations of inappropriate behavior with a shepherd, all fabricated by her family in order to justify her death, deeming it to be necessary in order to remove the stain on the family's reputation. As Khoury explains, Maria's death was falsely attributed to a case of honor killing, because this is the only instance in which a murderer is not prosecuted. As Nimah, an old villager, says, Maria was a kind young woman and an innocent virgin. Her murder was planned and orchestrated by her uncles and their wives, who resorted to the help of revolutionaries to kill her. Maria was shot in the back in El Khader, a place near an abandoned church. Maria's story turned into a local legend, and, over the years, people developed several different versions of how and why she was killed. Furthermore, there is a widespread rumor that, due to their calumnies against Maria, a curse struck all the members of her family and wiped them from the village.[39] A grotto, found in the ruins of an abandoned church, became Maria's grave and to this day the burial place continues to bear her name as a reminder of her innocence and unpunished murder. In voiceover, Khoury recalls the annual ritual of slaughtering a lamb on the day of the souls in El Khader, where she used to go as a child to commemorate the dead. A mournful soundtrack follows the director's voiceover narration as the camera takes the viewer through the quiet streets of the village.

The second victim of a brutal case of honor killing in this film is Hiyam,[40] a thirty-three-year-old Muslim woman from a different village, who died in September 2005. She was eight-months-pregnant when she was killed. Khoury explains that the man involved in such situations (sometimes a relative) either rapes the woman, or has a regular relationship with her with the promise of marrying her. In cases of rape, if the family knows the man, rather than killing her, they force the woman to marry him to cover up her story. In these situations the woman is victimized twice, first with sexual violence and second with a forced marriage. In the case of a relationship, however, if the man fails to keep his promise to marry the woman and runs away because she is pregnant, the woman is left alone to a fatal destiny.[41]

When her family realized that Hiyam was heavily pregnant out of wedlock, her brothers forced her to swallow poison (agricultural pesticide). The Legal Medical Institute provided forensic and medical evidence that Hiyam was killed (and did not commit suicide) because they found clear signs of violence to her jaw and around her mouth, confirming that she had been forced to swallow the poison. Hiyam's brothers are still free with no pending charges. Although no members of Hiyam's family agreed to be interviewed, Khoury explains that her mother became depressed and seriously ill shortly after her daughter's death and died within six months. The human tragedy and loss of life involved in the decisions made in the name of honor are usually concealed, because, as a female villager states, "there is nothing more important than honor."[42]

Meanwhile, another man, Mahdi, married and with three children, the son of the owner of the factory where Hiyam worked as seamstress for several years, was falsely accused of having a sexual relationship with Hiyam by her family. Such slander against him was used to cover for the man (possibly a close relative) who had in fact impregnated Hiyam (and presumably promised to marry her, otherwise she would have decided to have an abortion). Furthermore, her family, out of revenge, burned down six houses belonging to Mahdi's relatives, including his own, as well as the tailors shop. In slow-motion and blurred images, the camera leads the viewer through the inferno-like images of the burning buildings.[43] Khoury rushed to the scene, and started filming the destructive effects of the arson, but her equipment was severely damaged by the angry young men who were starting the fire. Unfortunately she lost most of the footage.[44]
The aftermath of the devastating fire is presented through a sequence of stills of the destroyed houses, and slow-motion images of collapsed walls, smoking ruins, and burning ashes amongst shafts of daylight coming in through the destroyed windows. No human victims were reported in the fires, but several families were left homeless. Thakla, Mahdi's mother, in despair, tells her son's story.

Following the fires Mahdi was held for six months under guard at a detention center, away from his family, due to fears for his own

**Figure 10.1** Photo poster of *Maria's Grotto*: Light coming into the burned house.

safety. While in custody, he was asked to take the DNA test, which proved that he did not father Hiyam's unborn child, and was not responsible for her death. Both Hiyam's and Mahdi's families were more preoccupied with determining who Hiyam had had a relationship with, rather than wanting to find out who had killed her. The man who impregnated Hiyam never claimed his responsibility for fathering her child and having a relationship with her.[45]

As the Ramallah police commissioner stated, under tribal law a reconciliation meeting was held in order to reach a peace agreement (Atwa)[46] amongst the two villages and the two families. Nonetheless, now under pressure from his society, stigmatized for being accused of having had a relationship with another woman, dishonored for having caused so much moral and material damage to his family, and disgraced in the eyes of the entire community, Mahdi decided to leave his hometown, and eventually the country, with his wife and children. With a discreet camera, Khoury films the tribal court meeting where the destiny of Mahdi was decided, while Hiyam's two brothers (their faces blurred) were set free, because they had killed to restore their family honor. In this case, a rigidly honor-based society produced innocent victims on both sides. The woman was killed, and the suspected man, who brought shame on the family, was forced to leave to avoid more violence.

The third story is about a woman (whose name is kept confidential) who survived repeated stabbing by her brother. She had been wrongly accused by neighbors of immoral behavior, so her brother, pressured by societal honor codes, had to kill her. The woman later married, moved to a different village, and had a child. However, she continues to live with the trauma of the violence and resentment for her brother's initial physical abuse, and later attempted murder, because he had believed the neighbors' slanderous gossip, rather than trusting her. The brother, on the other hand, after attempting to kill his sister, turned himself in to the police, and spent some time in jail. After failing to kill his sister, he is now haunted by remorse for giving in to the pressure to murder her put on him by the community, and he has fallen into a state of deep depression. Their mother expresses her own drama of when she was dealing with the pain of a son in prison and fearing for her daughter's life in the hospital. This story victimizes both siblings as a result of the pressures exerted on them to behave in a manner that is either socially acceptable or punishable, and brings to the fore the pain of the victims' mothers in situations of honor crimes. Khoury visits the family of the woman who survived her brother's stabbing and films in close-up, but her camera is remarkably respectful and blurs the family's faces to conceal their identity. Both the severely injured sister and the depressed brother revisit the episodes that led to the failed attempt to kill, and reflect on the trajectory of their doomed lives. Theirs are pain-stricken stories of family shame, confronting social exclusion from the community, enduring psychological trauma, and devising ways to heal emotional wounds as siblings.

The final story is about Abeer Zinati, an eighteen-year-old Palestinian hip-hop artist, a singer with the band DAM.[47] She is not afraid to write and perform songs about love and honor killing, but the leader of her group has been threatened by her cousins, so she could not perform publicly for several years. She had collaborated on the song *Born Here* and performing on stage would have been her moment of glory. At the same time her sister Ayah accidentally witnesses a woman being murdered in the middle of the day in the street of her village. With her sister's support and courage Abeer confronts the family threats by refusing to become a victim of her own society, while her mother expresses disapproval for her daughter's artistic choices and inappropriate lifestyle.[48]

*Maria's Grotto* has a circular structure and a cyclical narrative spanning over a seventy-year cycle (1936–2006), where each woman's story marks a different chapter in the spiral of violence fueled by the notions of honor and shame. The film's unadorned style intensifies the drama and highlights the interviews and encounters with the characters. The deliberate omission of clearly marked transitions between the four stories creates a flow of testimonies linked by common destinies that are scarred by slander, threats, revenge, and murder. At the heart of the film are intimate conversations with women and men, who tell old stories, offer information, share feelings, candidly express their views on "honor," and critically expose injustice.

Khoury visits a prison, a hospital, and people's homes, she films the tribal law reconciliation meeting, and interviews a Palestinian tribal law counselor, thus portraying a composite perspective of the cultural causes, ethical implications, irreversible psychological damage, and legal repercussions of honor killings on communities and individuals' lives. It is revealing and disquieting to listen to Mr. Abdullah Khalaifeh, the Palestinian Tribal Law Counselor, as he explains honor codes and honor-based legal justifications,

> The one who kills the woman in the name of honor and the one who orders her death are not punished…When someone's sister, God forbid, commits a shameful act, he will slaughter her. He will be in prison for two or three months, just for appearance because this crime was committed for the sake of honor, not just for the sake of murder. We will kill the woman so that others will take her as an example, and will steer away from shameful acts.[49]

The film's closing scenes show Mahdi unlocking Maria's grotto, zooming in on the open grave and exposing her remains. The director comes full circle to conclude her portraits of these women, with Maria's story becoming the unifying thread of injustice for all the victims in the film. A video of the hip-hop singer's performance, shown in the split screen alongside the closing credits, of a protest song against honor killings expresses the artistic energy and militant spirit of a young generation of women who confront diverse forms of challenges and choose a new language with which to fight against crimes of honor. Abeer's voice and rhymes, as an alternative form of resistance, shift the direction and tone of the film and give hope for a more proactive effort to bring change in women's lives. She sings,

> You should get used to seeing girls doing what they want…I don't want you, or your house or for you to marry me to protect me! I want to be listened and sing provocative Eastern hip hop…I can do what you do and more, I don't weaken in front of any man, nor be limited by traditions…I am the writer, I am the composer, I am the singer, and I will bring more girls to keep on going, if I am killed before I complete my song…[50]

# Conclusion

Men from honor-centered societies are constantly worried about their social status, as this is defined by (sexual) honor. They live in permanent anxiety over their women's sexuality and honesty, as the female *"hymen* is both a symbolic and real border" preventing association within the community (King 2008, 317). Önal (2008) writes extensively on the high cost that men pay to preserve honor in their groups. Perpetrators of the killings are themselves victims of social beliefs and cultural traditions as their families put the burden and pressure of the murder onto them. Mojab (2002) writes, "Honor killing is a tragedy in which fathers and brothers kill their most beloved, their daughters and sisters…Here, affection and brutality coexist in conflict and unity" (cited in King 2008, 320). No man or woman wants to kill a family member. Husseini explains that they do it "because of a mis-defined concept of honor that has been nurtured since birth" (2009, 216). But the psychological harm of murder leaves individuals tormented by guilt and "alienated by a community who cannot and will not help them come to terms with what they have done" (217). Önal adds that "honor killings cause a double tragedy for families. The girls lie in the cemetery while the boys or men are thrown into prison" (2008, 255). If a man chooses not to kill, he cannot continue a normal life and is belittled and humiliated by his community. Furthermore, families are often divided by opposing loyalties, especially when confronted with the process of assimilation and full participation in modern societies.

As the sociocultural, political, and legal fault lines of the next decade of the twenty-first century take shape, what will be the defining international politics on honor crimes? In the wake of an era of fast-paced transitions from traditional lifestyles to modernity and urbanization, of rapid changes in women's status and roles, one response could be a stronger worldwide political commitment to the recognition and protection of human and women's rights. The discussion in this chapter has explored the impact of decades of grassroots work, media information, legislative reforms, and educational programs on crimes of honor. The film analyses have illustrated the fatal consequences of individuals' rebellions against honor-based values and have demonstrated forms of violence in communities defined by marked gender inequalities and family divisions. Along with the more reported stories of female and male victims, different choices and reactions are already evident in the rise of new militant behaviors in urban areas. A different culture of honor will need to articulate socio-ethical codes that recognize human dignity, guarantee physical security, and attribute meaning and value to people's lives. The way in which societies give priority to these principles and the way in which people mobilize and react to the threats against them will shape the post-2010s honor landscape across the world.

# Notes

I thank director Buthina Canaan Khoury for her generous collaboration during interviews in preparation for the analysis of her film *Maria's Grotto*. I am also grateful to my students Mohona Siddique, Duygu Ula, Gabriella Wakeman (Wellesley College Graduating Class 2010), and Alexandra L. Brown (Wellesley College Graduating Class 2011) for their excellent work as dedicated research assistants.

1. The title of this essay has been adapted from William Shakespeare, *Much Ado About Nothing* (4.1.113). The play is set in Messina, a coastal city on the island of Sicily. Shakespeare tackles the themes of male social status and honor, sexual jealousy and anxiety over women's sexuality, and female honesty and chastity in the comedy *Much Ado*, in the tragedy *Othello*, and in the romance *The Winter's Tale*. He sets all three stories in Italy, and two of them, the comedy and the romance, in Sicily.
2. Radhika Coomaraswamy was appointed by the then U.N. Secretary-General Kofi Annan as Under-Secretary-General, Special Representative for Children and Armed Conflict, in April 2006. In this capacity, she serves as a moral voice and independent advocate to build awareness and give prominence to the rights and protection of boys and girls affected by armed conflict.
3. These single women are considered both dishonored and worthless because they will have no bride price if they marry.
4. In some countries, women are killed for reasons unrelated to their suspected sexual behavior. They are often murdered by their fiancé's family

members in retaliation for having insufficient dowries. Usually the woman is covered with kerosene and burnt alive, which explains the term "bride burnings" used for women killed over dowries.

5. These cause dreadful scarring of the face, hands, throat or any other exposed parts of the body. Often the victims are also blinded by the nitric acid thrown into their faces and eyes.

6. Bangladesh, Pakistan, Jordan, Syria, Palestine, Egypt, Lebanon, Iran, Iraq, Israel, Yemen, Morocco, Kuwait, Turkey, and Qatar (Coomaraswamy 2005).

7. United States: In the Atlanta suburb of Jonesboro in July 2008, Chaudhry Rashidm, a Pakistani man, strangled his twenty-five-year-old daughter, Sandeela Kanwal, with a bungee cord because she was determined to end her arranged marriage and started a new relationship with another man. In Upstate New York, a few weeks earlier, Waheed Allah Mohammad, an Afghani man, was charged with attempted murder after repeatedly stabbing his nineteen-year-old sister because she was going to clubs, wearing immodest clothes, and planning to leave her family for a new life in New York City. On New Year's Day in Irving, Texas, eighteen-year-old Amina and her seventeen-year-old sister Sarah were found shot in an abandoned taxi. Police issued an arrest warrant for their father, Yaser Abdel Said (Jacoby 2008). Canada: The murder of sixteen-year-old Aqsa Parvez of Mississauga, Ontario, by her father, hit the international news in December 2007.

8. Great Britain, Denmark, Holland, Germany, Italy, and Sweden. Government officials say that there are twelve honor killings a year in Britain. Police, doctors, and school teachers are being trained to recognize warning signs of possible abuse (Clark 2008). In London, a seventy-year-old woman and her son were convicted on July 26 for the honor killing of Surjit Kaur Athwal, who was murdered after she threatened to get a divorce. Both the woman and her son face life sentences in prison. The verdict came a week after a British court concluded proceedings in the sexual torture and murder of a Kurdish woman, Banaz Mahmod, at the hands of her father and uncle, who both received life sentences. A third man involved in the honor killing was sentenced to seventeen years in prison; two others are still free (*The Guardian* 2006). Twenty-year-old Hina Saleem, a Pakistani woman, was killed in Sarezzo, near Brescia in Northern Italy. Her father and uncle were charged with slitting her throat because she dated an Italian man and refused to conform to an Islamic lifestyle. The woman's body was found buried in the family's garden in Sarezzo. Hina had moved to her Italian boyfriend's house and had refused the arranged marriage with her cousin in Pakistan (Boskovitch 2007). Cases of honor-related violence are also prevalent in Sweden (Hellgren and Hobson 2008, Reimers 2007).

9. Brazil and Ecuador.

10. In Italy, Giovanni Morabito, a twenty-four-year-old member of a mafia clan in Calabria, shot his older unmarried sister in March 2006 for

having a child out of wedlock and for apparently wanting to leave the family after earning her law degree. "She had a child by a man she was not married to," Morabito told the police, "It is a question of honor. I am not sorry. On the contrary, I am proud of what I did" (Boskovitch 2007). Miraculously, she survived. The principle of honor, defined as a moral and social value, was an admitted legal defense until 1981 in Italy under Art. 587 of the 1931 Rocco Penal Code. Rocco (inspired by the former Zanardelli Penal Code 1890–1930) provided a reduced penalty of imprisonment of only three to seven years for a man who killed his wife, sister, or daughter to vindicate his or his family's honor. (For a fuller analysis, see Bettiga-Boukerbout 2005). This legislation was reversed by Law 442 of August 5, 1981, which recognizes honor killing as murder.

11. Diana Nammi, a refugee from Iran and founder of an Iranian and Kurdish women's rights organization, has long campaigned against honor killings.

12. Including the provisions of the 1979 Convention on the Elimination of All Forms of Discrimination Against Women (CEDAW), and the terms of the 1993 U.N. General Assembly resolution on the Declaration on the Elimination of Violence Against Women.

13. The two practices are strictly connected because when a woman refuses to marry the man chosen by her family she is automatically punished for disobeying, first with threats and attacks and ultimately with murder.

14. The European Union has been monitoring Turkey's progress on women's rights because failure to stop human rights violations could prevent the country's entry into the union.

15. "Families of disgraced girls are choosing between sacrificing a son to a life in prison by designating him to kill his sister or forcing their daughters to kill themselves," said Yilmaz Akinci, who works for a rural development group. "Rather than losing two children, most opt for the latter option" (Bilefsky 2006).

16. Yakin Ertürk is also a Member of the UNRISD Board. She has been a Professor in the Department of Sociology at the Middle East Technical University, Ankara, since 1986. She is currently the Chairperson of the Gender and Women's Study Programme at the same university. Professor Ertürk has held a number of international and national posts, including Director of the U.N. Division for the Advancement of Women, Department of Economic and Social Affairs, 1999–2001, and Director of the U.N. International Research and Training Institute for the Advancement of Women (INSTRAW), 1997–1999.

17. Asma Khader is coordinator of Sisterhood Is Global Institute / Jordan and Counsel on violence against women to the Permanent Arab Court. She is also founder and president of Mizan: The Law Group for Human Rights in Jordan. She is a member of the Arab Lawyer's Union, the Arab Organization for Human Rights, the Executive Committee of the International Commission of Jurists, and elected to the Permanent Arab

     Court as Counsel on violence against women. In 1990 she received an Award of Honor from Human Rights Watch for her role in defending human rights.

18. Rana Husseini has earned eight local and international awards, including a medal from HM King Abdullah II in 2007, for her reporting on honor killings. She founded the National Jordanian Committee to eliminate crimes of honor. She has also conducted several consultancies and advocacy for women's rights in the Middle East and Jordan with local NGOs and international organizations, and has worked as a regional coordinator and consultant for the UNIFEM, conducting research on human rights violations against women and children in the Middle East.

19. Ayşe Önal has reported on Turkish politics, organized crime, and conflicts in the Middle East. Whilst carrying out her work, she has been threatened by Islamic fundamentalists, placed on death lists, arrested, and shot. For ten years, she was blacklisted by the Turkish state and could not write or work for Turkish media until the political embargo was lifted in 2005. She won the IWMF's Courage in Journalism Award in 1996, and several other national and international awards.

20. www.stophonourkillings.com

21. *The Olive Harvest* (2003) by Hanna Elias.

22. Shelley Saywell started her career when she directed her first documentary *Shahira* in 1987. It is the story of a brave Egyptian woman fighting for the recognition and survival of a "lost" tribe of nomads called Bishari. Saywell named her company Bishari Films. Her choice of subject-matter has consistently been human rights issues, particularly those affecting women and children. Her most recent documentary is *Devil's Bargain* (2009), which tracks the global small arms trade. She has directed *Martyr Street* (2006), *Hamas, Behind the Mask* (2005), *Angry Girls* (2004), *Generation of Hate and Generation X-Saddam* (2003), *Streetnurse* (2002), *A Child's Century of War* (2001), *Out of the Fire* (2000), *Crimes of Honour* (1999), *Legacy of Terror: The Bombing of Air India* (1998), *Kim's Story: The Road from Vietnam* (1997), *Rape: A Crime of War* (1995), *Fire and Water* (1994), *No Man's Land: Women Frontline Journalists* (1993), *Shahira* (1988). Saywell is also the author of the books *Women in War* (Penguin Books, 1986), and contributing author to *Ourselves Among Others* (St. Martins Press, 1988). In 1997, after completing *Kim's Story: The Road from Vietnam*, she was awarded the UNESCO Gandhi Silver Medal for Promoting the Culture of Peace. Her film *A Child's Century of War* (2001) was short-listed for the 2003 Academy Awards.

23. The film was awarded an Emmy Prize. In 2000, a special committee of the United Nations held a private screening of the film at its New York headquarters. The original version of the film includes video clips of scenes of the stoning of two victims in Tehran. The two people,

presumably a young woman and her lover, huddle in the middle of a street covered only in a white sheet until stoned to death.

24. *Crimes of Honour*, VHS, Bishari Films, 1999.

25. Nadera Shalhoub-Kevorkian is a criminologist, clinical social worker, and specialist in human rights and women's rights. She is active in various Palestinian women's organizations, including the Women Studies Center in Jerusalem, the Jerusalem Center for Women, Women Against Violence in Nazareth, and Ma'an: the Forum of Arab Women's Organizations in the Naqab.

26. The film premiered at the 2005 Sundance Film Festival, was screened at the Tribeca Film Festival, and has won eight film festival awards across the globe, including Best Narrative Short at the Oscar-qualifying Nashville Film Festival, and the Women's Rights Award. On November 9, 2005 the film was screened before members of the U.S. Congress during the Congressional Human Rights Caucus on Honor Killings and it was later screened before members of the UNIFEM.

27. Danielle Lurie graduated from Stanford University in 2000 with a BA in Philosophy. While working as a production assistant on feature films, TV shows, and commercials, Danielle directed her first short films, *Nostrum* and *Harris Ranch*.

28. As Duygu Ula points out, while the film "is a fairly accurate representation of how honor crimes work within Turkish society, actors speak with a heavy American accent and as the credits prove, none of them are Turkish or have Turkish names. Also the song that the actress playing Derya hums, when doing the laundry, is not a Turkish song. A woman of her social class would most likely be humming a folk song or a pop song." (In a conversation with me on October 20, 2008).

29. Lurie states, "When I was casting this film, I look to cast only Turkish actors to play the roles because this film was in Turkish. But every Turkish actor who auditioned for me, when they found out the film was about honor killings, they said that they didn't want to do the film and they walked out of the audition" (Tehrani 2007).

30. The film won the CIDA Prize for Best Canadian Documentary on International Development at Hot Docs at the Toronto Festival in 2005, and the Quebec Film Critics Association's Best Medium Length Documentary Award in 2005.

31. Eylem Kaftan was born in Turkey and graduated in Philosophy at the Bogazici University in Istanbul. Then she completed her Master's degree in film at York University in Toronto in 2002. Her first documentary, *Faultlines* (2002), which investigates the aftermath of the 1999 earthquake that hit Turkey, won the Best Short Film and the Jury Prize at the Planet Indie Film Festival in Toronto. Her most recent film *Bledi, mon pays est ici / Bledi, this is our home* (2006), codirected with Malcolm Guy, is a dramatic and personal profile of those fighting Canada's deportation of "non-status Algerians."

32. Pinar Ilkaaracan is also cofounder of The Coalition for Sexual and Bodily Rights in Muslim Societies, an international network of NGOs and academicians working toward the promotion of sexual and bodily rights in the Middle East/North Africa and South/Southeast Asia. She has participated in various U.N. meetings and conferences on women's human rights both as a member of the Turkish delegation and NGO representative.

33. Comment by Duygu Ula in a conversation with me in October 2008.

34. *Maria's Grotto* was awarded the Silver Muhr Prize at the Dubai International Film Festival, the Jury Mention at Tatouan Film Festival, the Golden Hawk at the Rotterdam Film Festival, and Special Mention at Sguardi Altrove Film Festival.

35. Khoury received her Bachelor's degree in Filmmaking and Photography from the Massachusetts College of Fine Arts in Boston, in 1988. She is the first Palestinian woman to work as cameraperson, producer, and coordinator covering special events in the Middle East for the European Broadcasting Union (EBU) and several well-known European TV channels in Palestine. She has also worked as assistant director, documentary researcher, and cameraperson in the films *The Woman Next Door, A Woman of her Times: a Portrait of Hanan Ashrawi* (1995), and *Youth of Both Sides*. She established the Majd Production Company in Taybeh, Ramallah, in 2000. *Women in Struggle* (2004) is Khoury's first documentary as producer, director, and cameraperson. The documentary is about female Palestinian former political prisoners talking about their years of imprisonment and torture in Israeli jails. Screened worldwide, the documentary was awarded the Allsmalia Film Festival Prize, the American Muslim Women Association Award in Virginia, and the San Diego Film Festival Award in 2007. *Taste the Revolution* (2008) is a documentary about Khoury's family business, The Taybeh Brewing Company, in Palestine.

36. In the Q and A following the world premiere of *Maria's Grotto* at Wellesley College, as part of the international symposium *Visions of Struggle: Women's Filmmaking in the Mediterranean*, November 2–3, 2007.

37. Ibid.

38. Twenty kilometers East of Ramallah.

39. Interview with Khoury. Cambridge, MA, April 16, 2009.

40. This name means "love" in Arabic.

41. Interview with Khoury. April 16, 2009.

42. *Maria's Grotto*, DVD, Majd Production, 2007

43. The image below is from *Maria's Grotto*. Palestine 2007, Director: Buthina C. Khoury. Courtesy of the director.

44. Interview with Khoury. April 16, 2009.

45. In conversation with Khoury. Cambridge, MA, May 11, 2009.

46. Arabic word for a peace settlement in cases of honor killing and murder.

47. *DAM* (DA Arabian MC's), from the ghetto of Lyd city, is the first hip-hop band in Palestine.
48. In the past few years Abeer has become a popular and internationally famous rapper. She has also acted in the film *Slingshot Hip Hop* (2008) directed by Jackie Reem Salloum. The film chronicles the story of emerging Palestinian rappers.
49. *Maria's Grotto*, DVD, Majd Production, 2007.
50. Ibid.

# References


Bettiga-Boukerbout, Maria Gabriella. "'Crimes of Honour' in the Italian Penal Code: An Analysis of History and Reform." In *Honour. Crimes, Paradigms, and Violence Against Women*, ed. Lynn Welchman and Sara Hossain, 230–244. London: Zed Books, 2005.

Bilefsky, Dan. "How to Avoid Honor Killing in Turkey? Honor Suicide." *The New York Times*, July 16, 2006. http://www.nytimes.com/2006/07/16/world/europe/16turkey.html (Accessed on April 28, 2009).

Boskovitch, Angela. "Italy: 'Honor Killing' in Italy Spurs Quest for Justice." August 16, 2007. http://www.wluml.org/english/newsfulltxt.shtml?cmd%5B157%5D=x-157–555943 (Accessed on April 30, 2009).

Clark, Mandy. "Honor Killings on the Rise Worldwide." *VOA News*. February 5, 2008.

Coomaraswamy, Rodhika. "Violence Against Women and 'Crimes of Honour.'" In *Honour. Crimes, Paradigms, and Violence Against Women*, ed. Lynn Welchman and Sara Hossain, xi–xiv. London: Zed Books, 2005.

Eissenstat, Howard. "A Single Note for a Complex Social Tableau. Review of *In the Morning*." H-Gender-MidEast, HNet Reviews, July 2006. www.h-net.msu.edu/reviews/showrev.cg?path=788 (Accessed on March 22, 2008).

El Ouali, Abderrahim. "Islam is being misinterpreted to justify 'honor killings'; States Fuel 'Honor Killings.'" *IPS* (Latin America) February 1, 2008. www.lexisnexix.com.luna.wellesley.edu/usInacademic/delive (Accessed on February 18, 2009).

Filkins, Dexter. "Turkish Honor Killings Defy Efforts to End Them." *New York Times*, July 13, 2003.

Hellgren, Zenia and Hobson, Barbara. "Cultural Dialogues in the Good Society: The Cases of Honour Killings in Sweden." *Ethnicities* 8, 3 (2008): 385–404.

Husseini, Rana. *Murder in the Name of Honour*. Oxford: Oneworld Publications, 2009.

Jacoby, Jeff. "'Honor' killing comes to the US." *The Boston Globe*, August 10, 2008.

Jimenez, Marina. "Gay Jordanian Now 'Gloriously Free' in Canada." *The Globe & Mail*, May 20, 2004. http://www.glapn.org/sodomylaws/world/canada/canews021.htm (Accessed on May 2, 2009).

Khan, S. Tahira. *Beyond Honour. A Historical Materialist Explanation of Honour Related Violence*. Oxford: Oxford University Press, 2006.

Khoury, C. Buthina. *Maria's Grotto*, DVD, Majd Production, 2007.

King, E. Diane. "The Personal is Patrilineal: *Namus* as Sovereignty." *Identities: Global Studies in Culture and Power*, 15 (2008): 317–342.

Mojab, Shahrzad. "'Honor Killing' Culture, Politics and Theory." *Middle East Women's Studies Review* 17 (2002): 1, 2.

Önal, Ayşe. *Honor Killing. Stories of Men Who Killed*. London: SAQI Books, 2008.

Pamuk, Orhan. *Snow*. Translated by Maureen Freely. Oxford: Faber & Faber, 2004.

Reimers, Eva. "Representations of An Honor Killing." *Feminist Media Studies* 7, 3 (2007): 239–255.

Saywell, Shelley. *Crimes of Honour*, VHS, Bishari Films, 1999.

Simpson, Peggy. "Fifteen Years of Courage: Ayşe Önal." *International Women's Media Foundation*. www.iwmf.org/article.aspx?c=carticles&id=393 (Accessed on April 30, 2009).

Smith, Joan. "Introduction." In *Honour Killing. Stories of Men Who Killed*, by Ayşe Önal, 9–17. London: SAQI Books, 2008.

Tehrani, Bijan. "Danielle Lurie Plans a Feature Film on 'Honor Killings' of Women." *Cinema Without Borders*. 2007. www.digitaljournalonline.com/news/123/ARTICLE/1318/2007 (Accessed on March 12, 2008).

"Two charged with honour killing." *The Guardian*, Thursday, August, 17, 2006. http://www.guardian.co.uk/world/2006/aug/17/italy.mainsection (Accessed on April 28, 2009).

Welchman, Lynn and Hossain, Sara, eds. *Honour. Crimes, Paradigms, and Violence Against Women*. London: Zed Books, 2005.